AMERICA'S STANDARD GAUGE
ELECTRIC TRAINS

AMERICA'S STANDARD GAUGE

ELECTRIC TRAINS

Their History and Operation, Including
A Collector's Guide to Current Values

BY PETER H. RIDDLE

FOREWORD BY MIKE WOLF

Edited by Allan W. Miller and Gay Riddle

Antique Trader Books
A Division of Landmark Specialty Publications
Norfolk, Virginia

This book is dedicated to our son,
KENDRICK DAVID RIDDLE,
and to our daughter,
ANNE REBECCA MOGGY,
with great love and affection from Mom and Dad.

ISBN: 0-930625-22-6

Library of Congress Catalog Card Number: 98-71062

Published by Landmark Specialty Books, a division of Landmark Specialty Publications, Inc.

Editors:	Allan W. Miller and Gay Riddle
Assistant Editor:	Wendy Chia-Klesch
Copy Editor:	Sandra Holcombe
Design Coordinator and Cover Design:	Chris Decker
Designer:	Cynthia Dooley

Printed in the United States of America

To order additional copies of this book, or to obtain a free catalog, please contact:

Antique Trader Books
P.O. Box 1050
Dubuque, Iowa 52004

or call 1-800-334-7165

CONTENTS

FOREWORD

During the summer of 1972, when I was twelve years old, I began to pester a neighbor of mine for a job. Every day, I'd ride my bike over to his house to see what was happening in his backyard garage "factory." Inside this magical building, workers were busily engaged producing copies of a classic Lionel Standard Gauge steam engine: the 400E. It was a faithful replica of the original 400E that my family kept proudly displayed on our fireplace mantle, and it was an engine that had fascinated me for as long as I could remember. Eventually, the owner of that bustling neighborhood "factory"—Jerry Williams, of Williams Reproductions—relented to my badgering, and offered me a job on his Standard Gauge trains assembly line. This marked the beginning of a life-long fondness and appreciation for Standard Gauge electric trains.

Eight years later, while I was attending college and continuing to work as a production supervisor for Williams' firm, the entrepreneurial bug bit, and I decided to start my own electric toy train company. Housed in my bedroom at my parents' house, the aptly named Mike's Train House had its humble beginnings as a mail order business and train show retailer. Not long content with the limited scope of my new business, I soon began to plan for the day when I could expand into the actual manufacturing of electric toy trains.

My opportunity arrived in 1982, when Jerry Williams determined that there was no longer a significant market for his tinplate reproductions. With the help of my parents, who loaned me most of their life savings, I was able to purchase Williams' tinplate tooling. Soon thereafter, I found myself taking orders and employing friends and family to work in my very own basement "factory." Shortly after the sale of our first products, the loan from my parents was repaid, and my fledgling enterprise soon proved that it could successfully carry on the manufacturing tradition of tinplate electric toy trains. And the rest, as they say, is history!

Some twenty-five years have elapsed since I first fell in love with the toy train industry. Today, MTH Electric Trains offers an extensive and growing line of scale and semi-scale electric trains—including an array of nearly 80 detailed O

Gauge locomotive models released over the past decade alone, and a great many of our customers are attracted by these prototypical scale models. Still, my personal favorites continue to be O and Standard Gauge tinplate trains, and today my colleagues and I proudly produce more Standard and O Gauge tinplate toy trains than any other contemporary manufactuer!

Why my fondness for tinplate? Well, for one thing, I've always felt that the combination of colors, shapes, and sounds of tinplate toy trains creates something of an artistic impression for their owners. While some may prefer more traditional art forms—paintings that can be hung on walls, or statues that are placed on pedestals, for example—my preferred art form can actually be played with as well as admired. Tinplate toy trains—and especially Standard Gauge toy trains—truly are works of art as well as treasured artifacts.

The nostalgic charm of tinplate toy trains also appeals to me in a very personal way. Anyone who can recall turning off the room lights, firing-up a transformer, and lying flat on the floor with head nestled in arms for a close-up view of a gleaming toy train streaking around the base of a Christmas tree, will understand this emotion. I'm not really sure if it's their bright and shiny paint, their romantic squeaks and rumbles, the dancing reflections caused as illuminated passenger cars proceed on their imaginary journeys, or simply recollections of my own family's Standard Gauge tradition that I find so nostalgia evoking and heartwarming. But, of one thing I am very sure: Every time I see that beat-up old 400E on my parents' mantle, I'm continually reminded that there is something magical and wonderful about electric trains in general, and tinplate toy trains in particular. So, on behalf of all those who share a love for toy trains—whether from the past or the present—I invite you to experience a bit of the magic and the wonder!

Mike Wolf
President and CEO
MTH Electric Trains

ACKNOWLEDGMENTS

Many persons have provided assistance or contributed indirectly to the preparation of this book and have earned my undying gratitude. I sincerely thank them (and genuinely hope I haven't forgotten anyone): Joe Armacost, Gertrude A. Bull (whose home shelters the author's Standard Gauge layout), Jim Bunte, Harlen K. Creswell, John E. Harmon, Tony J. Hay, Mark Horne, Paul Johnson, Joseph L. Mania, Margaret McCoy, Maurice Weisblum, Nelson G. Williams, Mike Wolf, and Charles Wood.

Special thanks are due to Susan Childers, Manager of Richard & Linda Kughn's Carail Museum, and to John Lauter, who provided invaluable service to Gay and myself during our photographic session in the museum. We are also deeply grateful to Allan W. Miller, who served as both the driving force behind, and the final editor of, this book.

The majority of the photographs displayed herein (those which are not credited in the captions) were taken by the author, including those of the magnificent Carail Museum layout and collection. The camera used was an Olympus IS-3, loaded with Ilford XP2 black and white or Ektachrome Tungsten 64 color film, at various apertures and exposure times. The author created the technical drawings using DesignCAD 2D, marketed by the ViaGrafix Corporation. The names of photographers who contributed additional illustrations appear at the ends of the captions. The author is indebted to these photographers for their valuable assistance: Harlen K. Creswell, John E. Harmon, Ed Richter, Sean Smyth, Brad Varney, and Maurice Weisblum.

The trains and accessories pictured here are contained in several different collections, and these are also identified in the captions. The models without such identification are part of the collection shared by the author and his wife, Gay, who also served as the first reader and editor of the text.

INTRODUCTION

Setting the Standard in Toy Trains

by Allan W. Miller
Managing Editor, Landmark Specialty Books

Standard Gauge, as the term applies in model railroading, was conceived in 1906 by an enterprising young inventor and entrepreneur named Joshua Lionel Cowen, founding father of The Lionel Manufacturing Co.—an American institution whose name became synonymous with toy trains. Cowen had launched his electric toy train business in 1900 with large 2-7/8" Gauge powered gondolas and trolleys, but he soon opted to create a "Standard" size of electric train in an effort to preempt competition from other toy train makers, both in the U.S. and abroad. Lionel's Standard Gauge trains were big, much like their European counterparts, but the track upon which Cowen's trains operated measured a unique 2-1/8" between the running rails, thereby assuring that locomotives and cars produced by competitors would not be compatible unless they were re-manufactured to conform to his self-proclaimed "Standard."

Joshua Cowen's ploy worked, but only for a time. Standard Gauge dominance in the period before the Great Depression (including its emulation by major competitors such as Ives and American Flyer) gradually gave way to smaller and more affordable O Gauge trains in the years leading up to World War II. By the time that war ended, Standard Gauge had disappeared from Lionel's renowned consumer catalogs. And, by the 1950s—the period many hobbyists consider the "Golden Age" of toy trains— Standard Gauge was not only gone from hobby store shelves, it was also virtually forgotten by all but a few in the then-small community of avid collectors. No self-respecting boy of that time, regardless of his depth of immersion in model railroading, would have admitted to being a Lionel Standard Gauge (or American Flyer's equivalent "Wide Gauge") fanatic. Indeed, Standard Gauge was the stuff Dad might have had in his own youth, or, even more likely, that *his* dad would have had.

But today Standard Gauge trains are enjoying a resurrection of sorts, and these big trains continue to provide an active leisure-time pursuit for a growing number of enthusi-

asts. It appears that, in many respects, interest in collecting and operating toy trains has not only gone full circle—back to the toys of our respective childhood days—but, indeed, has been drawn even further back, to the formative years of the hobby itself.

But, what is it about Standard Gauge trains that has perpetuated interest in these objects even to the present day and, if current trends are any indication, well beyond? In this age of miniaturized computer-guided electronics and high levels of exacting detail in toys, why would anyone be drawn to massive, fanciful, noisy, and often unrealistically colored representations of outdated steam locomotives, streetcars, and the like?

If the truth be known, it's entirely possible that the same characteristics that so distinctively mark Standard Gauge electric trains as relics of the past are the very ones that also make them so appealing.

Standard Gauge electric trains are, indeed, big, boisterous, durable, and colorful. Originally manufactured in a time when many homes were spacious enough to accommodate large model trains operating on the living room floor or elsewhere, these mechanical marvels were truly designed to be admired as well as played with. Although they almost never faithfully duplicated the appearance or fine detail of the real locomotives and cars they supposedly represented, they more than compensated for this in other ways. They were constructed of heavy, tinplated metal, and were adorned with gleaming enamel paint and bright nickel or brass trim. Furthermore, they were powered by reliable, long-lasting motors that were easy to service and repair. Everything about these toys exemplified quality in the toy maker's art. In the world of toy electric trains, just about nothing else compares—then or now—to viewing a gleaming eight-foot-long Standard Gauge train set snaking its way along the track. It's an awe-inspiring sight to behold, and one that invariably appeals to youngsters and oldsters alike!

Another factor driving the continued popularity of

Standard Gauge trains is the American public's preoccupation with nostalgia. Collecting "things" is something of a national pastime, driven in large measure by an obsessive desire to seek out and preserve the artifacts of our past. In light of the role played by railroads in the nation's expansion and development in the nineteenth and early twentieth centuries, it's little wonder that railroad-related memorabilia, including toy trains, attracts such a devoted and persistent following. Because Standard Gauge toy trains actually look like toys from another era, and not at all like the rivet-for-rivet accurate scale models so often seen today, they are natural attractions for nostalgia buffs.

Finally, it can truthfully be stated that Standard Gauge never really did die. It's true that items produced in those first years—called the Early Period (1906-1923) by collectors—are increasingly difficult to find in good condition, and they may be extremely expensive to acquire. It's also true that even products made later, in what the collecting community knows as the Classic Period (1923-1942), are generally scarce and often quite costly. Nevertheless, as you'll dis-

A colorful and nostalgia-evoking scene on Richard and Linda Kughn's Carail Museum Standard Gauge layout. Richard Kughn is the former owner of Lionel Trains, Inc.— one of several corporate entities that have kept the tradition of railroading with Lionel electric trains alive for nearly a century.

cover in the pages of this book, a number of manufacturers, large and small, have kept the Standard Gauge tradition alive over the years by continuing to offer both innovative new items and superb reproductions of earlier models, often at reasonable prices. There's really no need to scour train shows and auctions in search of trains, track, or accessories for a Standard Gauge layout or display. Today, if you're so inclined, there are a good number of new and near-new items in the marketplace to choose from.

As Standard Gauge approaches its centennial anniversary, it can truly be said that these beautiful toy trains are not only alive, but that they're doing quite well for their age. And that bodes well for the future of these action-packed playthings from our past and present!

The earliest Lionel design, the No. 200 "Electric Express," was a simple wooden box mounted on a four-wheeled frame, powered by a simple open-frame electric motor located under the floor. (Reproduction by Joseph L. Mania, photograph by Sean Smyth)

1

JOSHUA LIONEL COWEN

and the "Standard of the World"

The name Lionel has been virtually synonymous with electric trains for most of the twentieth century. And yet when Joshua Lionel Cowen, the founder of the marque, created his first motorized toys, his initial intent was apparently not the manufacture of children's playthings. Judging by the focus of his advertising, he had something rather different in mind and must have been surprised to discover the clientele that his products were attracting.

Cowen was a talented amateur engineer, a workshop tinkerer with a flair for the unusual and the imagination to find new uses for the fledgling science of electricity. His training came not from formal schooling,[1] but from on-the-job experience while working for a small New York shop devoted to producing electric lamps and other devices. He was intrigued by the possibilities inherent in storage batteries, especially the new dry cell. On his own time he experimented tirelessly, seeking new uses for low voltage electricity.

His earliest inventions included a mechanism for igniting photographic flash powder, a rudimentary hand-held flashlight, and a small electric fan, for which he designed a successful direct current motor. At the turn of the century, these products held little promise for commercial prosperity, but Cowen chanced upon an adaptation for the flash powder

device that earned him a substantial contract with the United States Navy. Under the new contract, he produced an efficient and reliable electric detonator for explosive mines.[2]

With a substantial bankroll realized from the Navy venture, Cowen and an associate named Harry Grant set out to develop some type of merchandise on which to base a business, just as the twentieth century was being born. His primary stock in trade consisted of two patents in his name, a primitive design for an electric fan that had thus far attracted little interest among the public, and a seemingly unbounded optimism and faith in his own creative abilities. All he needed was a product.

With his miniature electric fan motor as inspiration, Cowen did not immediately turn to toys. Instead he envisioned a device that store owners might use to promote their wares and set about creating the first of what he referred to as "Miniature Electric Cars . . . For Window Display." His first design was extremely primitive, consisting of nothing but an open rectangular box mounted upon four flanged wheels and propelled by his electric motor which was connected to one of the axles. This "Electric Express" rode upon a circle of crude track, made from thin strips of steel embedded in slots in thick pieces of wood, like railroad ties. It was powered by dry cell batteries.

The Electric Express was made from stamped steel beginning in 1903. The original Ives No. 116 Station in the background, from the Joseph L. Mania collection, was made at about the same time as Lionel's 2-7/8" Gauge trains. (Reproduction No. 200 Gondola by Joseph L. Mania, photograph by Sean Smyth)

In an address to the New York Society of Security Analysts on June 10, 1949, Lawrence Cowen, son of the founder and at that time president of The Lionel Corporation, stated that "Early sales were largely for window display purposes. A train running around a circle of track in a store window was a great novelty and attraction in 1902 . . ."[3]

Joshua Cowen believed that animation would attract customers to products displayed in a shop window and took his first model to store owner Robert Ingersoll. He suggested that small items of merchandise be placed inside the "Electric Express," expecting that customers would be drawn first to the action, and then into the store to buy what the motorized car was carrying. It didn't quite work out that way. While the display did indeed attract customers, they did not come to buy the merchandise, but the clever animated container itself. Ingersoll immediately ordered half a dozen more.[4]

Other merchants followed suit, and Cowen and Grant found themselves in production.[5] By early 1902, the partners had begun to expand their product line and were successfully selling their toys, still promoted primarily as window displays, to buyers outside the New York metropolitan area. They incorporated under the grand title of the Lionel Manufacturing Company and issued a catalog advertising their line, now grown to include an electric trolley car, a bridge, a switch track, a crossing, and a bumper for the end of the line. The "Electric Express" was also offered without a motor; this version could be coupled to a powered model for a rudimentary "train," although the catalog did not use this word. The copy instead states: "These cars coupled together make a very interesting and entertaining outfit." Clearly, Cowen visualized his products only secondarily as toys, and the word "toy" appears only once in the text, almost as a sidelight in the promotion of

the "Electric Express."

Although toy trains were made almost as soon as the invention of steam railroads in Great Britain, they were mostly wooden pull toys, requiring no track and without motors. Cast-iron railroad toys became common in the latter nineteenth century, mostly still without track, but the concept of self-propelled toys was experimented with quite early. In Europe there were steam-powered toy trains being sold before 1850.[6] Such manufacturers as Marklin in Germany developed complex toy railroad systems in the 1890s, and in America, the Ives Corporation was producing a large quantity of cast-iron toy trains. While most of Ives' early designs were strictly floor toys, some of them were made to be pushed along a track, and the most elaborate even had clockwork (wind-up) mechanisms to power them.

The possibility of using electricity for self-powered toys was first successfully exploited in North America starting in 1896 by the firm of Carlisle & Finch of Cincinnati, Ohio.[7] Marklin soon followed suit in Germany (1898), but the problem of an adequate, safe and economical power supply relegated electric power to a very small segment of the toy market. The cost of these motorized novelties took them out of the toy category for most families.

For example, the 1902 Lionel catalog advertises dry cell batteries as $1.20 per pair. This outlay might be borne by a store keeper as an advertising expense, since the attraction of a motorized window display could be expected to lure customers and generate extra business. For the average household at that time in history, however, it was an astronomical sum. Dry cell batteries could not be recharged once exhausted, and few people could afford to spend more than a day's pay on a power source that would quickly be depleted and thrown away.

According to Cowen's son Lawrence, "the lack of available power lines and the mess caused by wet cell batteries was a great deterrent at the onset [of the company]."[8] Joshua Cowen attempted to address this problem in his early catalogs, and devoted four of the sixteen pages in his first catalog to power source options. In addition to the dry cells (a safe but very expensive solution to the problem), he offered components for a wet cell "plunge battery" that the purchaser could charge with "electric sand" obtained from a local supplier. For stores or households that enjoyed electric lighting, he also promoted wet cell batteries consisting of glass jars fitted with lead plates, intended to be filled with a mixture of sulfuric acid and water. These cells were charged by connecting them to the 110-volt current supplied by the local power company.

Although cheaper than dry cells, these alternatives threatened great danger, especially to young children. Responsible parents could hardly allow their offspring to play in the presence of open containers of sulfuric acid, and the hazard of potential electric shock kept most homeowners from tapping into the fabric-covered wires that powered their early lamps. Those lucky enough to have commercial power tended to be somewhat mystified by it, and therefore quite cautious in its use. Electric power was far from universal in those early years; metropolitan areas were serviced first, but only a relatively small percentage of homes were connected. In rural areas, widespread electric power was still many years away.

Despite this drawback, buyers almost immediately saw the primitive Lionel products as potential playthings, and the focus of Cowen's advertising began a slow but definite shift away from potential commercial customers and toward families. In the 1903 catalog, Lionel merchandise is, for the first time, described with the terms "locomotives" and "trains" in addi-

tion to the generic term "goods" first used in the 1902 copy. Significantly, however, the word "toy" is nowhere to be found in the 1903 catalog, although as in 1902, they are promoted as both "Window Display and Holiday Gifts."

Prominently featured in the new catalog were two additions to the line, a motorized crane and a box cab locomotive roughly modeled after a Baltimore & Ohio Railroad prototype. The appeal of these items as toys is immediately apparent, as the locomotive, while hardly a scale model, is at least reminiscent of the type of equipment seen on eastern railroads. The crane has real play potential, with its boom and operating crank and hook. Unlike the motorized gondola, the crane and locomotive were unsuited for displaying merchandise in a store window. And these new items looked like toys.

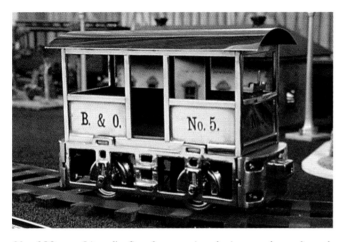

No. 100 was Lionel's first locomotive design, and was based on a Baltimore & Ohio tunnel electric engine. (Reproduction by Joseph L. Mania, photograph by Sean Smyth)

Joshua Lionel Cowen offered this No. 500 Derrick in an unpowered version, to be pulled by a locomotive, or in a self-propelled motorized version. (Reproduction by Joseph L. Mania, photograph by Sean Smyth)

Cowen Goes His Own Way

Inhibiting the use of these early Lionel "trains" as playthings, however, was the cumbersome system of track supplied for operation. This consisted of slotted wooden ties into which lengths of 3/8" steel were inserted. The ends of these steel straps were bent into L-shaped hooks, to allow them to be joined together. It must have been a laborious and time-consuming feat to form even the simplest loop of track, requiring sixty separate ties, a total of thirty feet of rail, and a fair amount of patience and dexterity. (At this time, other manufacturers were already producing sectional track, pioneered by Marklin in Germany in 1891,[9] and not

unlike the familiar toy train track still sold by Lionel and other manufacturers today.)

There is a significant clue to be found to Joshua Cowen's personality and his attitude toward competition in the configuration of his first system of track. When inserted into the ties, the rails measured 2-7/8" inches between them, corresponding to the width of the wheel and axle sets on the trains. This dimension was almost unique to the Lionel product.

In Europe, Marklin and other German manufacturers had developed a system of numerical track gauges for toy trains of various sizes.[10] The most common were No. 0, No. 1, and No.

The 2-7/8" Gauge track required laborious assembly from wooden ties and thin strips of steel. The No. 800 Boxcar was self-powered and is often called the "jail car" because of its barred windows. A version without a motor carried the catalog number 900. (Reproduction by Joseph L. Mania, photograph by Sean Smyth)

2, measuring 1-1/4", 1-3/4", and 2" between the rails respectively.[11] In America, the most prominent maker of clockwork toy trains, the Ives Corporation of Bridgeport, Connecticut, adopted both No. 0 and No. 1, and Carlisle & Finch used 2" Gauge track (No. 2).

Instead of adopting one of these existing standards, Cowen went his own way. Although his 2-7/8" Gauge had been occasionally used by early British toy makers and was close to the obscure No. 4 Gauge used rarely in Europe at that time, no North American manufacturer employed this gauge. It is likely that Cowen was unaware of the similarities to the remote continental gauges, and deliberately chose the measurement to ensure that his products would be distinctive.[12] This independence of spirit, as we shall see, manifested itself again in his creation of the then absolutely unique gauge of 2-1/8" in 1906. Just two years later, Cowen arrogantly proclaimed his trains to be the "Standard of the World" on the cover of the 1907 catalog, and the name stuck. Standard Gauge was born.

The adjective "arrogant" is not an exaggeration when applied to Joshua Lionel Cowen. As a promoter, he was aggressive and pretentious, and often given to gross overstatement in his advertising campaigns. In the 1903 catalog, he described his box cab locomotive as "a faithful reproduction of the 1,800 horsepower electric locomotives used by the B&O RR for hauling trains through the tunnels of Baltimore. Every line is carried out to the proper proportions."

Such hyperbole has never been uncommon in the advertising trade, and while Cowen's locomotive captured the general proportions and appearance of the B&O prototype, it was still a caricature of the real thing, rather than a "faithful repro-

duction" as the catalog asserts. The engine was reasonably realistic, especially for a toy, but it was hardly the highly detailed scale model that the ad copy seems to suggest.[13] In later years, Cowen would develop the art of embellishment and misstatement in his advertisements to such a high level as to embarrass even the most flamboyant used car or life insurance salesman.

The expanded 1904 and 1905 catalogs suggest that Cowen's company was at least moderately successful and that the promotion of the products as playthings was assuming greater and greater importance. The 1905 version begins with an assertive attack on the competition, and for the first time the word "toy" is stated first in the copy, achieving precedence over the "show window display" segment of the market. In large, double-underlined letters it reads: "A FACT," followed by "If you want a miniature electric car to work satisfactorily as a toy or for Show Window Display," and then a bold-faced, capitalized attention grabber in quotes: **"YOU MUST GET A LIONEL"**.

By this time, however, Cowen must have been having trouble believing his own sales material. Although his Lionel products had achieved modest acceptance in the marketplace, he must have seen the limitations that their overall design placed upon their potential for growth and continued acceptance as realistic and easy-to-use toys. The awkward track components, dangerous and expensive power supply options, and ungainly size of the trains made them barely competitive with the more realistic offerings of other manufacturers, especially the high quality clockwork (wind-up) trains being sold by Ives.

In 1905 the principal manufacturer of toy trains in the United States was the Ives Corporation, but toys imported from Germany formed a very large percentage of the market, and both Marklin and the Bavarian firm, Bing, were producing large quantities of high-quality trains for consumers in North America. Beginning around 1890, the German toy makers had made substantial gains in the American market. Their small and nicely detailed sheet-metal and cast-iron steam-outline locomotives performed well, powered by dependable clockwork motors and pulling several lithographed coaches or freight cars around loops of easy-to-assemble sectional track.

The first serious competition for these imported toys came from Ives, following a major fire in their manufacturing facility in 1900. The company quickly reorganized, and in 1901 began producing a line of O Gauge trains that closely imitated the European designs.[14] Due to the company's rigid adherence to high quality standards, the advantage of being produced domestically, and an established network of distributors for its other toys, Ives achieved a strong degree of success with this new line and gave the foreign firms their first serious competition in North America.

These "Made in America" O Gauge offerings were so successful that in 1904 Ives expanded the line to include a larger series of locomotives and cars for No. 1 Gauge track. These products were well engineered, very realistic in appearance, and ran well with their sturdy wind-up mechanisms, and the management at Ives resisted the growing movement toward electrically-powered toys. For a few years, at least, this decision seemed to be the right one, and their products sold reasonably well.

By contrast, Lionel's primitive trains and trolleys had achieved a measure of success primarily through the novelty of electric power, but their designs were not universally familiar. With the exception of the B&O locomotive, they were patterned after New York City's street railway designs, and were relatively unfamiliar to people living outside the Northeast. By 1905, Joshua Lionel Cowen had recognized that different designs were needed to make his company truly competitive nationally against Ives and the well-established European manufacturers. The decision was made to abandon the 2-7/8" line in favor of a completely new system that was destined to dominate the field until the years of the Great Depression, building the foundation of a reputation for the trademark "Lionel" that remained unsurpassed for many decades.

The "Standard of the World"

The 1906 Lionel catalog was a major departure for the company, not only in the design of the products, but in the promotional approach of the advertising copy. With typical bravado, Joshua Lionel Cowen tackled head-on the major shortcomings of his earlier products. Recognizing the perception of danger inherent in his previous technology, he stressed the safety of electric power on the first page, asserting that "it is totally impossible to experience the slightest shock."

In those innocent days before the proliferation of public safety messages and liability lawsuits, such deceptions were common practice in advertising, but in truth the company had vastly improved its power systems. The acid-based wet cells were gone, and in addition to dry cell batteries, Lionel offered rudimentary transformers sealed in protective cases for both direct and alternating house current applications. While not foolproof, these units were substantially safer than their predecessors, although a carelessly connected wire or misplaced hand could still result in a nasty shock.

During the early years of the twentieth century, fascination with electric power was widespread among the general public, and Cowen made the most of it. After virtually guaranteeing the absolute safety of his products, he stressed the educational value of the toys and liberally sprinkled the copy with technical terms ("brushes," "commutator," "armature") that gave the catalog a learned and scientific flavor. Borrowing from his competitors, he presented a new line of sectional track, described in such a manner as to make it seem like a Lionel innovation. Finally, the trains themselves represented a great leap forward: long and graceful trolley cars and railroad coaches, a complete line of seven different freight cars, and two chunky sheet metal steam locomotives that compared favorably with the competition, at least in the catalog illustrations.

The most important change, however, received little attention. Instead of choosing one of the existing European gauges, as Ives had done in adopting No. 1 Gauge for its large trains, Lionel chose to go it alone once more. The track gauge measured 2-1/8",[15] thus establishing Lionel Trains as incompatible with all others. This was a bold move. Customers who already owned trains made by a competing manufacturer might be reluctant to buy the new Lionel products, once they discovered they could not be used with their existing toys.

There were actually four American manufacturers of electric toy trains during those early years that ran on 2" Gauge track: the Voltamp Company, Carlisle & Finch, Knapp Electric & Novelty Company, and the Howard Miniature Lamp Company. However, in 1906 none had achieved much market penetration, and the Ives No. 1 Gauge line of clockwork-powered trains was probably the most widely distributed.[16] Furthermore, these competing lines were not even compatible with each other, some using two-rail track and others using three-rail, all manufactured to different standards. Right from the beginning, it appears that Cowen was intent upon establishing a special niche for his Lionel products, and one suspects he hoped even then to make the competition follow his lead.

In fact, that is exactly what happened. When the new Lionel size appeared in 1906, both Ives and the German manufacturer Bing had their No. 1 Gauge trains reasonably well established in the American market. In less than two decades, the success of Lionel's 2-1/8" line would force both companies to convert their trains to that size. But that is getting ahead of our story.

In 1906, there was no such thing as a "standard" toy electric train. Although they shared certain similarities, the

The most impressive product in Lionel's early Standard Gauge line was the brass and nickel steamer, cataloged as either No. 6 Special or No. 7. (Reproduction by Joseph L. Mania, photograph by Sean Smyth)

products of the different manufacturers were actually quite disparate. Joshua Cowen wisely adopted the most successful features of the other makers, combining them with his own ideas in what he hoped would be a superior product. For example, the first operational electric headlight appears to have been introduced by Howard in 1905.[17] Just two years later, in the 1907 catalog, Lionel trumpeted this feature on its largest steam locomotive.

Lionel's early 2-1/8" Gauge locomotives were also reversible. The motors used in these toys were universal series-wound designs that could work on either alternating or direct current (AC or DC). A simple rotary switch mounted near the bottom of the frame could be thrown to reverse the flow of current through the field of the motor, thus reversing its direction. Lionel used this simple technology to good advantage by providing a mechanism that mounted on a section of track and that could be positioned to activate this reversing switch when the train passed beside it. This device caused the train to stop and back up (in an admittedly sudden and jerky fashion) automatically.

The new Lionel track was copied after the Ives and German designs, with three steel rails mounted firmly on steel ties. A substantial pin in one end of each of the rails could be inserted into the open end of a rail on an adjoining section, thus eliminating the difficult problem of assembling the separate rails and wooden ties supplied with the earlier 2-7/8" Gauge trains. In addition, the middle rail of each section was insulated from the ties by strips of fiber material, making electrical connections simpler and almost foolproof.

The 1906 trains seemed much more realistic to customers who were unfamiliar with the urban designs in the 2-7/8" Gauge line. In place of the powered gondola and odd box-shaped locomotive of the 1905 line, two steam-outline engines pulled trains of freight and passenger cars. Although somewhat crudely made from stamped and soldered sheet metal, these toys generally resembled the boxcars, tank cars, hoppers, cattle cars, and cabooses that children saw every day on real railroads. The passenger and trolley cars were very impressive, being massive in appearance with attractive raised roofs, end platforms, and rows of cut-out windows.

In the first year of the new line, two sizes of steam locomotive were offered. No. 5 was a short 0-4-0 design,[18] having four driving wheels under the boiler, but neither pilot wheels nor a trailing truck. Instead of a tender, it carried a small extension in back of the cab, simulating a coal bunker. The larger and more expensive No. 6 pulled its own large eight-wheeled tender, and had four pilot wheels in addition to the four drivers.[19] The locos were black with red trim. (In later years, Lionel would add a sloped-back tender to the No. 5, calling it first a No. 5 Special, and later a No. 51. The No. 6 later came in a polished brass finish rather than black, under the designation No. 6 Special or No. 7.)

Seven freight cars were offered, all mounted on a pair of swiveling four-wheeled trucks: flatcar, gondola, cattle car, boxcar, oil (tank) car, coal car, and caboose. These cars were numbered 11, 12, 13, 14, 15, 16, and 17 respectively. Two passenger cars were illustrated in the catalog, a No. 18 Pullman and a No. 19 Combine, but it is unlikely that they were actually produced until at least 1910.[20] There were also two sizes of trolley cars, two stations, a trestle bridge, a foot bridge (bought from German manufacturers for resale), a bumper, power supplies, and track products.

Lionel's 1906 and 1907 catalogs were undeniably attractive, and the advertising copy within was extravagant in its claims. In fact, the company had not yet begun producing all of the items pictured therein, and the early motors and drive systems were not fully perfected when the first models reached the market. However, Cowen was already beginning an assault on the competition that would soon convince the buying public of the superiority of his trains over all other brands. With unrestrained enthusiasm, the 1908 catalog proclaimed the new line of Lionel Trains to be the "STANDARD OF THE WORLD" a mere two years after their introduction.

The term "standard" applied to a product would usually suggest quality and reliability against which all others should be measured. In 1908, Lionel was still the "new kid on the block"—several years behind the more established Ives, Marklin, and Bing. Nevertheless, page 8 of the 1908 catalog claims that Lionel is "foremost in the manufacture of Miniature Electric Cars and motors, not only in the United States but in the world—quite a statement to make but we can prove it." In fact, the supporting text offered no such proof, but only elaborated on the original claims: braggadocio of the highest order! Four pages of copy proclaimed Lionel's supposed superiority, while belittling and misrepresenting the competition and its products. The claims of durability and superior performance could hardly have been proven in the short time the products had been on the market, but according to the catalog, Lionel was obviously the best, because Lionel said so!

The public, continually assaulted by this outrageous yet convincing advertising hype, bought into the myth and began buying Lionel Trains in substantial numbers. Cowen's new products were so successful that they soon came to be known by the term "Standard Gauge," borrowed from his "Standard of the World" slogan.

By 1910, in a period of great industrial expansion throughout the Western world, Lionel's growth rate far exceeded that of the nation's generally healthy economy. In the following decade, the firm expanded to employ seven hundred workers,[21] producing an ever-growing product line. But such success could not have resulted from advertising alone. To his credit, Cowen relentlessly strove to improve his toys, refining and upgrading them, and introducing new features. In 1910 the firm announced a brand new series of locomotives to complement the existing steam engine designs.

Early freight cars, such as the reproduction No. 11 Flat Car and No. 15 Tank Car shown here, were built in the proper proportions to match either of Lionel's two sizes of steam locomotive. In this photo, they are coupled to a No. 5. (Reproductions by Joseph L. Mania, photograph by Sean Smyth)

Based as it was in the New York metropolitan area, Lionel's largest market consisted of children (and their parents) who were as familiar with electric-powered trains as with steamers. Clean-running box cab locomotives that drew current from overhead wires pulled both passenger and freight trains into the crowded cities of the Northeast, where the smoke from coal-fired engines had been banished. Recognizing the advantages of capitalizing on this familiarity, Cowen introduced three new designs, all patterned after one locomotive used on the New York Central Lines, the S-2. Numbered 1910, 1911, and 1912 (from smallest to largest), these squared-off sheet metal locos were quite respectable interpretations of the real thing. The largest model, No. 1912, rode on eight large driving wheels.

It is interesting to speculate upon the choice of numbers for these new engines. While the earlier steamers carried the numbers 5 and 6 in the catalogs only, these new designs had their numbers stamped prominently on their sides. The use of numerals that also denoted years, present and future, might have been a subtle attempt to establish a sense of modernism, and therefore quality, in the minds of prospective purchasers.

By this time the line had been expanded dramatically, with three-car passenger sets available, consisting of a combine, Pullman, and observation car, as well as several sizes of trolley cars and a powered Interurban. There was even a set of miniature figures, designed to fit over pins on the seats of the trolleys. Only a few accessories were offered, as Cowen seemed to be concentrating primarily upon perfecting the trains themselves and their mechanisms. In this effort he was largely successful, for many of these vintage trains remain in operating condition today. In addition to track products, the 1910 catalog showed just three stations (similar to Ives products and presumably purchased from that firm for resale), and a tunnel.[22]

Two significant items appeared on page 16 of the 1910 catalog, although their debut received so little attention as to go virtually unnoticed. In Outfit No. 1910, the company offered a No. 1911 locomotive accompanied by two gondolas, priced at $6.25 (not an inconsiderable sum in those days, although well below the prices of most other items in the catalog). The gondolas were not numbered, but were described as being 7-1/2" long, and they could not be purchased separately, only as part of the set. (The only gondola described in previous catalogs was the higher priced No. 12, measuring 11" long. This larger car had been available since 1906.)

Further down the same page was an illustration of the larger No. 1911 locomotive, also pulling two freight cars of a design not seen before in any Lionel catalogs. Looking like small hopper cars, they were described as "dump cars" and measured 10" in length, whereas all previous Lionel freights were 11" long (plus an extra half inch for the caboose). This locomotive, with the two dump cars and a complete circle of track, sold for $8.25—a bargain when compared with the cost of the other more elaborate trains.

In fact, the early appearance of the diminutive gondola and dump car heralded the beginning of one of Joshua Lionel Cowen's most brilliant marketing strategies: the division of his products into two distinct price ranges. In 1911 these cars were again offered only in the outfits described above, but in the 1912 catalog they appeared in company with a full set of smaller freight cars. Finally they had their own numbers, No. 112 for the gondola and No. 116 for the dump car. The new caboose was No. 117, the cattle car was No. 113, and the boxcar was No. 114.[23] In general, the new line was more simply constructed and lighter in weight, requiring less material and slightly less assembly time, thus cutting production costs. The variety of smaller cars was somewhat restricted, with neither a tank car nor a flatcar available. They measured an average of 9-1/2" long, and were sold with a newly-designed small electric locomotive numbered 33.

The passenger car line received similar expansion in 1912. In addition to the large Nos. 18 Combine, 19 Pullman and 190 Observation cars available for the previous two years (although cataloged earlier), Lionel advertised three similar types, numbered 180, 181, and 182 respectively, which measured just 12-1/2" long each, four inches shorter (and a dollar cheaper!)[24] than their larger cousins. For the one dollar saving, the purchaser received a smaller car with somewhat simpler decoration, but still acquired a toy with Lionel quality and reputation.

From this time forward, most types of Lionel Trains would be offered in two or more different but complementary price ranges, distinguished by size, weight, and number of features. This marketing move made Lionel Trains available to a much larger segment of the buying public. While the price differentials seem minor today, in the second decade of the twentieth century a family would be considered comfortable on an income of just a few dollars a day. The difference between a small passenger train set at $7.00 and a large one at $20.00 was highly significant. By creating two similar lines, Cowen maintained his company's premium toys while attracting a whole new market, with one of the first "low priced" lines seen in American manufacturing.[25]

The 1912 catalog also illustrates Lionel's first significant venture into other toys, with the introduction of a pair of electric racing automobiles, running on their own special track. At a total of 36 pages, this catalog reflects the burgeoning prosperity of the United States in the years leading up to World War I. In little more than a decade, Cowen's upstart company had become a significant competitor to the more established firms, and the latter were taking notice. Lionel's principal competitor was the Ives Corporation, and the second decade of the twentieth century would witness an intense rivalry between these two companies for the toy-buying public's hard-earned cash.

chapter 1 Notes chapter 1

(1) Although Cowen enrolled briefly in two different colleges, he left before completing a degree.

(2) Ron Hollander, *All Aboard*, p. 25.

(3) Lawrence Cowen, as quoted in *The Train Collectors Quarterly*, July, 1988, p. 7.

(4) Hollander, *op. cit.*, p. 29.

(5) Harry Grant's association with Cowen was relatively brief. In his book *All Aboard* (p. 39), Ron Hollander reports that Grant was mechanically gifted but neither skilled at administration, nor inclined to complete projects which he started.

(6) Pierce Carlson, *Toy Trains, A History*, p. 9.

(7) Carlson, *op. cit.*, pp. 35-36.

(8) Cowen, *Ibid*.

(9) Louis H. Hertz, *Riding The Tinplate Rails*, p. 46.

(10) The term "gauge" today means the distance between the inside surfaces of the rails, whether referring to prototype railroads or to toys and models. In the late nineteenth and early twentieth centuries it was common to measure toy train gauges between the center lines of the rails, rather than the inside edges. To avoid confusion, all references to gauge in this book use the modern definition.

(11) Hertz, *op. cit.*, p. 47.

(12) Alternatively, he may have chosen this odd gauge out of ignorance. Toy trains were by no means widespread in the United States in 1906, and the issue of compatibility with other manufacturers' products was unimportant.

(13) The author admits the possibility of applying late twentieth century standards unfairly to Cowen's early efforts at producing accurate models. Maurice Weisblum contends that the B&O locomotive is a fairly good copy of the original.

(14) The European designation No. 0 ("number zero") for trains running on 1-1/4" gauge track is more commonly referred to today by the capital letter O, as in O Gauge. This nomenclature is used here for consistency.

(15) The early catalogs incorrectly describe Lionel Standard Gauge track as "2 inch Gauge", but all known samples (and the wheels of the trains themselves) reflect the 2-1/8" measurement. Later catalogs list the gauge at 2-1/4", which was accurate if measured between the centers of the rails instead of the inside surfaces. It may be that in the early years of Standard Gauge, Cowen was reluctant to call attention to the incompatibility of his products with those of other manufacturers. Or perhaps it was just considered simpler to round off the dimension by eliminating the extra eighth inch in print.

(16) Ives did not begin producing electric-powered trains in No. 1 Gauge until 1912.

(17) Hertz, *op. cit.*, p. 66.

(18) Steam locomotives are normally described numerically by their arrangement of wheels, under the Whyte system of classification. The first digit in the sequence is the number of small leading (pilot) wheels, usually located ahead of or underneath the cylinders. The middle number refers to the larger powered driving wheels, and the final number to the trailing wheels beneath the engineer's cab. When viewed from the side, a locomotive would appear to have only half the number of wheels stated, since those on both sides cannot readily be seen at the same time. An 0-4-0 loco has only four driving wheels, two per side. A 2-6-0 would have a pair of pilot wheels and six drivers; one pilot wheel and three drivers would be visible on each side. A 4-6-4 has four pilot, six driving and four trailing wheels. Each arrangement also carries a popular nickname, applied by railroad men over the years for convenience. For example, a 4-6-0 is a ten wheeler, and a 4-6-4 is a Hudson.

(19) In the 1906 catalog, No. 5 was offered at $5.50, while the No. 6 cost two dollars more.

(20) Donald S. Fraley, ed., *Lionel Trains, Standard Of The World, 1900-1943*, 2nd edition, p. 74.

(21) Hollander, *op. cit.*, p. 49.

(22) In later years, Lionel built a substantial part of its reputation upon a wide range of signals, buildings, tunnels, and especially a variety of clever operating accessories. In 1910, while such makers as Bing, Marklin, and Ives sold many accessories to accompany their trains, Lionel concentrated mainly on locomotives and rolling stock. At that early date, the operation of electric trains took precedence over scenic items in the North American market.

(23) Lionel numbered these new smaller freight cars by simply placing the extra digit 1 in front of the number for the corresponding larger car. Thus the two sizes of caboose were 17 (large) and 117 (small). The company continued to employ similar logic in numbering its products over the next half century, making it relatively easy for collectors to memorize the numbers of various items. There are exceptions, however. For example, the two-digit No. 19 Pullman and three-digit No. 190 Observation Car were both large cars. Possibly the addition of the zero for the latter might really have been meant to denote the letter "O" for Observation.

(24) The large and small Pullman cars were priced at $4.50 and $3.50 respectively, while the other two types (baggage and observation) were $5.00 for the large models and $4.00 for the small ones.

(25) This strategy would later be used to great advantage by the automobile industry during the Great Depression, where lower priced versions of respected luxury cars would be sold side by side with premium models in the same show rooms.

*An Ives 1134 locomotive and tender from 1930
pulls a set of large passenger coaches on the
author's Standard Gauge layout.*

2

IVES

America's Premier Toy Maker

Just three short years after the close of the American Civil War in 1865, Edward Riley Ives began manufacturing a modest line of steam powered mechanical toys in the small town of Plymouth, Connecticut. Two years later, at the age of thirty-one, Edward moved his business to the growing city of Bridgeport, and, in partnership with Joel Blakeslee, he established the firm of Ives & Company (later Ives & Blakeslee, then Ives, Blakeslee & Co.) and expanded the line to include clockwork mechanical toys. These early products usually took the form of miniature figures which were set in motion by gears and levers, powered by hand-wound spring mechanisms. Common examples included a child on a primitive tricycle, a rocking horse, or a swing. One of the earliest featured a man sitting in a rowboat and gripping a pair of oars, the motion of which could actually propel the boat on the surface of water.[1]

These tin novelties enjoyed considerable popularity, and as the company prospered, Ives developed the line to include a wide variety of vehicles, including horse-drawn wagons and chariots, musical toys, and especially the first of many miniature locomotives. By the mid-1870s, the quality of Ives, Blakeslee & Co. products had earned the company a central position among toy makers, and they soon outsold the competition.[2]

Elaborate and sophisticated clockwork and steam-powered toys were much more widespread in Great Britain, France, and Germany in the latter nineteenth century than they were in North America, and a number of successful European firms exported to the United States. Ives faced substantial competition from these quality imports, but met the challenge in three ways. First, the Bridgeport firm's designs were characteristically American in appearance. This was especially noticeable in the style of their steam locomotives, with typical western cabs instead of the open engineer's platform that was common to British and Continental toy trains of the period. Ives trains looked more familiar to children and their parents. Second in importance was a well-developed wholesale distribution system that ensured a steady supply of products to major retail outlets. And, finally, given that Connecticut was an important center of clock-making activity, Ives had access to much technical expertise and succeeded in maintaining high standards of quality.

The first Ives trains, dating from the early 1870s and fabricated from tin, were floor toys that required no track. They were not the first American clockwork trains, however. The George W. Brown Company, located in nearby Forestville, Connecticut, made wind-up trains as early as 1856,[3] but most railroad toys of the period were unpowered, made from either cast iron or wood. Cast iron proved to be much more durable than tin for children's toys, and in the early 1880s Ives added to its inventory locomotives made from this heavier material.

At about the same time, Eugene Beggs of Patterson, New Jersey, was selling a line of steam-powered trains that operated on a circle of track. These colorful sets, featuring American-style locos and brightly lithographed wood and paper cars, looked authentic and ran well, but they were extremely expensive. At a time when a dollar a day was considered good wages, these trains sold for ten to thirty dollars.[4] In order to increase the opportunity for sales, Beggs also sold his trains to other manufacturers, including Ives, who marketed them under their own brand names. The deal was mutually beneficial; Beggs' toys received greater exposure through Ives' vast distribution system, and the Bridgeport company could offer a premium line of trains without the cost of additional tooling and production.

Throughout the remainder of the nineteenth century, Ives toys prospered in the marketplace. The firm created a wide variety of tin and iron novelties, constantly adding new and clever designs; one locomotive even puffed smoke, courtesy of a lighted cigarette concealed in the stack. So successful was the endeavor that, in 1890, when they reorganized under the name Ives, Blakeslee & Williams Co., capital assets exceeded $100,000.[5] However, the great economic downturn in the middle of the decade crippled the firm, as it did so many others, and the business was forced into receivership in 1897.

Nevertheless, thanks to continued good management practices, prospects improved as the turn of the century neared, and the company appeared headed for recovery. But, just three days before Christmas of 1900, only nine days before the new century was born, the factory and all its assets burned to the ground. With the total loss of its patterns, tooling, and records, the company that Edward Ives founded was gone forever. Although its successor bore the family name, the extensive line of mechanical toys was mostly abandoned, and the products and purpose of the new Ives Manufacturing Company were redirected primarily toward miniature railroads.

A New Direction

After the factory fire, Ives quickly regained its competitive position with attractive O Gauge toy trains like this diminutive set. The locomotive was made in 1903, and the tiny coaches date from about 1905. All are in original condition, except for the tender, which is a reproduction (on original Ives wheels) made by Rulon Taylor (address in the Appendix). Ives cast-iron locomotives were very sturdily made and have survived in greater numbers than the more fragile stamped steel tenders.

Thanks to responsible management policies, the losses sustained in the fire of 1900 were substantially compensated by insurance, and Ives had the opportunity to take a fresh approach to manufacturing toy trains. De-emphasizing their line of trackless floor toys, the firm elected to follow the lead of European manufacturers. New tooling was prepared for a system of diminutive locomotives and cars to run on sectional track, powered by spring-wound motors. The choice of sectional track (pioneered in Germany by Bing and Marklin) ensured that an Ives train could be set up and operated easily by children. The choice of clockwork motors, rather than the new and somewhat primitive electric motors recently introduced by Carlisle & Finch and Lionel (in 1896 and 1901, respectively), demonstrated Edward Ives' philosophy of employing tested technology to ensure quality and dependability.

From the beginning, the new Ives trains were always identified as toys, while the fledgling Lionel Manufacturing

Company was still struggling to find an identity for its products.[6] Edward Ives accurately identified his principal competition as coming from the German toy makers, especially Marklin and Bing, whose products were, by that time, widely distributed throughout the United States. He wisely chose to produce trains that were similar to the European products, and therefore familiar to consumers. The choice of O Gauge, rather than the more expensive large sizes, predicted a greater volume of sales for Ives, at a time when the lower cost of German labor maintained attractive price levels for imported toys.[7]

Until 1907, when William Coleman and William Hafner established the American Flyer line of clockwork trains, Ives was the principal American manufacturer of toy railroad systems, offering the only significant alternative to the German products. The newly emergent Lionel company appeared headed in an entirely different direction, with its much larger and more expensive 2-7/8" Gauge trains that were powered by electricity. The new Ives trains were attractive and well made, and profits grew during the first decade of the century, but so did those of the European importers, as American families bought these ingenious toys in record numbers. In addition, new domestic firms were beginning to make inroads into the market, with Voltamp (1903), Howard (1904), and Knapp (1905) following Lionel's lead and choosing electric power for larger (No. 2 Gauge) trains.[8]

These new companies chose, like Lionel, to produce trains for the upper end of the market, a segment not covered by the Ives line. The Bridgeport firm was quick to recognize the threat these new products would create, and moved into the higher price range with a line of substantial and attractive No. 1 Gauge trains in 1904. These big toys were beautifully designed and priced to be competitive, but the conservative management of the company made one significant error in failing to recognize the growing importance of electric power for mechanical toys. They chose to continue with clockwork mechanisms alone, a decision that would ultimately lessen their competitive position significantly. Despite the relatively small market for electric toys when compared with those powered by clockwork, Lionel was probably seen by consumers as more innovative than Ives.

It is understandable that, given the excellent reputation and effective distribution system of the Ives company, the No.

1 Gauge trains were successful, albeit modestly. Nevertheless, the firm might have achieved total dominance among the larger gauges, possibly defeating the less well-funded companies (Carlisle & Finch, Howard, Knapp, and Voltamp), and even the aggressive but infant Lionel, had they moved to electric power. It is undeniable that the firms producing electric trains (especially Lionel) fueled this interest with their clever advertising. Buyers were quick to see the possibilities.

Despite the extra cost of dry cell batteries and the dangers inherent in the wet cell alternatives, electricity promised much greater and more realistic control of the toys. A clockwork motor ran at one constant speed for a relatively brief period, only to slow and stop as its spring wound down. An electric motor could be started and stopped many times by the operator, just by interrupting the current, and could keep running much longer than a spring-powered model. And it wasn't long before other benefits became apparent, such as having an electric headlight. Active imaginations were already conceiving other wonders.

In Ives' favor, however, was the exceptional quality and realism of the new No. 1 Gauge offerings. The first locomotive, a graceful steam-outline 4-4-0, was accurately proportioned and made from rugged cast iron. It was painted black, with red and yellow trim, and had bright metal boiler bands and bell. All of the prominent features of a real locomotive were captured, from the tall smokestack and steam domes to the working valve gear. By contrast, Lionel's earliest Standard Gauge steam-type locomotives seem like chunky and toy-like caricatures.

Similar care was taken to make the passenger cars seem authentic, with colorful lithography[9] that simulated wood-grained bodies, liberally decorated with authentic-looking names such as "Twentieth Century Limited Express" and "New York and Chicago" on their letter boards. The freight cars were well detailed with brake wheels, truss rods, and steps, and they carried real railroad heralds such as Santa Fe and the familiar Pennsylvania Railroad keystone. Although somewhat foreshortened to allow their use on the sharp curves of toy train track, these cars nevertheless convey a strong impression of reality.

At the time of Lionel's conversion to the new Standard Gauge in 1906, the Ives line was by far the most complete miniature railroad system being produced in North America. Following the European example, the inventory contained stations, signals, bridges, and tunnels that allowed a child to create the atmosphere of a real railroad. Covering all price categories, from the simplest tiny O Gauge sets to the most elaborate large-size toys, Ives seemed positioned to dominate the market for many years. But two factors mitigated against this.

The first was, of course, management's stubborn refusal to consider using electric power. (Edward Ives distrusted most forms of modern technology, and even avoided the automobile. He continued to travel by horse and buggy until his death in 1918.)[10] The first Ives locomotives with electric motors did not appear in their O Gauge line until 1910, by which time Lionel's Standard Gauge had gained a substantial following among technologically sophisticated toy buyers. Even slower to be updated was the No. 1 Gauge line. In 1912 Ives finally marketed an excellent model of a New York Central S-class electric locomotive, richly detailed and well proportioned in cast iron. However, by that time Lionel had already attracted considerable attention with its three sizes of electric-outline engines, all made of sheet metal and somewhat less realistic, but with a firm foothold in the marketplace.

At about the same time, the German firm, Bing, sought to improve its already substantial share of the American market by producing its own versions of the same New York Central S-class locomotives in both O and No. 1 gauges. They resembled the Ives models so closely (even carrying identical numbers) that some collectors still have trouble telling them apart. As a result, Ives and Bing were vying for the No. 1 Gauge portion of sales, and competing 2" Gauge trains were made by the smaller Knapp, Howard, Voltamp, and Carlisle & Finch lines, while Lionel had the 2-1/8" Standard Gauge market segment all to itself.

Ives did not produce an electric-powered No. 1 Gauge steam outline locomotive until 1915, fully nine years after Lionel's No. 5 and No. 6 appeared on the scene. In addition, the company seemed content to continue selling their large scale trains virtually unchanged from year to year, at a time when the aggressive Lionel management was introducing new and updated products annually. By the time the Bridgeport firm finally recognized the power of Joshua Cowen's competitive position, a majority of the nation's large-sized toy trains were riding not on No. 1 Gauge track, but on Lionel's audaciously named Standard Gauge.

Throughout the years leading up to World War I, Lionel continued to expand its offerings. To invade the low-price field where Ives and American Flyer had proven successful, Cowen introduced his own O Gauge designs in 1915. The company could now attract buyers at virtually all income levels, with the O Gauge trains being the most economical,[11] the largest Standard Gauge models appealing to the wealthy, and the smaller Standard Gauge line bridging the gap between.

With his keen sense of public taste, Cowen also kept his products current. As America drew closer to involvement in the war in Europe, Lionel designed a special armored locomotive, with olive-drab paint and turret-mounted guns. "PLAY WAR!" Lionel's 1917 catalog shouted. "Bring Up Siege Guns On Tracks! Another Triumph In Motor Car Construction." Joshua Cowen, in tune with real-life events, made his company's products seem the most modern and responsive to the times.

Lionel catalogs from these years also contain a series of assaults on the competition, most especially Ives. Large, substantial and pristine Lionel car bodies are compared in photographs to bent and battered Ives products, always the smallest and cheapest examples. Lithography is belittled as inferior to Lionel's enameled finish, despite the obvious realism of the fine detailing possible only with lithographed car bodies. And Lionel's production methods and machinery are touted as being the finest and most modern.

The most blatant and fundamentally unfair comparisons show two locomotives being dropped from a table. The sheet metal Lionel loco appears undamaged, although the caption states "The Lionel is only dented," while the cast-iron Ives equivalent is shown broken into fifteen pieces. It is unlikely that customers would ever duplicate this test with their toys to determine whether Lionel's claim of greater durability was valid. But the message was indeed powerful, and many people undoubtedly accepted it at face value. Two other photos show the locomotives and their motors on scales, with the Lionel product apparently having a heavier motor and a lighter overall weight. The inference is that these features are superior, but just exactly why this should be so is not explained.[12]

There was some truth to Lionel's claims, however. Each of their car bodies was made from a single steel stamping comprising sides, ends, and floor, then folded into a box shape and soldered together; this was a very sturdy design. Beginning in 1924, patented steel window frame inserts further strengthened the car sides. Lionel motors were indeed well made and reliable (but so were those made by Ives), and even if the enameled finish on a Lionel Pullman was somewhat less attractive and lacking the authentic representation of detail provided by lithography, it did withstand rough handling with less surface damage. Such was the brilliance of Lionel's advertising that a deficiency—the absence of fine detail that lithography provided—could be made to seem like an asset.

Lionel also maintained a competitive edge through its manufacturing methods. Lionel freight cars had fewer parts than comparable Ives models, and time-consuming hand work was further reduced by painting the parts in subassemblies before putting them together. All major components were carried on conveyors, dipped in vats of paint, then dried in ovens by an economical assembly-line process. Later, in the 1920s, the company's engineers further reduced assembly time by replacing soldered joints with mechanical attachments (screws, rivets, and metal tabs) to assemble the cars and locomotives.

At a time when Lionel's modern steel-stamping techniques were reducing the number of solder joints on each car, the more conservative Ives firm was slower to adopt new procedures. Each Ives car required a great number of solder joints for assembling the numerous body parts, a labor-intensive method that severely limited the number of toys a worker could produce in a given amount of time. Even after switching from lithography to enameled car bodies, Ives continued to paint its window frames and other decorative details by hand. (Lionel added a minimum of hand-painted details.) The results were attractive, but the cost in worker hours was very high. In order to keep its prices competitive with those of Lionel, Ives had to settle for a lower profit margin (and even a loss on some items), thus limiting the amount of money available for the development of new products.

The advent of World War I affected the North American toy train industry by creating an antipathy toward German-made products, and the sale of Bing and Marklin toys

The many soldered joints and hand-painted details, such as the rainbow-colored transoms on this restored 189-1 Observation Car, contributed to a poor profit margin for Ives through excess production time.

declined dramatically. Major retailers such as Sears & Roebuck discontinued their German trains in favor of American made products, and while Bing continued to export to the United States in greatly reduced numbers, Marklin abandoned the North American market completely.[13] Being denied the foreign toys, or eschewing them for political reasons, the public had only two major manufacturers to choose between, and they increasingly chose Lionel's Standard Gauge over Ives' No. 1 Gauge.

Lionel's magnificent color 1920 catalog promised a wonderland of toy train fun. The finely drawn illustrations depicted the trains to good advantage, and for the first time, accessories received almost equal attention. Two full pages were devoted to a new steel station and a selection of bridges in both O and Standard gauges. Two other pages illustrated a variety of semaphores, lampposts, and traffic signs, some electrically lighted and all colorfully decorated. Tunnels in three sizes filled another page, and "A Complete Miniature Railroad All Your Own" was advertised at a package price, including a locomotive, freight and passengers cars, a station, lampposts, signals, track, and switches.

Ives Capitulates

Sales of No. 1 Gauge trains had been declining steadily for over a decade, as the near withdrawal of the German products and Ives' late adoption of electric power served to strengthen Lionel's grip on the market. By 1920, the Bridgeport management realized that the vast majority of large scale toy trains in America were riding on Lionel's 2-1/8" Standard Gauge track. In an attempt to make its products more attractive to buyers who already owned Lionel trains, Ives converted the wheels and trucks on its No. 1 Gauge cars and locomotives from No. 1 Gauge to 2-1/8", allowing them to operate on Lionel track.

This was a much riskier move than Lionel's conversion from 2-7/8" to 2-1/8" Gauge in 1906. In changing the track measurement, Ives was abandoning all those customers who had purchased their No. 1 Gauge products since 1904. No longer could Ives owners add new cars and locos to their

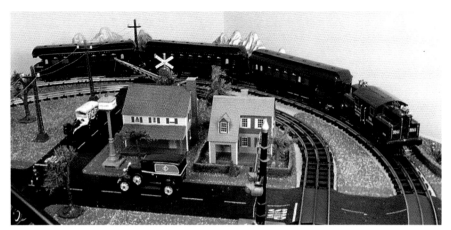

Ives' newest locomotives, such as this restored 3241 New York Central design (pulling a 187-1 Buffet Car, a 188-1 Pullman and a 189-1 Observation Car from 1922), were made with stamped steel bodies on cast-iron frames. Their No. 1 Gauge predecessors were entirely fashioned from cast iron.

virtually the same as the No. 1 Gauge designs, having received only new trucks and catalog numbers. The last of the beautiful early lithographed coaches vanished from the line. The largest passenger cars, Nos. 181, 182, and 183, had been painted rather than lithographed since their inception in 1912, and with the advent of the Standard Gauge trains, Ives dropped lithography altogether for its large sized models, although the process would be continued in the O Gauge line.

Despite the new locomotive designs, the 2-1/8" Gauge products were too little changed to attract the amount of attention from the public that Ives needed to guarantee an instant high volume of sales. There must also have been some confusion among consumers, since the new line was not advertised as "Standard" gauge. Lionel had created that term as it applied to toy trains, and used it proudly. Being reluctant to adopt their competitor's nomenclature (and probably unable to do so for legal reasons), Ives called their product "Wide" gauge to differentiate it from the O Gauge line with its narrower track. This was an ambiguous term that did not necessarily promise the desired operational compatibility with Lionel track.

In spite of these problems, sales of the Wide[14] (Standard) Gauge line improved over the No. 1 Gauge line, and for a time it seemed as if the conversion would prove successful. As the decade progressed, Ives introduced new, attractive, and very realistic locomotives, and demonstrated its technological expertise by introducing the industry's first reliable remote control reverse unit. No. 1 Gauge continued

layouts, and their loyalty to the product was now compromised. Ives was gambling that they could produce toys attractive enough to compete with Lionel on the Standard Gauge battleground, and thus gain a new customer base. Had the company followed through by introducing a complete line of modern and attractive trains, the gamble might have paid off. Without adequate financial resources to accomplish this, however, they had to settle for a face lift.

First, mechanical components were altered to accommodate the wider track. Ives engineers widened the wheel and axle sets, and redesigned the motors and car trucks. New models of the New York Central S2-type electric locomotive were introduced in economy, mid-priced, and deluxe versions under the catalog numbers 3241, 3242, and 3243. The sharp-edged bodies of these engines closely approximated the prototype. A Standard Gauge steam locomotive (No. 1132) also appeared, but it was very little changed from the earlier No. 1 Gauge design.

Unlike their cast-iron No. 1 Gauge predecessors, the electric-outline locos were fashioned from sheet metal like the Lionel designs (although the use of cast iron was continued for their frames through 1926, when steel frames replaced them). Lionel's advertising, in which cast iron was depicted as fragile and unnecessarily heavy, was apparently sufficiently forceful to make sheet metal construction appear to be superior, and Ives must have concluded that they could not fight this trend in public opinion.

Changes to the passenger and freight cars were minor, and not necessarily improvements. The freight designs were

Ives' 1921 and later Standard Gauge freight cars were little changed from the earlier No. 1 Gauge designs. They appear smaller and more primitive than competing products. Left to right: Ives 193 Stock Car, Lionel 213 Stock Car, American Flyer 4020 Stock Car, all restored.

to lose market share, as Bing, the only foreign player of any significance in the American market at that time, also converted its products to be compatible with Lionel.

For a brief period, Ives seemed to be regaining some of the ground lost during Lionel's dramatic growth and expansion during the previous decade, but Joshua Cowen's company was not standing still. During 1921 and 1922, his designers and engineers were hard at work on the first models for what would later be called Lionel's "Classic" period. When the 1923 catalog appeared, readers discovered two new locomotives and a set of large passenger cars that can only be called magnificent. Once again Ives was caught asleep at the switch, but the Bridgeport firm soon rallied, creating new designs of its own. To complicate matters even further, William Coleman's American Flyer introduced a new and attractive Wide Gauge line of its own, compatible with Ives and Lionel track and offering buyers yet another alternative. A year later an upstart New Jersey company which called itself "Dorfan" also joined their ranks.

The stage was set for a half decade of intense competition, at a time when world economic growth and prosperity was reaching previously unheard of levels. Incomes rose, business and industry flourished, and a vital economic engine—the stock market—tempted investors to ride the crest of a wave of easy riches. Toy trains became bigger, more powerful, more complex, and much more expensive, but the newly-affluent public bought them in ever-increasing quantities. And, as before, Lionel led the way.

Like Ives, German importer Bing converted its No. 1 Gauge line to Standard Gauge by altering the width of the trucks and wheel sets. Coaches like this Bing Pennsylvania Lines combine were a good match for small locomotives like Lionel's No. 5 shown here, but were quite undersized when compared with the largest Lionel and American Flyer locomotives.

chapter 2 # Notes chapter 2

(1) Louis H. Hertz, *Messrs. Ives of Bridgeport*, pp. 17-21.

(2) *Ibid.*, p. 26.

(3) Pierce Carlson, *Toy Trains, A History*, p. 16.

(4) *Ibid.*, p. 19.

(5) Hertz, *op. cit.*, p. 63.

(6) Lionel's earliest 2-7/8" Gauge trains were initially promoted primarily as commercial display devices.

(7) Bruce C. Greenberg, *Greenberg's Guide To Ives Trains*, Vol.I, p. 8.

(8) Carlson, *op. cit.*, pp. 46-47.

(9) The lithographic process involves printing on steel with ink-sensitive stone plates, and the results are characterized by very fine detail. It was a relatively inexpensive way to produce multicolored graphics and lettering.

(10) Hertz, *op. cit.*, p. 104.

(11) In later years, Cowen also divided the O Gauge line into two distinct price categories, giving the public even more options in the low price range.

(12) 1917 Lionel catalog, p. 10

(13) Carlson, *op. cit.*, p. 91.

(14) Despite Lionel's proprietary use of the term "Standard" as it related to its 2-1/8" Gauge trains, the word is used throughout this book to describe the trains of other manufacturers that ride on the same width of track. Other companies (Ives, American Flyer, and Dorfan) all used the term "Wide" Gauge. In the 1920s, only Boucher copied Lionel's word "Standard," apparently without consequence.

The author's restored 408E locomotive and 419 Combine dwarf the 126 Station as they round the end of a modest-sized layout. A photo of this locomotive before restoration appears in Chapter 10.

3

STANDARD GAUGE TAKES OVER

Joshua Lionel Cowen was the eighth of nine children born to Hyman and Rebecca Cohen, on August 25, 1877.[1] He grew up in Manhattan in a prosperous and intellectual atmosphere; although they were not considered truly wealthy, the Cohens were reasonably well-off, as Hyman succeeded in several business ventures.[2] The young Cowen appears to have been intelligent, creative, and possessed of a strong work ethic. By his early twenties, he had already patented several inventions, started his own company, and was well on the way to achieving personal economic security. Confident of his potential for success, he married the former Cecelia Liberman in 1904, and the couple had two children, Lawrence and Isabel.

Cowen possessed several talents which served him well in the early years of his New York company, most notably his mechanical aptitude and a gift for seeing the possibilities inherent in the new technologies that seemed to be multiplying as the twentieth century was born. He had a similar instinct for assessing public taste and for conceiving products that would appeal to the imaginations of children and their parents alike. And, he had a talent for creating erudite, convincing promotional prose in his catalogs. Although his claims and promises were more in the style of P. T. Barnum than Honest Abe Lincoln, the style and wording of his advertisements nevertheless were apparently perceived as truthful by his customers.

If his trains were not, in the early years, as superior to the competition as the catalogs declared, they were nevertheless of very good quality, and Cowen possessed those traits of the perfectionist that drove him to institute improvements on a regular and continuing basis. By 1910, the Lionel Manufacturing Company was well established, and its founder was earning nearly $57,000 annually.[3] Throughout the years preceding the outbreak of war in Europe in 1914, the firm enjoyed modest growth and secured a substantial share of the toy train market.

Cowen's principal competition came from the highly regarded Bridgeport, Connecticut, company headed by Edward Ives, and the German imports from Bing, Marklin, and Karl Bub of Nuremburg. The quality of the imported toys was very high, and their prices were very competitive. They enjoyed an excellent reputation, bolstered by support from such national retailers as Sears & Roebuck, which gave them prominent space in their catalogs. The First World War radically altered the competitive balance between these companies, however. The flow of German imports decreased dramatically, even though the United States did not become involved in the conflict for several years.

Lionel products from just before the First World War were well received by the public, and attracted many buyers. These common pieces (custom restored in a rare dark blue color scheme sold only by Montgomery Ward) are readily available to collectors, although rarely in excellent condition.

As home electrification became increasingly widespread, reliable low-voltage transformers became the most economical method of operating toy trains. Light bulb sockets preceded wall plugs, and early electrical devices came equipped with lamp-socket plugs as shown, instead of the more familiar two- or three-prong plugs in use today.

With their choices now limited to domestic products, toy train buyers in most parts of the country had only Ives and Lionel to choose from in the larger gauges. The 2" Gauge manufacturers were not widely distributed, and American Flyer was making only O Gauge at the time. Throughout the war years, sales of the larger Lionel products increased steadily at the expense of the Ives line, and by the end of the war, Lionel had emerged as the undisputed leader in the field.

By 1912, Cowen had established a diversified and desirable range of Standard Gauge products, and spent the next decade refining and perfecting the large trains. There were relatively few changes in the Standard Gauge line until 1923. The bulk of his company's engineering effort was directed toward the introduction of O Gauge trains in 1915, allowing Lionel to compete in every price category. Concurrently, Lionel's catalog instituted an all-out assault on the other train makers, most especially Ives. Six pages were devoted to what Cowen called "A Little Trip Through My Factory," and two additional pages presented detailed descriptions of his locomotive mechanism.

Throughout this presentation were glowing claims and photographs that presented Lionel trains as virtually indestructible, such as a picture of two men standing on a piece of track. In another pair of photos, a Lionel track section is shown with a 110-pound weight hanging from it without causing damage, while a 20-pound weight is shown breaking a rail from a competitor's track. The copy is further interspersed with unflattering shots of a badly dented, cheap tin passenger car, presumably an Ives product, and a broken

cast-iron locomotive, also apparently Ives. Lionel aggressively touted the superiority of sheet steel construction.

While Lionel Trains were certainly well made, the comparisons presented in the catalog were grossly unfair, with a large section of Standard Gauge track tested against what appears to be a much lighter piece of Ives O Gauge track. In general, the best that Lionel had to offer was compared to the cheapest offerings of the competition. The attack was inflated in the 1917 catalog, with a full ten pages devoted to the factory "tour." The derogatory photographic comparisons were now accompanied by an expanded series of shots showing nearly every step of Lionel's train-making process, in a modern factory turning out great numbers of toys.

The number of new products created during the war years and immediately thereafter was relatively small, although the O Gauge military set[4] reflected current world events (such as the Great War), and the previously neglected accessory category received some much-needed attention with the addition of new stations, bridges, and signals. With the continuing spread of electrification beyond city homes to rural areas, Lionel promoted its transformers heavily, and the public seemed by this time to accept the relative safety of electricity for powering toys. The first automatic accessory, the No. 69 Warning Bell, was introduced in 1921. It consisted of a simple lattice-work post with a diamond-shaped warning sign at the top, and an electric bell mounted on the back. When the train passed by, it completed an electric circuit through a special section of track, making the bell ring.

In general, these years provided Lionel with the opportunity to consolidate its position of leadership. Ives' market share declined precipitously, and Cowen dropped his aggressive advertising campaign beginning with the 1918 catalog. By 1921, the catalogs simply proclaimed "Lionel Trains Are Superior . . . They are guaranteed forever against defects in material or manufacture." Using the latest in printing tech-

niques, Cowen published catalogs featuring exquisite, highly detailed artwork in beautiful color. While the design of the toys was little changed from a decade earlier, subtle improvements, such as the addition of a second motor to the largest box cab locomotive (No. 42), made the line seem fresh.

Lionel Meets the Ives Challenge

The first locomotives of Lionel's classic period, the 380 St. Paul-type and the twin-motored New York Central-style 402, appeared in the 1923 catalog.

When Ives conceded the defeat of its No. 1 Gauge line and converted it to run on track compatible with Lionel's Standard Gauge, Cowen wasted little time in taking steps to insure against a resurgence of the Bridgeport firm. In 1923, he resurrected the unfair photographic comparisons of Lionel and Ives products which had been missing from the catalogs since 1917. The cover of the catalog presents an unmistakable quality-of-life image, portraying, in full color, a father and son engaged with their extensive Standard Gauge railroad.[5] But

most important, depicted inside the catalog was the first in an entirely new line of Standard Gauge electric-outline locomotives, powered by a new "Super-Motor," and much more colorful and more modern in appearance than its forerunners.

Interestingly, while the new models were beautiful and very sturdy, they were somewhat less realistic than the trains they would soon replace.[6] The older products carried authentic names and heralds, representing such railroads as the New York Central and the Pennsylvania, which had been

Many Ives freight cars, like this O Gauge Canadian Pacific box-car, carried authentic railroad heralds on their beautifully lithographed sides. This level of authenticity proved to be inconsequential in the marketplace, however. The public bought many more of the colorful enameled cars with brass plates.

rubber stamped on the enameled sides. The two new box cabs, a St. Paul style (No. 380) and a twin-motored New York Central design (No. 402), bore no such realistic designations. Instead, the name "LIONEL" and the model number were embossed on large brass plates that were part of a sheet forming the windows and door frames; these plates were visible through cut-out areas of the steel bodies.

Like the Ives 3241, 3242, and 3243 models, Lionel's earlier interpretations of the New York Central S-2 design (e.g., No. 1912) were rectangular and crisp in outline. The new No. 402 was patterned after the same prototype, but its softly rounded edges did not capture the flavor of the original.

This new method of lettering the trains announced the birth of the best-known railroad nameplate in the world, bigger than the Baltimore & Ohio, Pennsylvania, Southern Pacific, or even the mighty Santa Fe. Within a few decades, more trains would run under the banner "Lionel Lines" than all other railroads combined. While Ives continued to produce carefully detailed representations of authentic road names, Lionel established its own unique identity, creating in the eye of the public a new image for its toy trains. And, as in the matter of track gauge, Lionel would win this battle, too. When American Flyer unveiled its own line of Wide (Standard) Gauge trains in 1925, they too carried brass plates instead of railroad heralds, and Ives also soon replaced stamped lettering with brass plates for its entire Standard Gauge locomotive line.

The appeal of this new design concept was apparently aes-

thetic, for manufacturers soon discovered that brightly painted trains with a lot of shiny trim far outsold the somewhat drab but much more realistic earlier designs. Although true railroad enthusiasts would no doubt find these caricatures less than satisfying, the toy-buying public is normally less concerned with authenticity than with attractive appearance. And, the new Lionel locomotives were undeniably alluring, especially when shown with the new line of substantial passenger coaches as displayed across two full pages of the 1923 catalog.

Although the remainder of the Lionel line is portrayed in fine detail and full color, it suffers by comparison with the illustrations of the new products. The freight cars, especially, are shown to disadvantage, appearing foreshortened and toy-like, and lacking the appearance of quality that the large passenger cars convey. Although the older designs would not be completely phased out until 1927, the Lionel Corporation's[7] marketing strategy was clearly focused upon innovation, as almost the entire range of toys in both Standard and O gauges was replaced over the succeeding four years.

Ives and American Flyer were often forced to follow Lionel's lead in order to remain competitive. These locomotives (American Flyer 4644, left, and Ives 3236) have brass identification plates instead of the more realistic stamped lettering used by Ives up until the mid-1920s.

This Lionel 380 St. Paul-type electric locomotive first appeared in 1923 as part of a revised line of more substantial and modern looking trains that collectors call "classic."

Scale was apparently of little importance to the designers at Lionel. Most of the stations made prior to the Second World War, such as this No. 124 (center), were appropriately sized for Standard Gauge trains, but were also sold for use with O Gauge. At left is a kit-built prewar house marketed by the Skyline company, built to match O Gauge trains at 1:48 proportions; compare its windows and door with those on the station. The tiny Lionel bungalow (right foreground) is scaled at about half O Gauge size, but was sold to accompany Standard Gauge trains.

items that looked reasonably good with Standard Gauge trains (although they were actually too large even for these big trains), but when the O Gauge line was introduced, the same accessories were sold to go with this smaller size. Although the semaphores and lampposts towered far above the trains (and the imaginary engineers and passengers they supposedly carried), children didn't seem to mind, and these items were sold in great numbers for both gauges.

The same is true of the houses. In fact, their lilliputian dimensions probably served to increase sales, since a house built to Standard Gauge proportions would have occupied much more valuable layout space, at a far higher cost. Quite a few bungalows and villas could fit in a small area, and Lionelville real estate boomed. The company sold tens of thousands of them, both alone and mounted on fully landscaped scenic plots, with hedges, sidewalks, trees, lawns, and bushes already in place.

Other accessories broadened Lionel's appeal and advanced the concept of building a railroad, rather than just running toy trains. Two colored bulbs in a block signal (No. 76) announced the presence (red) or absence

Page 37 of the 1923 catalog announced the first of a very curious range of accessories, the first dwelling places for the tiny inhabitants of Lionelville. Three types were offered: a diminutive "bungalow" (No. 184), a mid-sized "villa" (No. 189) and a comparatively large "villa" (No. 191, today sometimes referred to as a "mansion" to differentiate it from No. 189). All were lighted by an interior bulb, although an unlighted version of the small bungalow was offered as No. 185. These houses came in a variety of lithographed and enameled color schemes, and featured such details as porches, "brick" chimneys, dormers, deck railings, and even lithographed trees, shrubs, and vines.

The main discrepancy, and it was a large one, was the size of these beautiful homes. They were sold without reference to the gauge of train they were meant to accompany, and in fact it is probable that just as many were bought for use with Standard Gauge trains as for O Gauge, but they were far too small for either, being approximately half the size of a properly proportioned O Gauge house.

This cavalier attitude toward scale was typical of most toy train manufacturers, however. The earliest Lionel accessories were signals and lampposts, large and substantial

These Lionel Villas, mounted on reproductions of vintage Lionel Scenic Plots, are only a quarter the size of scale dwellings in Standard Gauge. However, by grouping them as shown and using them in background scenes, they are surprisingly effective. Their small size creates the illusion of greater distance between them and the trains in the foreground. This illusion adds depth to even small layouts, although it takes a big room to accommodate a layout like the one shown here, at Richard and Linda Kughn's Carail Museum in Detroit.

Lionel's 1924 catalog cover. The boy-and-his-dog theme appeared on Lionel's catalog covers for three consecutive years in this decade.

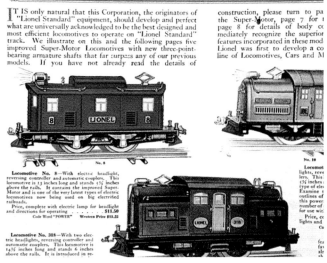

IT IS only natural that this Corporation, the originators of "Lionel Standard" equipment, should develop and perfect what are universally acknowledged to be the best designed and most efficient locomotives to operate on "Lionel Standard" track. We illustrate on this and the following pages five improved Super-Motor Locomotives with new three-point-bearing armature shafts that far surpass any of our previous models. If you have not already read the details of

construction, please turn to pa the Super-Motor, page 7 for 1 page 8 for details of body c mediately recognize the superior features incorporated in these mod Lionel was first to develop a co line of Locomotives, Cars and M

Locomotive No. 8—With electric headlight, reversing controller and automatic couplers. This locomotive is 13 inches long and stands 5½ inches above the rails. It contains the improved Super-Motor and is one of the very latest types of electric locomotives now being used on big electrified railroads.

Price, complete with electric lamp for headlight and directions for operating **$11.50**

Code Word "POWER"   Western Price $12.25

Locomotive No. 318—With two electric headlights, reversing controller and automatic couplers. This locomotive is 14½ inches long and stands 6 inches above the rails. It is introduced in re-

The first illustration of Lionel's new No. 8 box cab locomotive appeared in the 1925 catalog. It closely resembled the O Gauge 256 design, but it was never made this way.

(green) of a train on a specific length of track, thus supposedly serving as a warning to following trains. Lionel also introduced its first automatic crossing gate (no. 77).

The cover of the 1924 catalog was a masterpiece of design and advertising skill. On a huge array of Lionel track, reaching beyond sight to the far reaches of the room, speeding Lionel locomotives haul colorful passenger and freight cars, cheered on by two happy boys, one with his hand prominently placed on the throttle. At left, a terrified puppy (seemingly almost dwarfed by the trains), races to escape the huge eight-wheeled locomotive racing down the track. The scene is irresistible in its appeal.

Inside, there is a subtle change in the copy. While the first few pages extol all the reasons "Why Lionel Trains Are Supreme," the attacks on the competition are missing. By this time, Cowen apparently felt satisfied to let his products speak for themselves, and indeed, they had a lot to say. Three new locomotives appeared in the O Gauge line, along with an attractive set of passenger cars so huge as to be mistaken for Standard Gauge. However, the 2-1/8" Gauge trains received the major share of attention. Gone are the largest, but primitive, locomotives from the previous decade, and the only remnants of the earlier series of motive power are the lowest priced Nos. 33, 38, and 50. For the first time, there are no steam locomotives featured, only electric-outline designs of the type used on urban-centered railroads.[8]

Joining the Nos. 380 and 402 locomotives introduced the previous year, No. 318 was a mid-priced locomotive patterned

after a New York Central concept. Its body resembled that of the 402, but instead of the two motors and eight wheels found on its larger brother, the No. 318 had a single motor and four wheels. This new engine was offered in only one train set, accompanied by three new passenger cars in a complementary size (two No. 319 Pullman cars and a No. 322 Observation). The No. 380 was sold in sets with the older style freight and passenger cars, while the magnificent new large coaches (Nos. 418, 419, and 490) were reserved for use with the big No. 402. (Interestingly, the No. 402 is also shown in a small illustration with a set of seven old-style freight cars, and it looks decidedly out of place in such company.)

On the accessory pages, a new wonder was announced, the No. 78 Train Control Signal. Although it looked more like a traffic stoplight than a railroad block signal, its ingenious mechanism guaranteed its success. The signal could be wired between the power source (batteries or transformer) and an insulated length of track, and when the train entered that track, it would stop. A heat-sensitive circuit inside the signal then gradually closed a set of contacts, and after fifteen or twenty seconds, the train would start again. At the same time, the signal light changed from red (stop) to green (go). The signal mechanism then cooled and reset itself, so that the next time the train came around, it would repeat the stop-and-go sequence. This same device would later be adapted for use inside several different stations, causing a train to stop in a logical place to discharge and accept imaginary passengers, then start on its way again automatically.

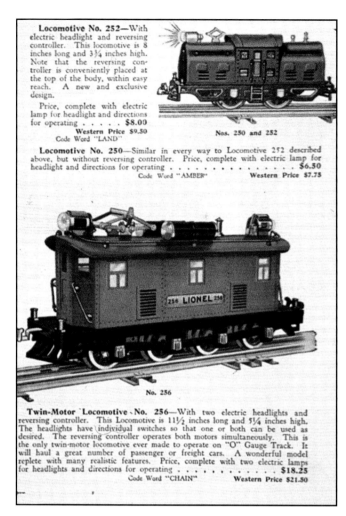

Locomotive No. 252—With electric headlight and reversing controller. This locomotive is 8 inches long and 3¾ inches high. Note that the reversing controller is conveniently placed at the top of the body, within easy reach. A new and exclusive design.

Price, complete with electric lamp for headlight and directions for operating **$8.00**
Western Price $9.50
Code Word "LAND"

Nos. 250 and 252

Locomotive No. 250—Similar in every way to Locomotive 252 described above, but without reversing controller. Price, complete with electric lamp for headlight and directions for operating **$6.50**
Code Word "AMBER"
Western Price $7.75

No. 256

Twin-Motor Locomotive No. 256—With two electric headlights and reversing controller. This Locomotive is 11½ inches long and 5¼ inches high. The headlights have individual switches so that one or both can be used as desired. The reversing controller operates both motors simultaneously. This is the only twin-motor locomotive ever made to operate on "O" Gauge Track. It will haul a great number of passenger or freight cars. A wonderful model replete with many realistic features. Price, complete with two electric lamps for headlights and directions for operating **$18.25**
Code Word "CHAIN"
Western Price $21.50

It is likely that the 1925 catalog illustrators borrowed the basic outlines of the O Gauge 256 locomotive when drawing the new No. 8 for the Standard Gauge line. Perhaps they did so out of ignorance, but it is also possible that Lionel planned to adapt the O Gauge body for a small Standard Gauge loco as an economy measure.

Operating accessories became an increasingly important part of Lionel's sales strategy over the next several decades. These signals, crossing gates, and later the marvelous mechanisms that loaded freight and set tiny figures in motion, greatly broadened the play value of toy trains. While electric trains had long been viewed as a staple of the Christmas holidays, the company's management realized the importance of promoting their products as year-round toys, in order to keep sales active during the other months of the year. Operating accessories were a primary means of maintaining this year-round interest, and in 1924 Lionel furthered the concept by packaging the first of its Scenic Railroads. Offered in both Standard and O Gauge, the Scenic Railroad package included everything a buyer needed to set up a complete, permanent railroad: trains, track, stations, houses, signals, landscaping, and a

Lionel 8E locomotive. (Carail Museum Collection)

background simulating the sky and mountains, plus a painted platform with the wiring already installed.

The cover of the 1925 catalog conveyed the same theme as the previous year's, this time with just one boy and his somewhat apprehensive dog, but also showing an inset of the same boy and dog in a full-sized locomotive cab, surely the stuff of a child's dreams.[9] After the usual hyperbole, and the introduction of a new O Gauge locomotive, the Standard Gauge pages revealed no trace of the earlier engine designs. In addition to the higher priced models from the previous two years, two new locomotives appeared, under catalog numbers 8 and 10.

The design of No. 8 deserves special attention. In the catalog it closely resembles the largest locomotive in the O Gauge line, the No. 256. This O Gauge box cab is loosely modeled after a style used on the New Haven railroad, which was later adopted by American Flyer for its lowest-priced Standard Gauge engine. It was pictured with a rounded roof that overhung each end, three windows per side, and simulated ventilators in the same locations as on the O Gauge No. 256. In fact, all No. 8 locos were built to more closely resemble a New York Central design, with a flatter roof that had no overhang. It looks much more like the second largest O Gauge Lionel engine of the same period, the No. 251.

Although no records survive to confirm it, it is likely that at the time the catalog was printed, Lionel engineers had not yet settled on the exact design of the No. 8. In order to have their promotional material ready for distribution well before the Christmas season, Lionel often printed its catalogs months before production actually began on new items.[10] Apparently both the New Haven and New York Central concepts were being considered, and lacking firm direction from management, the catalog designers opted to illustrate the former. This error was corrected in the 1926 catalog.

There is another distinct possibility regarding the design of No. 8, however, as suggested by the descriptions contained in the 1925 catalog. On page 17, the new No. 8 is specified as being 13" long and standing 5-1/4" above the rails. It is shown with a typical Standard Gauge frame and four large wheels centered under the cab. The body, however, appears virtually identical to the O Gauge No. 256 on page 11. Only small particulars differ, such as roof and handrail trim. The frame on the O Gauge No. 256 accommodates the eight-wheeled, two-motored drive system. The dimensions given are very similar to those of No. 8: 13-1/2" long and 5-1/2" above the rails.[11]

These similarities strongly suggest that the company was planning to save tooling costs by adapting the oversized O Gauge No. 256 body for use as the small Standard Gauge No. 8. The slight difference in

Lionel's low-priced St. Paul locomotive (No. 10) was sold in great numbers, mostly in sets of freight cars or with these similarly sized passenger coaches (Nos. 332, 339 and 342). The two-tone brown color scheme was used only on sets sold through some department stores, and not by regular Lionel dealers.

Lionel's early primitive freight cars remained available through 1926, three years after the first of the more modern classic era locomotives and coaches appeared. Shown here are two 112 Gondolas, a 114 Boxcar and a 117 Caboose.

advertised length could be accounted for by the substitution of the Standard Gauge frame, and Lionel did not give dimensions for the body alone. The quarter-inch difference in height could have been caused simply by the twin O Gauge motors in one model and the single Standard Gauge motor in the other.

When No. 8 finally appeared on the market, the design was unlike the No. 256, although the dimensions were similar, and all catalogs subsequent to 1925 pictured it more accurately. Whether Lionel truly planned to use the same body stamping for both O Gauge and Standard Gauge locomotives may never be determined, for no records are known to exist concerning this aspect of the design process. However, the possible savings in tooling cost would have helped the company keep the cost of No. 8 very low, thus giving it a great competitive advantage.[12]

The second new entry (No. 10), a low-priced version of the St. Paul-style No. 380, was introduced at $13.75, compared with the No. 8's price tag of $11.50, and was available in only one set. It pulled two newly-designed Pullman cars and an observation car (Nos. 337 and 338, respectively) that matched it in size. By contrast, the lowest-priced No. 8 came only with a set of early small freight cars, or as a two-car passenger set with the No. 35

Pullman and No. 36 Observation. These small coaches were the last of the early designs to persist in that catalog, lasting through 1926.

Another new design for 1925 was a baggage car (No. 320) to match the coaches that had come with the No. 318 locomotive the previous year. However, this new car was offered not with the No. 318 loco, but in a new four-car set (baggage, two Pullmans and observation) pulled by the No. 380 locomotive.[13] The No. 318 continued, as in the year before, to pull a three car set containing two coaches and an observation. Lionel now produced five distinct sizes of passenger coaches, in different price ranges and sized to match various locomotives. This unusual diversity gave the public a much wider choice and a greater diversity of prices, and probably gave the company a correspondingly larger share of display area in retail stores.

The line of freight cars had been somewhat neglected,

however. Although several new designs were introduced in the O Gauge lineup, Lionel continued to market the two sizes of out-dated Standard Gauge freights that had been designed before World War I.

Their comparatively primitive construction did not match the sophisticated lines of the new locomotives, and were inferior in appearance to the graceful designs offered by Ives. Lionel was planning a new series of Standard Gauge freight cars, but they would not be released until 1926.

Also in 1925, the management at American Flyer entered the lucrative Standard Gauge field, and the engineers at Ives were about to introduce a revolutionary new device that would temporarily improve their competitive position. Remote control was just on the horizon.

chapter 3 Notes chapter 3

(1) Cowen legally changed the spelling of his last name in 1910. In his book *All Aboard* (p. 47), Ron Hollander speculates that he may have taken this action to avoid anti-Semitic discrimination, although he was a public and practicing member of the Jewish faith throughout his life. Hollander further suggests that it may simply have been "an expression of his Americanism."

(2) Ron Hollander, *All Aboard*, p. 20.

(3) *Ibid.*, p. 47.

(4) This set, introduced in 1917 and advertised for only two years, consisted of an armored locomotive with turret-mounted guns and cars painted in military colors. It was not a big seller, and few examples exist today. This may have been the result of an isolationist attitude common among the American people that resisted involvement in the European war. Parents may have passed up the military set as being a bad example for their children.

(5) Cowen would continue to exploit this theme, alleging that the bond between fathers and sons is most firmly welded through their mutual enjoyment of Lionel Trains.

(6) Virtually all of the older designs were still being produced, and were featured prominently in the 1923 catalog.

(7) The name change from The Lionel Manufacturing Co. to The Lionel Corporation was made July 22, 1918.

(8) One sharp-eyed reviewer of this manuscript, Maurice Weisblum, notes that a tiny image of the No. 5 steam locomotive is visible in the Complete Railroad illustration on page 24. The No. 5 was available through 1924, although not listed for separate sale in the catalog.

(9) It would be many years before young girls would receive equal attention in Lionel advertising, although Ives advertising featured both boys and girls at an early date. However, the boys were always shown running the trains, while their sisters only watched, and the Ives slogan was "Ives Toys Make Happy *Boys*" (emphasis added). Nevertheless, someone in the Ives management may have felt some gender sensitivity prior to the twentieth century. Ron Hollander reports that one of the company's most popular toys in the 1880s was an animated suffragette (*All Aboard*, p. 41).

(10) Sometimes items that appeared in the catalogs were never produced. Examples include some of the O Gauge locomotives shown in the 1915 catalog—a big Hudson promised for 1946 but never made, and a No. 213 lift bridge that exists only in pre-production mockup form.

(11) As was often the case, Lionel catalogs misstated or exaggerated dimensions. No. 256 actually measures 11-1/2" long, while the No. 8, with a different body style, is 11".

(12) Lionel often modified existing tooling for a variety of different applications by interchanging parts of locomotives, cars, and accessories and adapting them to new uses.

(13) In the 1923 and 1924 catalogs, the No. 380 was shown only with the large Nos. 18, 19, and 190 cars of earlier design.

Lionel made two different models of the St. Paul electric locomotive, the large No. 380 (first sold in 1923) and the smaller, low-priced No. 10 introduced in 1925. Neither one was as attractive as the later versions made by Ives (No. 3237, left, in 1926 through 1930) and American Flyer (No. 4683 and other numbers, from 1929 through 1933).

4

SERIOUS COMPETITION

for the Industry Leader

Perhaps the most blatant advertising misstatement that Joshua Cowen ever printed, "LIONEL ALWAYS LEADS," appeared at the top of page 3 in the 1925 Lionel catalog. The accompanying copy lists an impressive series of innovations and features claimed to be industry firsts, but just a year earlier, Ives had scooped its more popular rival with an invention so clever it was used in toy trains for more than half a century afterward.

In 1924, the Ives Corporation introduced the world's first commercially successful remote control reverse unit for toy trains.

Prior to that time, toy trains could be made to run either forward or backward by means of a switch mounted somewhere on the locomotive frame. While agile fingers might be able to manipulate this switch while the train was in motion, it was easier to accomplish with the locomotive standing still. And, it still required the operator to touch the train. The only system of remote control reverse then in use was the track-trip device, a projecting lever that contacted the train's reverse switch as the locomotive passed by, causing a screeching halt and an immediate reversal to the opposite direction, hardly a realistic maneuver.

The Ives remote control reverse switch was an ingenious electrical mechanism that enabled a young engineer to stop the train gradually, allow it to stand in neutral in the station with all of the car lights shining, then move smoothly into reverse, all without having to leave the transformer. The secret to this device was a small rotating drum, fitted with a set of electrical contacts. When an operator turned on the track power, a magnetic solenoid pulled a small ratchet that rotated the drum a quarter turn, aligning the contacts and directing the electrical power through the field windings of the motor. Any momentary interruption of the current, such as could be accomplished by moving the transformer's control handle to an "off" position, released the solenoid and ratchet, and when current was restored, it rotated the drum another quarter turn.

Each quarter turn of the drum realigned the contacts to one of four sequential positions: forward, neutral, reverse, and neutral again. In the neutral positions, no current flowed through the windings of the motor field, but current from the track still lighted the passenger cars and the loco's headlight bulbs. In forward mode, current flowed through the field in a specific direction, causing the train to move ahead. The reverse position caused the current to enter the field from the opposite end, making the motor run backwards and causing the train to back up. Every momentary interruption of current by the operator cycled the reverse unit to the next position in a predictable forward-stop-backward-stop sequence, giving a young engineer complete control over the train without ever touching it.

This clever device was fundamentally simple in design and reliable in operation. It must have seemed almost magic to children in those technologically naive years. In the face of Lionel's claim always to lead, Ives should have been able to capitalize on their invention to regain a major share of the toy train market. The company's approach to advertising, however, had always been much lower key than that of Lionel, and their announcement of remote control reversing was too restrained and conservative to attract the kind of attention that would generate a high volume of sales. Once again Joshua Cowen's grasp of the power of the printed word turned his competitor's creation to his own advantage.

The Ives Corporation patented its new device, and although Lionel's engineers immediately tackled the problem of developing a competing remote control reverse unit, they were only partially successful. Ives could not patent the magnetic solenoid itself, as this pre-existing technology was applicable to a much wider range of products than toys. However, their patent covered not only the ingenious rotating drum itself, but the concept of rotation as it affected the alignment of electrical contacts. Lionel could not use a similar design without facing an infringement lawsuit.

Lionel engineers finally fabricated an inferior imitation of the Ives unit, using a solenoid for its power, but containing a pendulum-type mechanism that had only two possible positions, forward or reverse. Each interruption of track power activated the solenoid, which pushed the pendulum alternately right or left; there was no neutral position, and a Lionel locomotive could not stand still with its lights blazing, as an Ives locomotive could.

This defect may not seem too significant, but the superiority of the Ives system soon became apparent to operators. If an Ives train suffered an accidental interruption of track power while running, such as could be caused by dirt on the rails, the locomotive would cycle into neutral and coast to a stop. If the same interruption occurred on a Lionel layout, the locomotive motor would immediately begin to run backwards. This instant reversal slammed the entire train into a screeching halt, and sent it careening off in the opposite direction. The greater complexity of the Lionel reverse unit also led to adjustment and maintenance problems. Friction or improper lubrication sometimes impeded the action of the pendulum, and if track power fell below a certain point, the solenoid sometimes failed to move the pendulum fully, leaving the electrical contacts between positions. An operator would then have to reset the unit by hand.[1]

Buyers who took the time and trouble to investigate the two competing systems could not help but recognize the superiority of the Ives design. However, Cowen turned his own product's deficiencies into an apparent advantage through the use of

clever promotion in his 1926 catalog. On page 3, he presented "The New Lionel 100% Electrically Controlled Railroad" as if it were a brand new invention. The Ives competitive unit was ignored, and the wording of the copy suggested, without actually saying so, that the Lionel device was the first such remote control unit ever created. In the grand tradition of advertising, it wasn't a lie, but it avoided telling the whole truth.

The "LIONEL ALWAYS LEADS" page was brazenly reprinted from the 1925 catalog, along with the usual glorifications of components and construction techniques (five colorful pages of them!), but page 17 was new, a cleverly worded description of "The New Electrically Controlled Locomotives" in the Standard Gauge line. The copy is littered with words like "desirable" and "dependable," but is intentionally vague or misleading on the matter of just how the unit worked. Instead of describing it as having just two positions, forward and backward, the copy says "they may be started, stopped, reversed and operated at various speeds from any distance."

Having been unable to achieve the desirable lights-on neutral position, Lionel engineers did incorporate one new feature not duplicated by Ives locomotives. By outfitting the reverse pendulum with an extra set of contacts, they created a directional headlight circuit, and the catalog touted this highly. On an Ives train and on earlier Lionel locomotives, both headlights (front and rear) were illuminated whenever the train ran in either direction. The Lionel design lit only one headlight at a time, depending upon the direction of travel. This feature further complicated construction of the mechanism, however, and made it more susceptible to failure when it became dirty through use.

Near the end of the copy on page 17, Cowen takes oblique aim at Ives: "The construction throughout is dependable, and must not be confused with so-called 'Automatic Reversing Locomotives'." In fact, the Ives device was exceedingly dependable, and much less prone to malfunction and cause unexpected reversal than the Lionel unit. But the reputation of the Lionel brand name was so powerful that its claims were believed by the majority of the public, and the new "Electrically Controlled Locomotives" were an instant success. In another attention-getting maneuver, all descriptions of locomotives with the remote reverse unit were boldly printed in red.

Like Ives, Lionel sold its locomotives in both manual and remote control reverse versions. The automatic reverse unit commanded a substantial premium. The low-priced No. 8 with manual reverse sold for $11.50 in 1926, and the remote control version was $5.00 more at $16.50, an increase of more than 40 percent. That extra five dollars could have been used to purchase several accessories or a new freight car, with change left over. But the promise of such sophisticated operation enticed many buyers to sample the new remote

The dramatically improved 200-series freight cars bore little resemblance to Lionel's pre-1926 offerings. Shown here are the early lightweight 116 Ballast (dump) Car, with simple lever-operated hopper doors, and the very heavy 218 Dump Car with a substantial worm gear mechanism.

control technology, and the expensive option soon became a best seller.

In 1926, Lionel also introduced a new line of modern freight cars in both O and Standard gauges, some new accessories, and an important advance in operating technology: remote control track switches. These new switches further enhanced the "hands-off" concept of operation that was begun by remote control reversing. Previously, all track switches (devices that allow a train to move from the main line onto a siding, for example) were operated by a hand lever, requiring the operator to move to wherever the switch was located on the layout. The new switches were operated by solenoid, and could be controlled by an electrical contact lever placed next to the transformer. Now an engineer could send the trains anywhere on the layout without ever touching them or the track, or even moving away from the throttle.

As had happened before, Joshua Cowen's imagination, and that of his talented staff of designers, had expanded upon the ideas of a rival company. Having not only remote control reversing, but also remote control choice of train route, Lionel owners moved from simply playing with trains to running their railroads in prototypical fashion. In 1927, Lionel adapted the remote reverse and switches to its O Gauge line, further improving its competitive position against Ives. And in 1928 the copy writers coined a clever catch phrase, "Distant-Control," that seemed to sum up the superiority of Lionel products in the minds of consumers. But by 1928, the competitive balance of power had already shifted, with Ives facing bankruptcy and the new American Flyer Wide (Standard) Gauge trains attracting increasing attention on the retail market.

Although American Flyer entered the Standard Gauge field comparatively late, it quickly produced very competitive designs. The "President's Special" coaches (lower shelf) were half an inch longer than Lionel's famous "Blue Comet" cars (top). There were some important differences between the two lines. For example, Flyer's cars were more expensive to produce, due to the extra detail installed on the underframes and the many separate window frames that were installed by hand. (Lionel's patented window frames were a one-piece insert.) Lionel never made a baggage car or combine in a size comparable to this Flyer Club Car (combine).

A new line of O Gauge clockwork trains appeared in 1907 under the brand name American Flyer, made by the Edmonds-Metzel Manufacturing Company of Chicago.[2] The line was founded by William O. Coleman and William Hafner, who later left the firm and began marketing his own line of O Gauge clockwork trains under the Hafner name. Like Ives, American Flyer avoided electric power in the early years, preferring the simplicity and relative economy of wind-up power, but around the end of World War I, some electric-powered locomotives appeared in the line. From that time onward, electric motors would come to dominate American Flyer production.

The success of Lionel's Standard Gauge line prompted William Coleman's company to enter the large train market, and the first of his Wide (Standard) Gauge trains appeared in 1925. The line was not fully developed at the time of introduction, and consisted of just one locomotive design and matching lithographed passenger coaches.

Interestingly, for a Chicago-based company, American Flyer chose a New York Central design for its first locomotive, similar in concept to Lionel's No. 8 but larger and more impressive. Sold initially under two different catalog numbers, 4000 and 4019, these engines had a four-wheeled motor and were advertised to have an automatic reverse. The device was actually a variation on the old track-trip concept, whereby a lever contacted the reverse switch of a passing locomotive. Beginning in 1927, Flyer added an electro-mechanical remote control reverse unit that, like the Lionel unit, provided directional headlight operation but had no neutral position.[3]

Unlike its two major competitors, who offered each of their locomotives in a variety of colors under one catalog number, American Flyer assigned different numbers according to color. Thus the No. 4000 was always a green locomotive, while the No. 4019 was finished in maroon enamel. Other details often differentiated them, such as a single headlight on the No. 4000 and dual directional headlights on the No. 4019. All Flyer Standard Gauge locos were made with stamped-steel frames; only Ives continued to use cast iron.

The earliest passenger set consisted of three cars, a No. 4040 Mail and Baggage Car, a No. 4041 Pullman, and a No. 4042 Observation. They were lithographed in either green or maroon to match their locomotives, and had contrasting lettering, window frames, door panels, and rivet detail. Like the Lionel products, and unlike Ives, they carried no railroad heralds, but were instead lettered "AMERICAN FLYER LINES" above the windows. Nor were the locomotives identified with the New York Central railroad, instead carrying brass plates with the catalog number and the toy company's name. The cars measured 14" long.

In order to give its various trains a sense of identity in the catalog, American Flyer applied descriptive names to each of its Standard Gauge sets. In the first year of production, both of the introductory sets (one with the green No. 4000 and matching cars, the other in maroon with loco No. 4019) were labeled "The All-American." In subsequent years, each set would have its own title. The maroon set became "The All-American Limited"; the green set was "The Sesquicentennial Special."[4]

In 1926 the Chicago company expanded its line by producing the first of a series of sets named "The President's Special." It was touted as being a conception of a train that might be used by the American president, and the catalog claimed it was built using New York Central Railroad blueprints.[5] The locomotive was numbered 4039, and was identical to No. 4019 except for some additional trim and a tan paint scheme. While the locomotive was not significantly different or improved, as might be expected for such a grandly named set, the cars that accompanied it were very impressive. Substantially longer at 19", "The President's Special" coaches were richly lithographed in tan with gold-colored trim, making a massive train. The proportions of these coaches seemed more realistic than Lionel's higher, chunkier designs, although the shiny enamel on the Lionel product probably appeared to better advantage on store shelves.

With only one style of locomotive and three train sets in the catalog, American Flyer's Standard Gauge line was off to a rather modest start. The company was busily working on a series of freight cars, but they were not ready for the 1926 season. In order to fill this gap, the company purchased from Lionel four of their older style 10-series freight cars, stamped them with American Flyer catalog numbers, and sold them under their own brand label. At that time, Lionel was nearing the introduction of their greatly improved 200-series freight cars, and the management probably determined that allowing its outdated products to be sold by their small rival would do them no competitive harm. Apparently not many of these cars were sold by Flyer, as very few with that company's rubber-stamped numbers have survived. They didn't go well with the large New York Central locomotive, and their primitive hook couplers mated poorly with American Flyer's own spring-loaded design.

Lionel also provided a few of its accessories to be resold by American Flyer—notably the No. 77 Crossing Gate and the No. 78 Train Control Block Signal—but like the freight cars, examples of these items with American Flyer catalog numbers stamped on them are relatively scarce.

American Flyer's new Standard Gauge line began modestly, but quickly grew in numbers and variety. The first locomotive was patterned after the New York Central's simple rectangular box cab design, mounted on a basic four-wheeled frame. The same body, however, was used on a huge twelve-wheeled frame for the "President's Special" sets shown here. Lionel did not interchange different size frames with any one body style, as both Flyer and Ives did. The lithographed coaches measured 19" in length, larger than any Ives or Lionel passengers cars except for the latter company's 21-1/2" State cars.

The Chicago-based design staff was not idle, however, as the 1927 catalog would reveal. Featuring twice the number of sets as in the previous year, the 1927 lineup introduced a new "President's Special," this time with a magnificent new locomotive truly worthy of the name. Although using the same New York Central body style, the new No. 4687 measured a full four inches longer over the frame, 18-1/2" compared to the No. 4019 and its siblings at 14-1/2". Whereas the first locomotives rode on just four driving wheels, this new entry had a modified frame and an extended pilot truck at each end, for a total of twelve wheels. The frame was black, while the body was enameled a deep rich blue with gold trim and brass plates. The same color was applied to the 19" passenger coaches, with three new catalog numbers (4090, 4091, and 4092), making a truly handsome set.

Although shorter and having fewer wheels than the New York Central locomotive after which it was patterned, the No. 4687 captured the general concept and massive propor-tions of the prototype quite well. It also introduced Flyer's new electro-mechanical remote control reverse unit, and sported a generous amount of shiny brass and nickel trim. This premium priced outfit replaced the former "President's Special" headed by No. 4039, but that set was continued in 1927 under a new name, "The Chief," and the locomotive (now numbered 4677) was upgraded with the new remote control reverse. Flyer continued to offer "The All-American Limited" set, and added a similar but somewhat fancier train called "The American Legion Limited," featuring remote control reversing and a shiny red color scheme. The locomotive was numbered 4667.[6]

More important to the company's marketing strategy was the introduction of a new locomotive design, created to compete with Lionel's low-priced No. 8 and the Ives No. 3235. The design is unique among Standard Gauge locomotives of this period, being patterned after a design used on the New York, New Haven and Hartford Railroad. In fact, it looks very much

The smallest Standard Gauge locomotive in Flyer's line, the New Haven box cab, powered a variety of low-priced sets, such as this three-car freight.

4023 Log Car, and a red No. 4006 Hopper Car (scarcest of all the American Flyer freights) appeared in 1931.

All of the American Flyer freight cars were 14" long, compared with 12-1/2" for Lionel's new line, the 200 series, introduced the same year. In appearance they are more graceful and better proportioned than the chunky Lionel product or the smaller Ives holdovers from the No. 1 Gauge years. Like Lionel, American Flyer stamped its cars from heavy-gauge steel, and assembled them mechanically (rivets for the Flyer cars, metal tabs for the Lionels). Mechanical construction techniques were much faster and required fewer steps than soldering, which was the method still employed by Ives, whose products were increasingly more expensive to produce, while still remaining outdated and old fashioned.

An especially beautiful example of the toy designer's art is Flyer's No. 4021 Caboose, having a massive body with six windows per side and a wealth of brass trim: window frames, ladders, steps, railings on the sides, roof and ends, and a smokestack. Similarly impressive is the No. 4010 Tank Car, loaded with brass and painted a glowing yellow with a dark blue frame.[8] The first two sets to contain these freight cars appeared in the 1928 catalog. One was the economical "Trail Blazer," a

like the concept that Lionel introduced for its No. 8 locomotive in the 1925 catalog, a design that was never produced. Measuring 12", the New Haven loco was smaller than the New York Central style (but a competitive inch larger than Lionel's No. 8), and it had less trim. The first ones were numbered 4643 (green) and 4653 (orange), and several other catalog numbers would be used through 1933.

The New Haven loco headed many different sets in succeeding catalogs, each with an identifying title. First among these were "The Eagle" and "The Commander" in 1927, each containing one 14" Pullman and a matching observation car. Future Flyer sets would be named "The Statesman," "The Brigadier," and other romantic sounding titles. All of the sets advertised in 1927 contained passenger cars, but a new line of freight cars also entered production that year. Dropping the Lionel-made cars, Flyer created the first in a series of long and well-proportioned cars that many collectors consider to be visually more realistic and attractive than those of either Lionel or Ives.

First to appear were a gondola (No. 4007) that the company unaccountably called a "sand" car, not a term familiar to most railroad enthusiasts; a No. 4008 Boxcar; a No. 4012 Flat Car; and a No. 4011 Caboose. The following year these cars received new catalog numbers (4017, 4018[7], 4022, and 4021, respectively), and were joined by a massive tank car (No. 4010) and a No. 4020 Stock (cattle) Car. In 1934 the No. 4022 Flat (machinery) Car received a removable load of wood and was sold as the No.

Extra cash bought a lot of brass trim on American Flyer Standard Gauge locomotives, as on this 4678 New York Central type (right), compared with the more economical 4644 New Haven-type.

American Flyer's 4010 Tank Car (right) was much bulkier and more heavily detailed than either Lionel's 212 (center) or Ives comparatively spartan 190 (left). The Lionel design, however, was more realistic. The Ives tanker was updated only once after the conversion from No. 1 Gauge, and its smaller size and lack of detail made it much less attractive to buyers than the competition.

two-car set (sand car and caboose) pulled by the economical No. 4644 New Haven locomotive. The other set, "The Mountaineer," had a sand car, flatcar, boxcar, tank car, and caboose, and was pulled by Flyer's newest locomotive design: the No. 4637, based on a St. Paul-style prototype.

With a raised center cab and a lower rounded hood on each end, the St. Paul-style locomotive differs sharply from the more boxy New York Central and New Haven types. Based on a Milwaukee Road prototype, the Flyer version was made in two sizes, 13-1/4" and 15". Under four different catalog numbers (Nos. 4633, 4635, 4683 and 4685), it came painted red in the shorter versions, or in a special brown version sold by the Spiegel department store chain.[9] Those with catalog numbers ending in the digit 3 also had operating ringing bells. These intriguing devices were geared to a ratchet on the motor, as well as to a rod projecting through the cab and connected to a decorative bell on the hood. As the internal bell rang, the decorative bell swung back and forth in a realistic manner.

The largest and most impressive of the St. Paul locos was also the first to appear. It was nicknamed the "Shasta" and it came in a medium shade of green with a tan frame. The engine was cataloged in 1928 with "The Mountaineer" freight set and "The Pocahontas" passenger set, which contained four 14" coaches painted tan with green roofs. Another impressive set to use the 14" cars was "The Hamiltonian," pulled by a premium New York Central loco-

motive (No. 4678), some of which were equipped with the ringing bell feature.

In 1928, all locomotives offered by Lionel and American Flyer were electric designs, with only Ives among the major manufacturers offering a steam locomotive (No. 1132) in the years since 1924, but plans for new steamers were nearing the production stage. Enjoying the overheated economy of the latter 1920s, an increasingly prosperous American public had an unprecedented amount of surplus cash to spend on amusements, and toy trains were exceptionally popular. The smaller New Jersey firm of Dorfan entered the Standard Gauge arena in 1926, and Lionel designers were about to unveil their new No. 390 steamer. The economically troubled Ives had introduced a

Perhaps no other cars produced by these three manufacturers differed more significantly than their cabooses. The Ives model (foreground) was complexly and expensively constructed, with many separate soldered pieces and a lot of hand-painted detail. Largest was Flyer's 4021 (right), covered with a huge amount of brass (window frames, handrails, etc.) and enameled in a vivid shade of red. Lionel's simpler and more modern design (left background), similar to the style used by the Reading Railroad, had many fewer parts and was therefore more economical to produce, yielding a greater margin of profit. All are undeniably handsome; a buyer's choice was a matter of taste.

revolutionary steam loco drive system a year earlier, contained in a long and graceful steamer numbered 1134. They followed it in 1928 with a magnificent interpretation of a Milwaukee Road Olympian electric design.

As the decade neared its end, Lionel was experiencing unprecedented success with its so-called "Classic Period" designs, and American Flyer had established a complete Standard Gauge line and a secure economic base. The older manufacturers of 2" Gauge trains had declined, but Dorfan was attracting attention with a new technique of die casting, and another firm, Boucher, Inc. of New York, was producing a small number of trains to Standard Gauge specifications.[10] Except for Ives, whose expensive manufacturing techniques and inferior promotional strategies had crippled the company, the future looked bright.

The ringing bell feature was unique to American Flyer's more expensive locomotives. The decorative brass bell swung back and forth in a realistically slow manner, while the internal bell sounded at just the right point of its swing.

American Flyer's two more expensive locomotive types are strikingly different from each other, although both are heavily trimmed in brass. The St. Paul model (right) has a raised center cab and rounded end hoods, while the New York Central type is a more simple box. Both are shown stopped in front of Lionel's 437 Switch Tower.

chapter 4 Notes chapter 4

(1) Collectors who operate their trains often replace the pendulum reverse with modern versions of the original Ives design.

(2) The corporate name became American Flyer Manufacturing Co. in 1910.

(3) This heavy and complex mechanism is prone to stalling without proper lubrication and adjustment, and must have caused much frustration for young owners, just as it does today for operators of vintage trains.

(4) Alan R. Schuweiler, *Greenberg's Guide To American Flyer Wide Gauge*, p. 18.

(5) Jack McLaren, "American Flyer Wide Gauge—1926," *The Collector*, Vol. 19, No. 2, p. 12.

(6) Jack McLaren, "American Flyer Wide Gauge—1927," *The Collector*, Vol. 19, No. 3, p. 24.

(7) Flyer referred to this design as an "automobile" car, probably to give it an identity separate from the "box" cars advertised by Lionel and Ives. Similarly, the No. 4022 Flat Car was called a "machinery" car.

(8) An all-blue version was also made in smaller numbers.

(9) Schuweiler, *op. cit.*, p. 29.

(10) Boucher took over the Voltamp line of 2" Gauge trains in 1922, and widened their gauge slightly to match Lionel's track.

The designs created by Lionel during the mid-1920s are highly valued by collectors today. The massive 400E steam locomotive and twin-motored 408E electric-type pulled the most expensive sets in the catalog during the 1930s.

5

LIONEL'S CLASSIC PERIOD

*C*lassic: " . . . of acknowledged excellence; remarkably typical, outstandingly important . . . harmonious, well proportioned, and finished, in accordance with established forms . . . ."[1]

Train collectors have come to refer to the years between 1923 and the onset of World War II as Lionel's Classic Period, and the adjective is certainly appropriate when applied to Standard Gauge trains manufactured then. These Lionel products came to symbolize quality and substance at a time when American mechanical expertise, respect for excellence, and regard for value were at a high level. And, despite the severe economic restraints that nearly destroyed his company in the mid-1930s, Joshua Cowen never deviated from his devotion to the highest possible standards of quality.

In the highly competitive toy market of the 1920s, Cowen and his staff of talented designers and engineers seem to have cut few corners in order to save money. The locomotives, cars, and accessories from this period were substantially built from quality materials such as heavy-gauge steel. Their motors were designed for efficiency and built to last, with machine-cut reduction gears, bronze bearings, and replaceable but nevertheless long-lasting brushes. Glossy enameled finishes were baked on for durability, and shiny brass and corrosion-resistant nickel trim was lavishly applied. (Classic period Lionel Trains exhibit outstanding durability, and even badly worn or rusted examples may be restored to use.)

Toy manufacturers of the second half of the twentieth century are frequently criticized for the disposable nature of their products—their toys' tendency to break down (or break up!) after only minimum amounts of play. Lionel Trains, by contrast, have earned a reputation for unusual longevity, and in a great many families successive generations of children have inherited them from their parents and grandparents, finding them still to be serviceable and fascinating toys decades after they were made.

Few other toys have earned such a reputation for durability. There are examples, such as A. C. Gilbert's famous Erector sets and the Tonka line of heavy steel construction vehicles, that are almost as well known as Cowen's famous product, but no other brand name has achieved the same level of consumer respect and acceptance as Lionel Trains in the 1920s and 1930s.

After the successful introduction of the Nos. 380 and 402 locomotives in 1923, Lionel expanded the line over the next four years to include modern versions of all its motive power and rolling stock in both Standard and O Gauges. The old-style freight cars were shown for the last time in the 1926 catalog, and they appeared at great disadvantage, side by side with the new 200-series cars. The new freights were priced substantially higher than the older type but represented an enormous improvement in realistic design, quality construction, and inherent value.

Lionel maintained consistency in its numbering system by simply adding the digit 2 in front of the catalog numbers used for the older freight cars. Thus the number for a caboose evolved from 17 to 217, the number for a tank car from 15 to 215, etc. Only the two new designs, the No. 218

Dump Car and the No. 219 Derrick (crane) Car received entirely new numbers.

Unaccountably, the catalog described the new cars as being 11-3/4" long, while all examples actually measure 12-1/2", surely marking one of very few times when Cowen understated his products' features. Heavy-gauge steel was used throughout, and these cars have proven to be extremely resistant to damage. Even when subjected to rough play, they do not dent easily. A total of nine designs were offered: flat, box, cattle, tank, and hopper cars, a gondola and a dump car, and a magnificent derrick with a huge boom and three

Lionel designs were dramatically revised after 1923. The earlier dark colors and simple construction (No. 33, left) gave way to brighter but less realistic enamel and a huge amount of shiny brass and nickel trim (No. 408E, right).

The new large Lionel freight cars were much more massive and heavily constructed than the competing Ives products. Lionel's 216 Hopper lacked the prototypical lettering and hand-painted detail of Ives' 194 model, but soon outsold its Bridgeport rival. Size and a substantial feel gave the 200-series freights an aura of quality in the eyes of consumers.

Unlike real locomotives and rolling stock, Lionel's classic period trains were aggressively colorful. Despite their unrealistic brilliance, they far outsold the earlier, somewhat more drab colors that more closely resembled actual trains. The 318E locomotive shown here is painted in two-tone Stephen Girard green, and the white 514R Refrigerator Car has a bright blue roof, hardly an authentic choice. The impressive double 67 Lamppost in the center is over a foot tall; the Switch Tower at right is a reproduction 438.

The largest Lionel freight car was this 219 Derrick, an operating model that could actually lift heavy rolling stock with its boom and hook. A heavy bracket mounted beneath the frame could be clamped to the track, thus keeping the crane from tipping over when loaded. Although expensive, this car was sold in substantial numbers, as it had a considerable amount of play value.

Lionel's two sizes of freight cars complemented the various sizes of locomotives. First to appear in 1926 were the large models, such as this 215 Tank Car (right), meant to be pulled by the 402 and 380 engines. The 515 (left) was introduced a year later to go with such locos as the smallest 8 and 10 electric types.

hand-turned knobs for operation, all accompanied by a substantial new caboose.

A tenth design, the No. 214R Refrigerator Car, was added in 1929. It looked very much like the No. 214 Boxcar, except for the substitution of a pair of smaller hinged doors in place of the sliding doors on the latter. The last in the 200 series to appear was the No. 220 Floodlight Car, a simple frame supporting a low platform, on which were mounted two swiveling searchlights.

In line with its policy of covering all price ranges, Lionel introduced a new line of large O Gauge freights at the same time, and in 1927, smaller versions appeared in both gauges. Initially there were only six of the smaller Standard Gauge models (called the 500 series): a flatcar, gondola, cattle car, refrigerator car, tank car, and caboose, (numbered 511, 512, 513, 514, 515, and 517, respectively). They were described in the catalog as being 11-1/4" long, a quarter-inch understatement, while the larger 200-series cars were still understated at 11-3/4", which seems like a fairly insignificant difference.[2] Nor do the catalog illustrations even hint at the difference in their sizes. However, the prices quoted for the 500-series cars are considerably lower ($3.35 for a No. 17 caboose, for example, compared with $5.35 for a No. 217).

When the actual cars are viewed side by side, however, the difference is considerably more significant. The 200-series cars appear much bulkier, with very large trucks and wheels, and more substantial trim. These bigger models were designed primarily for use with the massive Nos. 380 and 402 locomotives, while the 500-series cars look best with the No. 10 or No. 8 engines. It may be that the illustrations in the catalog were deliberately planned to de-emphasize the size difference, in order to promote the new smaller series. Despite their lesser mass, the 500-series cars were still very handsome and well made, and were properly proportioned to match the smaller Standard Gauge locomotives which they were intended to accompany.

In 1928, Lionel added the No. 516 Hopper, and in 1929 the refrigerator car was renumbered 514R, bringing its nomenclature in line with its 214R companion. The number 514 was applied to a new boxcar, similar in design to the No. 214R, but with sliding doors instead of the reefer's hinged ones. Last to appear was the No. 520 Floodlight Car, for a total of nine different designs in the series.

In 1928, North America was riding the crest of unprecedented world-wide economic expansion, and the Lionel catalog reflected this prosperity. At 46 pages, all with beautifully detailed, full color art work, it represented the best in contemporary printing technology. Pages 23 through 25 were especially impressive, a central fold-out section approaching three feet in width. Stretched out full length was a photo of the massive "Outfit No. 409E—Lionel Twin-Super Motor De-Luxe Special—the World's Finest 'Distant-Control' Model Train."

During the Classic Period years (1923 until the Second World War), Lionel sold passenger cars in ten different sizes, offering consumers the widest choice of styles and price ranges of any manufacturer. (By comparison, Ives and American Flyer each made just two sizes of coach in Standard Gauge). Some were carry-overs from early production, such as the small 10-1/2" 36 Observation Car (center background), and were discontinued after 1927. The other observation cars shown here are (left to right): 490 (17-5/8" long, 1923-1932); 341 (12" long, 1925-33); and 312 (13-1/4", 1926-1940).

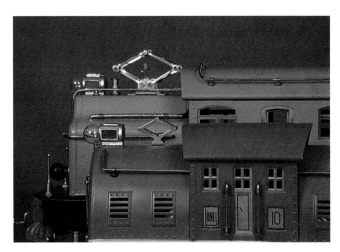

A simple one-piece pantograph decorated the inexpensive No. 10 locomotive (foreground), but the top-of-the-line 408E had a complex hinged pantograph that could be raised and lowered.

The four passenger cars in this impressive set were the Nos. 418, 419 and 490 that first appeared in 1923, plus a new type, the No. 431 Diner. Although outwardly similar to the 418 Pullman, the diner had a special interior. Most Lionel coaches were fitted with interior details consistent with ordinary passenger cars, such as the two-piece, swiveling, stamped-metal seats in the No. 18 Pullman. The diner, however, received special treatment, in the form of tables, chairs, and a neatly detailed kitchen area. Three car sets (without the diner) were still featured in the catalog at a lower price, and the diner is much less commonly found today than the other three designs.

At the head end of this impressive train came Lionel's top-of-the-line locomotive, the No. 408E. Introduced the previous year, this model was an upgraded version of the No. 402, powered by the same twin-motor drive system, but with some attractive additions to its trim. Instead of the simple stamped-steel pantographs of its less expensive companion, the No. 408 sported large collapsible pantographs, realistically fashioned from shiny brass and in much better proportion to the size of the engine. And at each end, a pair of running lights (most often one red, the other green) flanked the doorway, down low on the body and just above the frame.

Lionel's 408E locomotive (lower shelf) has larger pantographs and additional low-level running lights to distinguish it from the slightly less expensive 402E (upper shelf), which appeared in the catalog four years earlier. Both locomotives are followed by 419 Combines. (Carail Museum Collection)

Joshua Cowen shrewdly invested his company's capital in the development of modern fabrication techniques aimed at reducing the number of worker hours required to produce a given item. Through the use of assembly-line techniques, sub-assemblies of parts, and its patented car-side inserts, Lionel sharply limited the amount of handwork necessary, keeping production costs well under control. Further savings were realized by arranging some design and tooling contracts with a firm in Naples, Italy, where labor costs were lower.[3] Management could have reduced costs even further, and realized a greater profit or better competitive pricing, had they elected to use less costly materials (such as lighter-gauge steel, for example). However, Lionel Trains were selling at an all-time record rate, and given the general level of prosperity in America at the time, Lionel wisely chose to maintain high standards of quality and durability.

William Coleman followed a similar approach, combining the use of high grade materials with modern manufacturing techniques. His modest line of American Flyer Standard Gauge trains enjoyed considerable success, even in the face of giant Lionel's dominance of the market. The same could not be said of the Ives Corporation, however. Saddled with conservative management policies and badly outdated assembly techniques that required immense amounts of handwork,[4] Ives' profits dwindled throughout the 1920s, and the company filed for bankruptcy on July 7, 1928.[5] (An examination of the failure of the Ives Corporation appears in Chapter 6.)

Although its volume was far less than Lionel's, Ives was selling a respectable number of trains. However, in order to remain competitive, the company priced some of its pieces below the cost of manufacture. Ironically, the more they sold, the more money they lost.

The assets of the Ives Corporation were subsequently purchased by Lionel and American Flyer, acting in concert. Just why these two firms decided to gain control of their rival is open to speculation, but two probabilities exist. First, by acquiring the contents of the Bridgeport factory and all of its records and patents,[6] Cowen and Coleman could ensure that no other firm (possibly one with deeper pockets than the Ives

management had) could revitalize the line. This would account for American Flyer's interest. However, it is more likely that Joshua Cowen had a different motive.

Among the properties controlled by Ives was a patent that Cowen had coveted since 1924, the ingenious sequential remote control forward-neutral-reverse unit that was superior to Lionel's two-position imitation. There is no doubt that, in spite of his advertising bravado, Cowen recognized the limitations of his own company's reverse unit, as well as the inviolability of the Ives patent. Within a few years after the takeover, the Ives device was adapted for use in all Lionel O and Standard Gauge locomotives, and Lionel's own pendulum reverse was abandoned forever. To allow this valuable invention to fall into competing hands would have relegated Lionel to second place in remote control technology, a situation intolerable to the man who claimed that "Lionel Always Leads."

It may be asked, then, why Lionel entered into partnership with American Flyer, rather than making an independent bid for sole ownership of Ives. The records are not clear, but it can be hypothesized that neither Cowen nor Coleman felt financially capable of assuming the entire burden of maintaining operations at the Bridgeport plant. Although the cost of purchasing the assets was only $73,250,[7] Ives was losing money. It is probable that both the Lionel and American Flyer management teams had no plans in place that would ensure revitalization of the Ives line into a profit-making operation. Although the general financial outlook was still bright during the year preceding the stock market crash of October 1929, acquiring an ailing company must have seemed a risky venture, best shared between two healthy corporations.

The new owners would soon take positive steps to remedy this situation, but when Ives first came up for sale in 1928, it is likely that neither Lionel nor American Flyer had yet formulated firm plans for keeping their old rival afloat. By joining forces, they kept Ives out of the hands of any potential rival, but shared the burden of expected losses between them. (The attempts to turn Ives into a profit-making company are described in Chapter 6.)

In the long run, Lionel's broader economic base allowed it to purchase American Flyer's share, and Cowen became sole owner of Ives by early 1930, just as the Great Depression was about to begin. Even after the stock market crash in October 1929, no one could predict just how long the world-wide economic collapse would last, or how manufacturers of non-essential goods, such as toys, would have to struggle just to maintain solvency. In the four years following the Ives takeover, American Flyer would expand and refine its Standard Gauge line, while Lionel created an abundance of magnificent toy trains, reaching the pinnacle of its Classic Period production.

The 1928 catalog contained more new products than had ever before been introduced by Lionel in a single year. First came the introduction of two entirely new Standard Gauge locomotives, the giant Olympian No. 381E,[8] after a Chicago, Milwaukee, St. Paul and Pacific Railroad prototype, and a large No. 9 box cab loco somewhat similar to the small New York Central-inspired No. 8. As an added bonus, these engines were also sold disassembled in "Bild-a-Loco" kits, which buyers could put together with a screwdriver. (A similar model, No. 4, applied the Bild-a-Loco concept to the O Gauge No. 254 locomotive.)

The list of accessories continued to grow, and two items in particular stand out. The No. 300 Steel Bridge captured the essential flavor of the Hellgate bridge across New York City's East River. Measuring 28-3/4" long and close to a foot in width and height, the Hellgate was originally designed to accommodate Standard Gauge locomotives, although many have been used on O Gauge layouts as well. The end towers and the design of the girders produce the illusion of an elevated span, but the roadbed of the bridge actually lies flat, so that, unlike some earlier Lionel bridges, it is not necessary for the trains to climb up an approach ramp in order to cross (although it is fun to watch an early Lionel train tilting upward to cross one of the early bridges, this motion could hardly be classed as realistic.)

Also introduced in 1928 was Lionel's most massive structure, the No. 840 Power Station. At 26" by 21-1/2", and standing a full foot-and-a-half tall, this expensive toy ($20.00 in 1928) had dozens of separate window frames, towering smoke stacks, and an array of six operating knife switches that could be used in wiring a layout. The interior had room to conceal two of Lionel's largest transformers, and the central area was lighted.

With no hint that the booming economy might falter, business and industry continued the rapid rate of expansion that had been building for nearly a decade. The Cowen family was not immune to the lure of easy riches promised by the amazing growth of the stock market. Joshua's son, Lawrence, aspired to a financial career, and after a few years working for a brokerage concern, he gained a seat on the New York Stock Exchange, reportedly purchased for him by his father for the staggering sum of $585,000.[9]

The problem, of course, was that far too much of the wealth represented by the stock market existed only on paper, rather than in real assets. Although there were predictions of imminent economic collapse, the vast majority of the populace ignored the warnings. Normally a prudent businessman, Joshua Cowen was caught up in the fervor of the times, and poured ever-increasing amounts of capital into creating extravagant and expensive toys for a public that couldn't seem to get enough of them.

The 1929 catalog introduced the first Lionel steam locomotive since old No. 5 had disappeared after 1926. The new No. 390 could be purchased with either manual or remote control reverse, and was much more modern in design than the earlier efforts. The steamer could be purchased in four different freight and passenger sets, but, impressive as this debut was, the centerfold of the catalog displayed the largest,

Four of Lionel's impressive 300 Hellgate Bridges are visible in this view of the mountainous region of Richard and Linda Kughn's Carail Museum layout. The red-roofed structure in the center is a 438 Signal Tower, and to the right can be seen the top of the revolutionary 78 Train Control Block Signal, with its automatic stop-and-start circuit.

most magnificent train set any child could imagine. Headed by the huge, twelve-wheeled Olympian locomotive (No. 381E), the "Transcontinental Limited" contained four 21-1/2" coaches, each riding on a pair of six-wheeled trucks, and containing the most detailed interior fittings ever seen on a toy train.

Now called the "State Set" by collectors, after the names inscribed on the individual cars,[10] the "Transcontinental Limited" was enameled in two-tone green, with brass plates and trim. In addition to seats, the elaborate interiors boasted fully equipped washrooms, even including movable toilet seats. So heavy were these cars that the single-motored locomotive could pull them only with difficulty, and in future years the State set would be powered by the twin-motored No. 408E instead, in a new color scheme of two-tone brown. Recognizing the dissatisfaction that some customers felt with the first year's underpowered set, Lionel offered to exchange a new 408E for a customer's 381E at no charge. (Future sets powered by the single-motored No. 381E contained just three of the heavy State cars instead of four.)

The featured accessory for 1929 was an elaborate elevated terrace, designed as a base for a No. 124 Station. A set of broad steps led to an elliptical platform measuring 31-1/2" by 18", fitted with lattice-work railings and six die-cast lampposts. At either end were simulated grass plots, one containing a flower urn and the other supporting a flag pole with a cloth 48-star American flag. The station itself was lighted inside, and had two hanging lamps under the eaves. This huge and flamboyant accessory sold for $26.25, and the number that survive attest to the wealth of a significant portion of the public in those affluent, but all too temporal, times. In many ways, the grandiose 1929 Lionel catalog symbolizes an era that abruptly ended with Black Friday, that notorious day in October when thousands discovered just how tenuous the foundations of their fortunes had become. Seduced by the

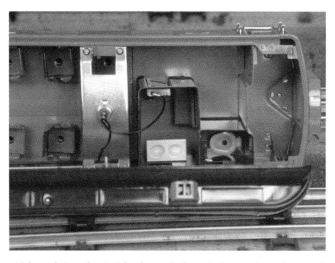

Although barely visible through the windows when the coaches were on the rails, the interior features of the State cars included fully equipped washrooms. Only with the roof removed could one appreciate this extra detail. (Carail Museum Collection)

get-rich-quick promises of a seemingly safe and solvent stock market, naive and gullible investors failed to realize that their equity was all too often underwritten by as little as 10 percent in hard assets. Having used the value of one stock as collateral to buy another, they were unable to produce the hard cash needed to support their holdings, and the whole house of cards came tumbling rapidly down.

As calamitous as the stock market crash seemed at the time, its long term effects were not felt immediately. Over the next several years, the economy steadily declined, despite the efforts of business and industry to regain a sound financial footing. As the public's buying power shrank, products that had earlier seemed in short supply now languished on the shelves for want of purchasers. This forced companies to reduce their work forces, and the resulting unemployment further curtailed consumption.

In a long, downward spiral, unemployment eroded purchasing power, which in turn forced further unemployment. The governments of the day, lacking the tools of economic manipulation that were developed during and after Franklin Roosevelt's administration, seemed powerless to assist a leaderless economy. Public confidence withered. Fearful of the future, those who still enjoyed employment sharply reduced their discretional spending, and this, in turn, jeopardized the viability of manufacturers of all but essential products.

Lionel designers spared no expense in detailing the State cars with partitions and seats, as seen in this reproduction Pullman. (Carail Museum Collection)

However, in the months immediately following Black Friday, the importance of the impending economic collapse was not fully realized, and many firms attempted to continue with business as usual. Many people, and one suspects Joshua Cowen was among them, expected an imminent return to the prosperity of the 1920s. Although Lionel's profit of $82,000 in 1930 was less than a quarter of 1929's $383,700,[11] the company was not yet in the red. Cowen tried to maintain the momentum that had built during the previous decade by introducing ever more elaborate additions to his company's line of products.

Following the successful return of steam locomotives (No. 390) in 1929, Lionel announced a second, more economical engine in Standard Gauge, numbered 384, as well as two new steamers for O Gauge buyers. The 1930 catalog was just as elaborate as in the previous year, and tucked away on page 26 was the first appearance of perhaps the most famous train set in Lionel's history, the "Blue Comet." Headed by a 390E locomotive decorated in two-tone blue (the standard version was black), this three-car passenger train was inspired by a Jersey Central prototype and featured coaches second only to the State cars in size. Measuring 18-3/4" long and numbered 420, 421, and 422, these impressive toys had the same interior detail as the State cars, although there were fewer passenger seats. The design of both sizes was very similar.

Lionel's 1931 catalog courageously stated: "So great is the demand for Lionel Electric Trains that it takes 3 large modern factories to produce enough trains to supply the boys of America." Indeed, the prosperous 1920s had created just such an enormous demand for these magnificent toys, but in 1931 that demand was rapidly eroding. Nevertheless, Lionel announced its most ambitious locomotive design to date, the huge twelve-wheeled No. 400E steamer. Offered in both black and two-tone blue, it replaced the No. 390E as motive power for the "Blue Comet," and was also offered for separate sale and in a seven-car freight set.

The introductory price for this giant locomotive was $42.50, and while many successful businessmen and professionals might have had the cash for such an extravagant purchase a few years earlier, this was not the case in 1931. In his book, *All Aboard*, Ron Hollander brings the No. 400E's price tag into perspective, suggesting that $42.50 in 1931 dollars could buy a three-piece suite of bedroom furniture, or even a good used car.[12] There is no doubt that the high quality of this Lionel masterpiece justified its cost, but there were just too few customers for toys in that price range, and Lionel posted not a profit, but a substantial loss at the end of the fiscal year.

This reversal of fortune was in part due to the continued diversification of the Lionel inventory. Yet another series of passenger coaches appeared in the 1931 catalog, the 16" Nos. 424, 425, and 426 Stephen Girard cars. This brought to five the number of distinctly different passenger car sizes offered that year.[13] With sales dwindling, the volume of sales for each type, especially the largest and most expensive ones, fell below the profitable level. Still, the company struggled to maintain the diversity and quality of its products. To complement the trains, there appeared a new and modern station design in two sizes, patterned after Grand Central Station in New York City. And the price of a complete Lionel Standard Gauge railroad was advertised at $350.00, as unattainable for most families as a king's ransom.

Cowen must have had a particular love for his large-scale trains. Given his proven business acumen, he surely must have realized by 1932 that such majestic toys were no longer viable in a depressed market, yet he continued to expand the line, and the investment in new tooling further depleted his capital. In 1932 and 1933, two new locomotive designs appeared, first the ten-wheeled No. 392E (only a few inches shorter than the top-of-the-line No. 400E), and a more moderately priced but still expensive eight-wheeled loco (No. 385E) the following year. Then in 1934, the latter was offered in an economy version under number 1835E.[14] These engines were the last major investment by Lionel in the Standard Gauge size, however, as by 1934 the company's losses forced it into temporary receivership.

As the Depression years deepened, Lionel bravely continued to promote its prohibitively expensive Standard Gauge giants to a public whose purchasing power was shrinking day by day. While a toy train empire like this Carail Museum display might have appeared attainable in the late 1920s, by 1931 it must have seemed an empty dream.

In 1932, subtle changes began to appear in the catalog presentations, with the beginning of a gradual shift in emphasis away from expensive Standard Gauge trains and toward O Gauge models.
Management must finally have realized that future prosperity depended more upon volume sales of sensibly-priced trains than upon the higher per-unit profits of such costly locomotives as the Nos. 400E, 408E, and their accompanying sets. Pages 14 and 15 of the 1932 catalog carry the following bold headlines: "THE LOWEST PRICED LIONEL TRAINS—WONDERFUL VALUES" and "NEVER BEFORE SO FINE A LOCOMOTIVE IN THIS PRICE CLASS." This attention to price is further reflected in the revised cost of the complete Lionel Standard Railroad—a much more modest array of items than offered the previous year, and reduced by a huge percentage from $350 to just $150.

In a move to generate much-needed capital, Cowen invaded the low-price toy market in two ways. In order to avoid having the Lionel trademark associated in any way with inexpensive or lightweight trains, he used his Ives subsidiary to sell economical O Gauge clockwork and electric locomotives with lithographed cars, all somewhat smaller than the regular O Gauge offerings. In a corollary move, he created the Winner Toy Corporation to make and sell truly tiny lithographed electric trains that nevertheless ran on O Gauge track. Having simple, lightweight motors and virtually no trim, Winner trains were made with absolute minimum production costs. At just a few dollars per set, the Ives and Winner products outsold both the regular O Gauge line and the Standard Gauge giants, and Cowen managed in this way to maintain the image of quality associated with the Lionel name, at least temporarily.

As an economy measure, Lionel had already closed the Bridgeport, Connecticut facility and moved production of Ives trains to the main plant in Irvington, New Jersey. It soon became apparent that there was little advantage in prolonging the fiction of a separate identity for Ives. Parts of that line were renamed "Lionel-Ives" in 1933 and "Lionel Junior" the following year, and were shown in the regular

Lionel's best-known operating accessory, the 45 Gateman, first appeared in 1935 and has been produced in a variety of colors and materials almost every year since.

Lionel catalog. (In 1932, there were separate catalogs for both Ives and Winner products.) A substantial amount of catalog space was devoted to the small lithographed clockwork and electric trains, shown in full color. There was also a subtle de-emphasis of the regular line, with pages depicting the O and Standard Gauge locomotives printed in black and white instead of color, as a means of reducing printing costs.

Although Standard Gauge trains continued to appear in the catalog through 1939, they increasingly received less attention from both company engineers and their promotional staff. New and impressive accessories were introduced, including a substantial Standard Gauge-sized No. 440 Signal Bridge and the most famous of all, the No. 45 Automatic Gateman. However, these items were promoted just as heavily for use with O Gauge trains, and throughout the 1930s, only the smaller-sized line benefited from research and development efforts.

As the 1930s progressed, few new items were added to the Standard Gauge line. Lionel's first streamlined train, a copy of the Union Pacific "City of Portland," appeared in 1934 in O Gauge size, and two new and fairly realistic locomotives—a New York Central-style "Commodore Vanderbilt" and a Milwaukee Road "Hiawatha"—came along the next year. Although Standard Gauge was still prominent in the 1935 catalog, it was the O Gauge line, with its lower per-unit cost and consequent higher volume of sales, that was expanded. Lionel created imaginative new technology to make its trains more appealing to serious operators and model railroaders, but just one such feature—the remote control whistle of 1935—was incorporated into the Standard Gauge line. Only O Gauge received remote control couplers, motorized freight loaders for coal, logs, and scrap metal, and an impressive operating lift bridge.

As the company inched slowly toward economic health once more, Cowen confirmed his commitment to O Gauge by producing the first mass-produced scale model locomotive for three-rail operators: the No. 700E Hudson. Instead of making it from sheet metal like most other toy trains,

Lionel die cast the boiler using highly detailed molds.[15] The result was the most realistic model locomotive ever to come from a major manufacturer, and it forever changed the public's perception of model railroading. By comparison, all previous locomotives seemed to be toy-like caricatures, and over the next several years, right up until World War II forced a halt to toy production in favor of the war effort, Lionel introduced a whole line of high, medium and lower-priced locomotives manufactured by the die casting process, in O Gauge only.

For all practical purposes, Standard Gauge was dead by 1940. Both American Flyer and Dorfan had already abandoned these large trains, and the small demand for them that still existed was easily met by Lionel's left-over inventory. It is probable that no Standard Gauge items were produced after 1939, and Lionel consolidated its offerings into just two distinct price ranges: the premium O Gauge and the economy O27 line, which had originated as Lionel Junior products.

Although generally of lighter weight and more economically produced (such as with lithographed decoration instead of enamel), the O27 trains could operate interchangeably on O Gauge track.

Recognizing the growth of small-scale model railroading as an attractive hobby for adults as well as children, Lionel produced a limited line of trains in OO (double-O) Gauge from 1938 to early 1942. Just a bit larger than today's familiar HO models, these trains were highly detailed and close to scale, but sales were insufficient to justify expansion of the concept, and only one locomotive design—a lilliputian version of the famous No. 700E Hudson—was produced, along with six different freight cars. But when train production resumed after the war, the only Lionel Trains to reappear rode on O Gauge track and its lighter weight O27 counterpart. It seemed as if the big trains were gone forever.

Construction Features

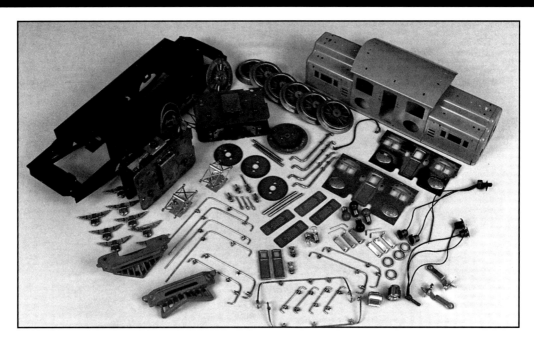

Lionel Trains of the classic period were engineered to last, and the premium Standard Gauge items were amazingly complex pieces of machinery, especially considering that they were intended primarily as playthings. Each locomotive contained an astonishing number of separate pieces, all of which were carefully designed to fit together with a minimum of assembly time. The following series of photographs illustrates the assembly of the largest box cab electric locomotive: the No. 408E.

Above: This array of parts only hints at the complexity of the twin-motored giant 408E. In this photo, the motors and automatic reverse unit are already assembled, shown at left and slightly above center in front of the massive frame. One wheel is shown with its gear in place (the other three gears are seen at center), and all of the handrails are already fitted with the many brass stanchions that secure them to the body. In addition, the main components of the body shell are shown soldered together.

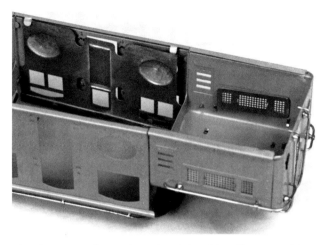

One important factor in maintaining Lionel's competitive edge was the use of these multipurpose inserts, a patented feature that other manufacturers could not use. Whereas an American Flyer worker, for example, had to install separate doors and window frames in all the body openings one at a time, the same task at Lionel involved installing just two brass parts, one within each side of the cab. Lionel's labor costs were correspondingly lower.

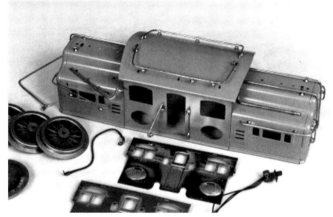

Trim pieces are shown in various stages of the assembly process. Two tabs on each of the tiny stanchions fit into slots in the body, and are then bent over inside to secure them. A skilled assembly line worker could install them quite quickly, although reasonable care was necessary to avoid scratching the paint. The large number of trim pieces explains, in part, the high prices charged for Lionel's largest locomotives. The smaller, more economical models were much less heavily trimmed, cutting down considerably on labor. Two brass inserts (lying in front of the body) contain the window frames, doors and brass identification plates; installation of these parts is shown in the next photo.

Most of the trim is in place in this view, with only the ornamental grill work still missing from the end hoods.

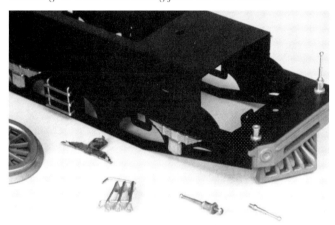

Not only the body was trimmed. Simulated springs and journal boxes (the shiny pieces resembling an eagle's wings), five-piece brass ladders (center foreground, and at upper left on the frame) and flagpole sockets (lower right) adorn the frame. The pilot (right) is also a separate piece, made from heavy cast iron.

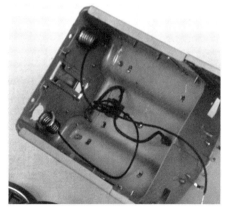

Each end of the 408E had three light sockets, one (the main headlight) on top of the body, and two (the running lights) low down on the end panel of each hood. The running light sockets (left) are fastened to the body with bend-over tabs. The die-cast headlights are held in place by small screws. The simple wiring harness connects these sockets to a power source terminal on one of the motors.

The motor at left is shown during insertion of the axles. On the other motor, the heavy bronze axle bearings are visible. The high quality of these components assured long life.

Each wheel set contains a plain wheel and a geared one. The brass gears were punched to fit over raised bosses on the back of one wheel in each pair.

Double reduction gears made Lionel motors powerful and smooth running. The single automatic reverse unit, mounted in the end of the motor at left, is wired to both motors to ensure that they always operate in tandem. The couplers are seen projecting from slots in the pilots, held in place by a screw hidden behind the cowcatcher spokes.

Each motor is suspended inside the frame, held in place by a heavy cotter pin in such a manner as to allow it to swivel freely to follow the curves in the track.

With both motors in place and the body fully trimmed, all that is required to complete the assembly is connection of the headlight wires and insertion of two screws through the end hoods into the frame. Expert engineering and careful attention to detail gave Lionel products great consistency, and made them easy to repair.

Each motor is suspended inside the frame, held in place by a heavy cotter pin in such a manner as to allow it to swivel freely to follow the curves in the track.

chapter 5 Notes chapter 5

(1)   J. B Sykes, ed., *The Concise Oxford Dictionary of Current English*, p. 171.

(2)   The actual measurements are 11-1/2" (500 series) and 12-1/2" (200 series).

(3)   Ron Hollander, *All Aboard*, p. 96.

(4)   Lionel car bodies were stamped from large sheets of steel, then folded and locked in place with sturdy metal tabs, or soldered in just a few locations. Ives workers laboriously fabricated bodies from many separate pieces, each one requiring one or more soldered joints. It has been suggested that some Ives trains were sold at prices below the cost of manufacture, in order to be competitive.

(5)   Bruce C. Greenberg, *Greenberg's Guide To Ives Trains*, Vol. I , p. 15.

(6)   Bruce Greenberg reports (*Ibid.*, p. 16) that the factory itself was not included in the sale. It presumably reverted to the mortgage holders, who subsequently leased the premises to the new owners.

(7)   *Ibid.*

(8)   Lionel used the suffix "E" to designate locomotives fitted with remote control reversing. Therefore a No. 10 had a manual reverse unit, while a No. 10E contained the Distant Control device. Ives used the suffix R. After acquiring the Ives unit, Lionel continued to employ its own letter designation. Collectors therefore commonly use the term "E unit" when discussing Lionel's reverse mechanism, but the heritage of the device is Ives.

(9)   Hollander, *op. cit.*, p. 102.

(10)   Pullman cars No. 412 California, No. 413 Colorado, No. 414 Illinois, and observation car No. 416 New York.

(11)   Hollander, *op. cit.*, p. 127. Sales declined less precipitously during the first year of the Great Depression, from $2,278,000 in 1929 to $1,932,000 in 1930.

(12)   *Ibid.*, p. 128.

(13)   Similarly, buyers had a choice of five different size coaches in the O Gauge line.

(14)   In 1932, the No. 392E was introduced at $35.00, while the price of the No. 400E had risen to $45.00. In 1934 the No. 385E appeared at $28.50, and the No. 1835E was priced at $25.00.

(15)   Tooling costs for the Hudson have been reported at $75,000, a record at that time for any toy product.

Boucher called both this locomotive and its more premium model a "Pacific," but with its 4-6-0 wheel arrangement, "ten wheeler" is the correct designation. However, their more expensive version did have the Pacific's 4-6-2 configuration. (Photograph by Brad Varney, Nelson G. Williams Collection)

6

BOUCHER, DORFAN
AND THE
DECLINE OF IVES

Among America's pioneer manufacturers of electric trains, only Lionel, Ives, and American Flyer achieved a high volume of sales and national distribution. Based upon the number of trains that survive, Carlisle & Finch was the most successful of the early smaller firms, but discontinued its train production around the beginning of the First World War. The Howard Miniature Lamp Company and the Knapp Electric and Novelty Company introduced 2" Gauge lines in 1904, but the former dropped its trains in 1907, as did the latter in 1913.

Somewhat more successful was the Voltamp Electric Manufacturing Company, which began making two-rail, 2" Gauge trains in 1903. Although never sold much beyond the Baltimore, Maryland area, Voltamp's elegant models achieved a fair measure of local popularity and continued in production until 1922.[1] In that year, Voltamp sold its train division to the Boucher Manufacturing Company of New York, a firm already well known for its model boats.

Boucher both widened the gauge of the Voltamp designs and added a third rail to match Lionel's then-dominant Standard Gauge, but otherwise changed the trains very little, retaining the former owner's primitive wood-and-steel construction techniques. With only a very limited offering of freight and passenger cars and locomotives, Boucher's sales were quite small. The trains remained in production only through 1929, when the firm elected to concentrate upon its more successful line of boats.[2]

The 1923 Boucher catalog is smaller at sixteen 6" by 9" pages than those printed by the larger companies. Nevertheless, it is very attractive and professional in appearance, with color illustrations and copy carefully worded to present the trains in the best light. Especially effective is a center fold-out page that presents a large image of the premium passenger set, plus two other sets, one freight and one with three differently-colored coaches.

On the back of this fold-out page are two freight sets and a photograph of the locomotive mechanism. This latter view suggests the simpler, more primitive design and construction features that did not compare well with contemporary Lionel technology. Boucher did not manufacture any railroad accessories. Instead, a limited number of items identified as Lionel products were offered in the catalog. These included semaphores, a telegraph post, a block signal, a lamppost, and a crossing gate.[3]

Boucher's track differed greatly from the all-steel track of its competitors, according to the catalog description: "Laid on a wood base 3/16" thick by 3-1/8" wide; this track provides a solid road-bed. The rail is securely fastened to wood sleepers[4] and the whole assembly reinforced by longi-

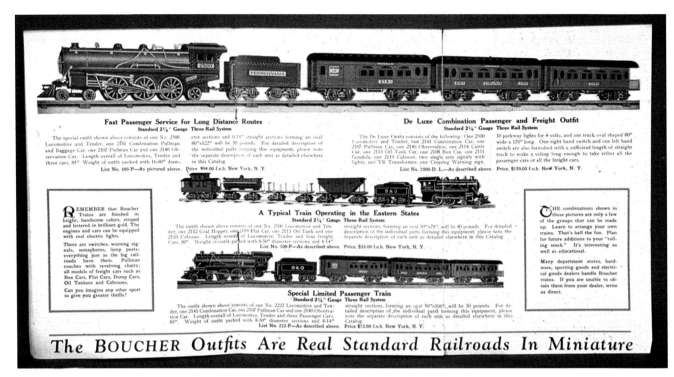

Fast Passenger Service for Long Distance Routes
Standard 2¼" Gauge Three Rail System

The special outfit shown above consists of one No. 2500 Locomotive and Tender, one 2141 Combination Pullman and Baggage Car, one 2107 Pullman Car and one 2140 Observation Car. Length overall of Locomotive, Tender and three cars, 85". Weight of outfit packed with 16-80" diameter sections and 6-14" straight sections forming an oval 80"x122" will be 50 pounds. For detailed description of the individual parts forming this equipment, please note the separate description of each unit as detailed elsewhere in this Catalog.

List No. 500-P—As pictured above. Price $104.00 f.o.b. New York, N. Y.

De Luxe Combination Passenger and Freight Outfit
Standard 2¼" Gauge Three Rail System

The De Luxe Outfit consists of the following: One 2500 Locomotive and Tender, one 2141 Combination Car, one 2107 Pullman Car, one 2140 Observation, one 2114 Cattle Car, one 2113 Oil Tank Car, one 2108 Box Car, one 2111 Gondola, one 2110 Caboose, two single arm signals with lights, one YR Transformer, one Crossing Warning sign, 10 parkway lights for 4 volts, and one track oval shaped 80" wide x 170" long. One right hand switch and one left hand switch are also furnished with a sufficient length of straight track to make a siding long enough to take either all the passenger cars or all the freight cars.

List No. 2500-D. L.—As described above. Price, $159.00 f.o.b. New York, N. Y.

REMEMBER that Boucher Trains are finished in bright, handsome colors, striped and lettered in brilliant gold. The engines and cars can be equipped with real electric lights.

There are switches, warning signals, semaphores, lamp posts; everything just as the big railroads have them. Pullman coaches with revolving chairs; all models of freight cars such as Box Cars, Flat Cars, Dump Cars, Oil Tankers and Cabooses.

Can you imagine any other sport to give you greater thrills?

A Typical Train Operating in the Eastern States
Standard 2¼" Gauge Three Rail System

The outfit shown above consists of one No. 2100 Locomotive and Tender, one 2112 Coal Hopper, one 2109 Flat Car, one 2113 Oil Tank and one 2110 Caboose. Length overall of Locomotive, Tender and four freight Cars, 80". Weight of outfit packed with 8-30" diameter sections and 4-14" straight sections, forming an oval 50"x78", will be 40 pounds. For detailed description of the individual parts forming this equipment, please note separate description of each unit as detailed elsewhere in this Catalog.

List No. 100-F—As described above. Price, $55.00 f.o.b. New York, N. Y.

THE combinations shown in these pictures are only a few of the groups that can be made up. Learn to arrange your own trains. That's half the fun. Plan for future additions to your "rolling stock." It's interesting as well as educational.

Many department stores, hardware, sporting goods and electrical goods dealers handle Boucher trains. If you are unable to obtain them from your dealer, write us direct.

Special Limited Passenger Train
Standard 2¼" Gauge Three Rail System

The outfit shown above consists of one No. 2222 Locomotive and Tender, one 2141 Combination Car, one 2107 Pullman Car and one 2140 Observation Car. Length overall of Locomotive, Tender and three Passenger Cars, 85". Weight of outfit packed with 8-30" diameter sections and 8-14" straight sections, forming an oval 50"x106", will be 50 pounds. For detailed description of the individual parts forming this equipment, please note the separate description of each unit as detailed elsewhere in this Catalog.

List No. 222-P—As described above. Price $73.00 f.o.b. New York, N. Y.

The BOUCHER Outfits Are Real Standard Railroads In Miniature

Boucher's premium passenger set stretches attractively across the center fold-out pages of the 1923 catalog. This illustration, and the smaller freight and passenger sets shown below it, show the trains to be similar to the early Lionel Standard Gauge offerings in style and construction. However, the Lionel catalog of the same year introduced the first of the modern designs that would set the pace for toy train production throughout the 1920s. As Lionel (and to a lesser extent, Ives) upgraded and innovated, and as American Flyer entered the market with new and substantial products, Boucher's old-fashioned designs began to appear more and more obsolete.

Boucher's locomotives and freight cars were handsome and well made, but the company failed to update the antiquated Voltamp designs when competing firms introduced their more modern products, beginning in 1923. A reproduction 2113 Oil Tank Car (made by John Harmon) accompanies this 2222 locomotive and tender. (Photograph by Ed Richter, Nelson G. Williams Collection)

tudinal strips of wood which eliminate warping or twisting and enable the track to be securely fastened. The appearance of this track is most realistic."[5] Lionel and Ives rails, mounted on metal ties, might have been less realistic, but production costs were certainly lower.

Boucher's train sets could be purchased either with or without track, and two different diameter curves were offered. Lionel made all its curved Standard Gauge track sections to form a 42"-diameter circle, excepting only the short-lived 36"-diameter track introduced in 1906 and soon abandoned. Boucher's regular line was described in the catalog as having 50"-diameter circles. In addition, wide radius track (80" across a circle) was sold separately and packed with the premium sets that were pulled by the large 4-6-2 Pacific locomotive. Such broad curves required a lot of floor space, and Lionel's sharper turns, while not as realistic, gave a customer the potential for more operation in a given amount of space.

Evidence of the widespread acceptance of Lionel's 2-1/8" Standard Gauge is found on page 9 of the 1923 Boucher catalog: " . . . Boucher cars can be used on tracks which you may have already or you can add Boucher equipment to what you have already purchased, even though it is of other make." This sentence was probably intended to encourage sales to customers who already owned Lionel or the recently converted Ives Standard Gauge trains, and who knew of the Voltamp heritage of the Boucher line. However, even though Boucher trains could run on Lionel or Ives track, their couplers would not work with products made by either of the latter two.

When Dorfan and American Flyer entered the Standard Gauge market shortly thereafter, they too each had unique couplers. As a result, by the mid-1920s there were five separate companies making trains that ran on 2-1/8" Gauge track, but none could easily be coupled to any of the others. An owner could not purchase pieces of Ives, Dorfan and Boucher rolling stock, for example, and expect to pull them with a Lionel or American Flyer locomotive.

Boucher's commitment to, and interest in, toy trains might have developed, had initial performance in the marketplace been better after the takeover of Voltamp. However, a combination of high prices and outdated construction kept the line from being really competitive, and sales were disappointing. The company elected to invest neither in significant improvements nor in new additions to the line. In the face of rapid expansion and development by the larger toy train corporations, Boucher's stagnant line withered and vanished after only seven years.

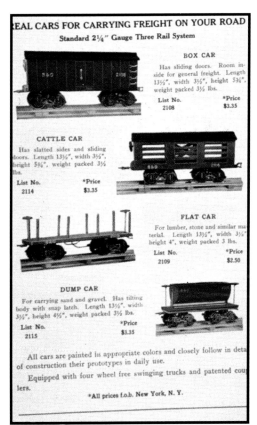

Above, left: Boucher Standard Gauge freight cars were adapted with very few changes from the Voltamp No. 1 Gauge line. They are distinctively different from the Lionel and Ives products of the pre-1923 era, but exhibit the same unsophisticated construction and foreshortened bulkiness. They could not compete with the new Lionel and American Flyer freights that would dominate the market after 1925.

Above, right: Least modern in appearance were the stock car and flatcar designs pictured in the 1923 Boucher catalog, but to many collectors they convey a delightfully toy-like character.

Dorfan and the Die Casting Revolution

Only one other company challenged the three large manufacturers with any degree of success, and in so doing contributed significantly to an infant technology that would in the future produce the world's most highly detailed mass-produced toy trains: die casting. Milton and Julius Forchheimer were part of the German toy making firm of Joseph Kraus & Company, owned by their cousin and well-known for the Fandor line of trains. In 1923 the brothers emigrated to the United States and the following year opened a factory in Newark, New Jersey.[6]

By reversing the syllables of the Fandor trade mark, the Forchheimers created their Dorfan Company to manufacture a new line of miniature railroads. Just exactly how they funded the enterprise is not entirely clear, but it was probably underwritten by Joseph Kraus. Although not as large as either Bing or Marklin, Kraus' Fandor trains were successful and highly respected in their native Germany. It is likely that Kraus looked with envy at the huge potential market for toys in 1920s America. However, with the memory of the Great War still fresh in people's minds, even mighty Bing was having difficulty reestablishing itself in the face of adverse public opinion. It is conceivable that Kraus sponsored his cousins' foray into the American market, believing that a domestic brand, built and distributed in the United States, would have a better opportunity for acceptance than a competing German import.

The Forchheimer brothers established their individuality early by using an entirely new method of construction. While cast iron and stamped steel had long dominated the field, Dorfan cast its locomotives from a newly-developed zinc alloy. This pioneering and adventurous use of an unfortunately unperfected technology would exert great influence upon Lionel and other toy makers in succeeding years. However, unforeseen difficulties with the process seriously marred the new company's reputation.

Die casting in the 1920s involved the formation of parts from hot liquid zinc alloy, which was poured into molds (called dies) and allowed to cool. Dorfan locomotives were cast in two halves, and had far fewer parts than the competition's steel designs, thus making their production more economical. Instead of having a separate frame, the box cab designs had bearings and supports for the motor parts molded into the interior walls of the castings. Dorfan locos were sold ready-built, or in kits (called "Take Apart Engines" in the catalogs) that could be assembled with a screwdriver.

Dorfan advertised its new state-of-the-art process as producing unbreakable trains, subject neither to denting nor

Very few of these Dorfan 3930 locomotives have survived in running condition. Dorfan had stopped making Standard Gauge locomotives by the time the problems with their die casting procedure had been properly addressed, and most of their Standard Gauge locomotives have suffered some degree of deterioration. (Photograph by Brad Varney, Nelson G. Williams Collection)

shattering as steel and cast iron were. Unfortunately, the early zinc alloy mixtures were contaminated by impurities and deteriorated after only a few years due to oxidation.[7] Since the slow failure of the alloy was not noticed immediately, a considerable number of trains had been sold to the public before the trouble surfaced. As soon as the problem became apparent, Dorfan's management strove to improve their product and offered customers replacement of their cracked locomotive bodies at no cost. This public relations effort, while expensive, did help to preserve some measure of the company's reputation, although it cut deeply into profits.

The first Dorfan trains were similar in size to other manufacturers' O Gauge products and operated on the same size track. The company quickly became known for its clever innovations. In addition to die casting and the take-apart feature,[8] Dorfan introduced tiny passengers to some of its coaches. The medium-priced cars contained strips of lithographed figures (heads and upper bodies only) mounted inside and visible through the windows. On the most costly sets, the figures were made of hand-painted, three-dimensional castings. Other innovations included ball bearing motors and an automatic reversing system, using rectified direct current, that was simpler and more positive than the electro-mechanical reverse units made by Ives, Lionel, and especially American Flyer.

By 1926, the Dorfan O Gauge line was well enough established to permit the company to expand its offerings. The zinc alloy defects had not yet surfaced, and the Forchheimers used their profits (and probably additional funding from Germany) to develop their own "Wide Gauge" trains, built to the same 2-1/8" Gauge as Lionel Standard track. Convinced of the educational and promotional value of its "Take Apart" O Gauge feature, Dorfan introduced two large "Loco-Builder" designs, a twelve-wheeled imitation of a Pennsylvania Railroad electric locomotive in 1926, and an interpretation of the St. Paul electric style a year later. While the latter design resembled locos already made by Lionel and Flyer (and later Ives), the distinctive Pennsylvania engine was unique to Dorfan.

All Dorfan locomotives, both Standard and O Gauge, are relatively scarce, since so many fell victim to deterioration of the zinc alloy castings. The Standard Gauge engines are the least common for two reasons. The company produced O Gauge trains from 1925 through 1933, but Standard Gauge production started a year later and was discontinued after 1930, due primarily to the rapid decline of the market for expensive toys during the Depression. Secondly, the fragility of the zinc alloy was just becoming evident shortly before the decision was made to discontinue Standard Gauge trains. Improvements in the die casting process extended the life span of later Dorfan O Gauge locos, those made in the last several years of production. Most Dorfan engines which are found in good condition today come from this latter period.

The 14-1/2"-long twelve-wheeled Pennsylvania-type locomotive, being the most expensive in the catalog, was sold in lesser numbers than the more economical St. Paul design. So few exist in running condition today that they may be classified as truly rare. They were sold under at least three different catalog numbers (most were No. 3930), depending upon such features as the presence or absence of ball bearings in the drive components. In the 1930 catalog, Dorfan advertised this engine at $24.25 with manual reverse, or at a $6.50 premium for its "Distant Remote Control" feature.

Less expensive at $16.75 in 1930, the No. 3920 St. Paul-style measured 13" in length, came with Distant Remote Control for an additional $6.50, and is somewhat more commonly found than its large sibling, although relatively few have survived without some degree of decay. These prices were roughly comparable to those charged for the St. Paul locos from Lionel, American Flyer and Ives.

Dorfan made only 14" passenger coaches in Standard Gauge, but differing trim options were available. While giant Lionel offered five distinct lengths of coach at the same time, Dorfan saved a considerable amount on tooling costs by making just one size. Least expensive were the lithographed coaches, riding on tinplate wheels in simple stamped-steel trucks, and lacking either handrails or steps. The more expensive cars carried this extra trim, and were mounted on handsome die-cast trucks and wheels, which were unfortunately subject to the same decay as the locomotive bodies. These trucks are rarely found intact today. Most of the premium cars were enameled, rather than lithographed, and some also had the clever little passenger figures in the windows.

The coaches were extremely rugged. Made with heavy-gauge steel and riveted together, they could withstand all but the roughest mishandling. Each of the stamped-steel sides contained six window openings, flanked by two doors. The company installed individual window frames and doors, painted in contrasting colors and held in place by bend-over tabs. Many of the cars, excepting only the least expensive, had simulated air tanks mounted beneath the floor. Some versions were lighted, again depending upon cost.

During the first year, only Pullman cars were made; Dorfan did not alter the tooling to make an observation car until 1927. As a temporary substitute, the company installed two round window frames in the ends of some 1926 cars, and fitted them with red glass. The interior lights shone through these portholes in imitation of the red lanterns sometimes used as marker lights on the ends of real trains when traveling without an observation car. In 1928 a true observation car was created by shortening each coach side, thus eliminating one door

Although the bodies are the same, the premium Dorfan coach at right displays many more costly features than its economy sibling at left: die-cast trucks, brass handrails and steps, glass portholes in the ends, and a rugged enamel finish.

Dorfan freight cars: 801 Boxcar (left) and 800 Gondola. (Photograph by Brad Varney, Nelson G. Williams Collection)

Dorfan freight cars: 806 Caboose (left) and 805 Hopper Car. (Photograph by Brad Varney, Nelson G. Williams Collection)

Dorfan 3930 Locomotive, the company's largest, with a complete set of six freight cars. (Photograph by Ed Richter, Nelson G. Williams Collection)

Lithographed details and brass trim contribute to the handsome appearance of this Dorfan 804 Tank Car. (Photograph by Brad Varney, Nelson G. Williams Collection)

and one window. The open observation platform that resulted was encircled by a brass railing.

Following the trend of the day toward bright rather than authentic paint schemes, Dorfan coaches came in a variety of colors, and carried descriptive names such as "Mountain Brook" or "Pleasant View." Others were named after cities, including "Chicago" and "San Francisco." The lettering was either part of the lithography, or added as decals on the enameled cars.

Dorfan also made six different Standard Gauge freight cars. Five of them were lithographed: a gondola (No. 800), boxcar (No. 801), tank car (No. 804), hopper car (No. 805) and the No. 806 Caboose, which had an interior light. All were first cataloged in 1928, and are especially handsome, being well proportioned and lavishly decorated by the lithograph process. Although not as heavy as the coaches, they were nevertheless very well built and resistant to denting, but the surfaces are easily scratched. However, they appear much more realistic than the freight cars made by the competition, thanks to their many fine printed details. Only the relatively scarce lumber car (No. 809) was enameled instead of lithographed, and, since it was introduced some time after the others, fewer were made.

The catalog shows the freight cars with die-cast trucks, although they were sometimes sold with the less expensive stamped-steel versions. All had 14" frames, the same as the coaches, but the catalogs describe them as being 15-1/2" long. This dimension includes the couplers, a somewhat dishonest way of advertising them as larger than the competition. Still, the freight cars are well proportioned, although the passenger cars seem somewhat stubby by comparison.

Dorfan neither cataloged nor produced a steam locomotive in Standard Gauge, but did sell a specially painted version of the Ives No. 1134 in 1929 and 1930. This locomotive is widely recognized to be the most graceful and authentic design made by any manufacturer prior to Lionel's scale No. 700E Hudson in 1937. The revolutionary Ives loco was die cast, and had a powerful motor mounted in the cab rather than between the wheels, which allowed more realistic detailing of the area under the boiler than either Lionel or American Flyer had accomplished. Two versions were offered by Dorfan under the same catalog number (1134), one in black and the other in an unfortunate shade of pea green that is indeed distinctive, but hardly realistic. Both were trimmed in red.

Considering the small size of the company, Dorfan produced a remarkable number of accessories. In addition to a line of signals, lampposts, bridges, and stations, the firm made an impressive motorized crane (No. 70), mounted on a steel girder platform and standing just four inches short of two feet high. Almost as striking were a large die-cast signal bridge (No. 419) and a well-detailed No. 427 Station.

Dorfan catalogs were never as large or as colorful as those published by Lionel or American Flyer, and their advertising strategy was subtly different. The cover bore the slogan "DORFAN modern ELECTRIC TRAINS" in 1930. The lower case letters used for the second word drew attention to it by a sort of reverse emphasis, suggesting that the products described inside were somehow more advanced than those of the longer-established companies (as indeed they were, in some respects). The copy inside stresses modern engineering principles and is somewhat reminiscent of Lionel's approach. There is also a carefully worded appeal to a parent's vanity: "Talk it over with your Dad, and tell him you want a real train in miniature, not a toy; explain Dorfan's wonderful features to him—he'll understand." The implication is that any intelligent father would instantly recognize the superiority of Dorfan's innovations.

The Standard Gauge portion of Dorfan's production did not survive beyond the first year of the Depression, and the O Gauge line lasted only through 1934. There are probably several reasons for this. First is the deterioration of the die-cast locomotives, the replacement of which cut deeply into profits already reduced by the failing economy. Second was falling demand. As discretionary income dropped, large companies such as Lionel and American Flyer suffered reduction in sales just as Dorfan did, but they still enjoyed much greater overall volume. Dorfan's already small share of the market shrank almost to invisibility.

A third reason is suggested by the company's parentage. As already proposed, financing for the Dorfan line most probably originated with Fandor in Germany, but in the 1930s it is certain that any possibility of continued support from abroad disappeared. Germany was already suffering runaway inflation, and the political climate that would eventually result in World War II was quickly developing. The New Jersey-based Dorfan Company lacked the resources to continue, and although they continued to make toys for other manufacturers until about 1938, tooling for the trains was sold.[9]

Although Standard Gauge Dorfan locomotives in operating condition are hard to find, their freight and passenger cars may be used with other manufacturers' engines, with just a little adaptation of the couplers. Here an American Flyer New Haven box cab pulls a string of lithographed Dorfan coaches.

The Decline of Ives

As the decade of the 1930s began under a deepening economic cloud, only two influential manufacturers of Standard Gauge trains, Lionel and American Flyer, seemed capable of sustaining profitable production. Boucher and Dorfan sales were minuscule, and Ives now existed in name only, being a part of the Lionel Corporation and rapidly losing its individuality.

Ives' Standard Gauge trains of the latter 1920s were beautiful, well constructed and engineered, and sold reasonably well. With the sole exception of the revolutionary remote control reverse unit, however, Ives followed Lionel's lead in most areas. When Lionel moved from dark colors and rubber-stamped lettering to brightly painted cars and brass plates, Ives soon did the same, and with the success of the new Lionel locomotive designs, Ives felt pressured to try to compete. But they always seemed to be one step behind Cowen's company.

In an effort to regain the advantage, the Ives management invested much of the company's thin profit margin in two exceptional locomotives. Up until 1925, there were just

two electric-type designs offered: the small square-bodied economy model and the larger, New York Central-inspired, S-type cab. Both were offered in varying trim options, for a total of five different price categories. In 1926 a new design appeared: the No. 3237 St. Paul.

The Ives interpretation of this well-known style, also produced by Lionel and American Flyer, is easily the most handsome and realistic of the three. The body is exceptionally well detailed, with hatches on the hoods, rows of louvers, bright brass journal boxes on the frames, and attractive shiny trim on top. Its proportions were realistic and pleasing to the eye, and it came in both manual and automatic reverse versions.[10]

Although it seems strange in retrospect, this attractive locomotive was not particularly successful for the company, and fewer were sold than was expected. That may be due in part to its size. The public was accustomed to equating size with cost, partly due to Lionel's practice of building so many different sizes of locomotives and cars and pricing them accordingly. The No. 3237 was almost exactly the same size as the less expensive (though less handsome) New York Central style (No. 3241 and 3242). It was also built for a shorter period of time, and is much less commonly found by collectors.

Even scarcer is a larger locomotive that used the same cab. Just as Ives had created a premium version of the four-wheeled No. 3241 by placing it on a huge twelve-wheeled frame, the company placed the St. Paul body on twelve wheels to create its No. 3245. This version appeared in 1928 and was joined a year later by an even more impressive loco

on which the end hoods were lengthened, but bearing the same catalog number. (Collectors differentiate between the two No. 3245 locomotives by calling them short cab and long cab.)

These magnificent engines might have become best sellers, and could have helped the company's financial situation, had they been introduced earlier. By the time they debuted, however, Ives' financial failure had forced its sale to Lionel and American Flyer, and the original management was no longer in control of its destiny.

The First Modern Standard Gauge Steam Locomotive

The final contribution by Ives' innovative engineers and designers was also their most influential. In 1928, just prior to the company's failure, they introduced the first No. 1134 die-cast locomotive, a 4-4-2 design with a graceful tapered boiler, extensive rivet detail and bright metal trim, and a new, highly efficient drive system that made it the most realistic toy locomotive to date. It came with a similarly well-proportioned, die-cast coal tender, and was usually painted black, although a smaller number of copper and nickel plated versions were also produced.[11]

Unlike Lionel, Ives produced a steam locomotive design every year of the 1920s after its conversion to Standard Gauge. The first was No. 1132 in 1921, an 0-4-0 design with a cast-iron boiler that was sold with a stamped-steel tender. A second cast-iron loco was created in 1927, and numbered 1134. With its 4-4-0 wheel arrangement and updated cab design, it was handsome, but still somewhat toy-like in appearance. Ives called it "President Washington," after a locomotive then running on the Baltimore & Ohio Railroad.[12]

When the new die-cast design was ready, it assumed the same catalog number (1134) as the discontinued "President Washington." The new design boasted a motor that was mounted in the cab, connected to the driving wheels by a long shaft. At that time, neither Lionel nor American Flyer was making steam locomotives in Standard Gauge, and the earlier Lionel designs, discontinued after 1926, had their motors located between the wheels. The new Ives design was much more authentic in appearance. On a prototype locomotive, the boiler is separated from the frame and wheels, so that there is open space visible in between. The cab-mounted motor provided this realistic touch. Although it was a minor detail that went largely unnoticed by the public, it demonstrated Ives' continuing attention to authenticity, and set the pattern for scale model manufacturers in the future.

To accompany the new locomotive designs, Ives planned a new series of passenger coaches which, at 21-1/2" long, would have been equal in size to Lionel's State cars. Although they were advertised for sale in 1928, production was canceled when the company declared bankruptcy, and only one sample is known to exist.[13]

As outlined in previous chapters, the failure of Ives was due to several factors, including outdated designs, expensive production methods, and a conservative advertising strategy that was overshadowed by Lionel's aggressive campaigns. It is also apparent that Ives management overextended resources by such endeavors as the new No. 1134 steam locomotive design, which required very costly tooling. By 1928, so much was owed to creditors that bankruptcy and reorganization seemed the only way to preserve any portion of the company and its reputation. As a result, Lionel and American Flyer jointly purchased Ives' assets at a bargain-basement price (see Chapter 5) and began to restructure the entire line of products.

To provide continuity, the new management coalition retained the services of some key Ives personnel, including Chairman of the Board Harry C. Ives, son of the founder Edward. However, it is evident that policy and decision-making authority was not left in the hands of the former conservative (some would say reactionary) directors. Under Lionel-Flyer administration, cost-cutting measures were immediately imposed. The new and impressive passenger car designs were canceled and replaced by the first of many products that would compromise the distinctiveness of Ives trains.

Since only one hand-made sample is known to exist, probably no new tooling had been ordered for the planned 21-1/2" coaches, and a substantial outlay of cash was avoided by adapting existing American Flyer car bodies instead. They were mounted on Ives trucks and given Ives couplers, so as to match existing locomotives, and they received new colors and

Unlike competitive locomotives made by Lionel, the Ives 1134 design had a realistic separation between the boiler and drive wheels.

The high foreshortened freight cars in the Ives line suffered by comparison with the long and graceful designs introduced by American Flyer in the mid-1920s. Despite the realistic subdued coloring and elaborate lettering on the Ives 192 Merchandise Car at right, buyers were more attracted to the bright enamel and shiny brass plates of the American Flyer 4008 and 4018 Automobile Cars and other large rolling stock.

Perhaps no phase of the former Ives operation was more in need of revision than its freight car division. These antiquated designs were hand-soldered and required many labor-intensive steps to produce, and little time was lost in replacing them. All but the hopper car, flatcar, and Ives' unique coke car (No. 191) were dropped in 1928. The more economical American Flyer caboose, boxcar, gondola, tank, and cattle car bodies replaced the Ives designs, but were fitted with Ives trucks and couplers to ensure continued compatibility for previous customers.

In spite of these economy measures, the new management endeavored to support the Ives line through the introduction of a new and attractive product, an elaborate circus set, headed by the new No. 1134 steam

catalog numbers, (No. 241 Club Car, No. 242 Parlor Car and No. 243 Observation), but otherwise they were identical to Flyer's 19″ premium cars.

locomotive. The set featured a standard boxcar and cattle car with special lettering for "THE IVES RAILWAY CIRCUS," as well as wheeled animal cages carried on flatcars, and a coach

The American Flyer caboose in the foreground came with Ives trucks, couplers, and identification plates, in a special combination of handsome colors (dark red, deep maroon, and peacock blue) that many collectors consider better looking than the standard all-red Flyer model (background).

Lionel production of the Ives 3236 locomotive (top) used a Lionel 8 body with an extra sheet metal strip around the bottom to give extra internal clearance for the Ives motor. Earlier 3235 and 3236 models shared the same Ives body stamping (bottom).

to transport the performers. Included with the trains was a cardboard cut-out circus tent scene, obtained from the Coca-Cola Bottling Company.

In 1929, before the October stock market crash and the onset of the Great Depression, it must have seemed to the new management that Ives could be made profitable once more. Having much greater resources than its temporary partner, Lionel bought out American Flyer's share and became sole owner of Ives.[14]

As part of the dissolution agreement, both companies retained rights to certain Ives designs. Most notably, Lionel became the sole patent holder for the superior Ives remote control reverse, while American Flyer obtained rights to the beautiful No. 1134 locomotive. Finally in complete control, Lionel then began the process of reducing the Ives line, abandoning many accessories, cars, and locomotives, and replacing them with existing Lionel designs, retaining only the Ives trucks and couplers.

This conversion process was hastened even further by the collapsing world economy in late 1929 and throughout 1930. Lionel freight and passenger car bodies were sold with Ives nameplates and numbers, and the last of the Bridgeport locomotive designs were phased out. Unable to maintain a separate factory in 1931, Lionel moved the Ives operation from Connecticut to its main plant in Irvington, New Jersey. As a final blow to Ives' identity, all of their trains in 1931 and 1932 came equipped with Lionel couplers, making them incompatible with earlier Ives products.

Lionel must have known that this step would alienate Ives' former customers forever, and cripple whatever small amount of sales potential the Ives name still generated. It is tempting to assume that management deliberately planned to sabotage the Ives division, thus justifying its total elimination. Whether it was, in fact, a calculated action, this is exactly what happened, for production of Ives Standard Gauge ceased after 1932, but curiously there was one apparent attempt to revive interest in the line. While most other Ives trains and accessories were virtually identical to Lionel's in 1931 and 1932, the company introduced one entirely new set exclusively under the Ives trademark. The No. 1764E locomotive and its accompanying passenger cars (Nos. 1766, 1767, and 1768) were made from new tooling and differed from anything ever before produced in Standard Gauge.

The locomotive was patterned after a New Haven Railroad prototype and rode on a twelve-wheeled frame, but it was substantially smaller than the old Ives Nos. 3243 and 3245. The body was a simple box cab, riding low on the frame and sparsely trimmed. The cars were built to a similar low profile and lacked any fancy decoration, but they were well proportioned and economical to produce. When the Ives nameplate was abandoned after 1933, Lionel incorporated these cars into its own line, but the locomotive was dropped and is consequently quite rare today.

The appearance of this last Ives set as late as 1932 remains a mystery, for it is questionable whether Joshua

Cowen was ever committed to maintaining the Ives name. His brief stewardship of the venerable company seems not to have been motivated by genuine respect; his efforts to crush his Bridgeport rival during the previous two decades suggest differently. It may be that Cowen's only goal was to achieve control of the one Ives patent that he coveted, the automatic sequence reverse unit. Even before the economic collapse of 1929, steps were well under way to weaken Ives' individuality and distinctive presence in the market. Had the Depression not occurred, it is still likely that this highly respected pioneering toy train trademark would have been quietly pushed into obscurity by its powerful new owner. Such was Joshua Lionel Cowen's stance toward the competition. It wasn't enough that "Lionel always leads"—he wanted Lionel always to win.

chapter 6 # Notes chapter 6

(1)   Dallas J. Mallerich III, *Greenberg's American Toy Trains*, p. 283.

(2)   Pierce Carlson, *Toy Trains, A History*, pp. 110, 125-126.

(3)   Lionel management probably saw the provision of their accessories to Boucher for resale as good advertising, and that the smaller company was not a serious competitive threat.

(4)   Curiously the British term "sleepers" is used in place of the American "ties".

(5)   Page 11 of the 1923 catalog.

(6)   Carlton McKenney, *Early American Toy Trains*, p. 165.

(7)   *Ibid.*, p. 166.

(8)   It is probable that Lionel copied the Dorfan concept when introducing its first Bild-A-Loco kit in 1926, a year after the smaller New Jersey company announced its first take-apart locomotive, the O Gauge No. 51.

(9)   McKenney, *op.cit.*, p.166. Mr. McKenney reports that the Unique Art Manufacturing Company of Neward bought Dorfan's dies, but only the largest O Gauge passenger car body was ever used again.

(10)   Ives identified its automatic revers locomotives by adding the letter "R" to the catalog number, just as Lionel used "E". Thus, an automatic No. 3237 is listed as "3237R", both in the catalog and on its brass plates.

(11)   While the innovative No. 1134 appeared about the same time as the Lionel/American Flyer takeover, it was undoubtedly created by the Ives engineering staff. It differs greatly in concept and construction from any loco ever conceived by Lionel. Also, the time required to create tooling for such a complex design suggests that it was planned and executed well before the bankruptcy.

(12)   In 1928, the "President Washington" loco was offered in an uncatalogued version under catalog No. 1132, previously used for the early 0-4-0 type. While Lionel always used a new number for revamped products, Ives reused the same numbers when introducing new designs.

(13)   Bruce C. Greenberg, *Greenberg's Guide to Ives Trains*, p. 78.

(14)   Bruce Greenberg suggests (*Ibid.*, p. 42) that American Flyer personnel differed with Lionel over the investment in new tooling for the Ives line, and that this disagreement may have contributed to Flyer's decision to sell out.

American Flyer made just one size freight car (14") in Standard Gauge, whereas Lionel offered both large premium and somewhat smaller economy models. The Flyer 4017 Sand Car (gondola, left) compared favorably with Lionel's big 212 Gondola (foreground), but the relatively inexpensive Lionel 512 Gondola (right background) was less expensive and a big seller. The 512 replaced the 112 (center) in 1927.

7

LIONEL'S FORMIDABLE COMPETITOR

American Flyer's success and diversity of products were second only to those of Lionel in the Standard Gauge field. The line of large trains made by this Chicago-based company was distinguished by unusually well-proportioned freight cars and a series of graceful and substantial 14" and 19" passengers cars. These coaches and their accompanying locomotives carried a wealth of shiny brass trim, making their fabrication somewhat more expensive than comparable Lionel products, but giving them a handsome appearance and a strong sense of identity and individuality.

One indicator of the company's secure financial position is the succession of handsome catalogs that appeared in the Standard Gauge production years. While advertising by the cash-strapped Ives was quite modest, American Flyer's catalogs were richly printed in full color, and at forty-eight pages in 1929, they equaled in size those issued by Lionel.

William O. Coleman, founder (with William Hafner) of the American Flyer line of trains, was no stranger to the toy-making craft when his company entered Standard Gauge production in 1925. He had been producing clockwork O Gauge trains successfully since 1907, and a few years after his partner left to form the Hafner Manufacturing Company

in 1914, Coleman decided to expand the line to include electrically-powered locomotives.[1] The first American Flyer electric trains appeared late in 1918, and consisted of cast-iron steam locomotive shells modified from clockwork designs, and mounted on a four-wheeled electric motor frame.

Over the next two decades, Coleman's designers created the widest range of steam locomotive types available from any company in O Gauge. There were at least seventeen different steam loco boilers, eleven styles of tender, and a variety of wheel arrangements ranging from 0-4-0 to the first 4-6-2 Pacific-type ever made by a high-volume maker in O Gauge.[2] Box cab electric locomotives were added in 1920, and again, the variety was very great. They ranged from tiny 6-1/2"-long lithographed examples to big New York Central-inspired locomotives with twelve wheels, enameled bodies, and lots of trim. At least eight cab styles were made, and an even greater number of different frames.

By 1925, with his O Gauge toys selling well, Coleman decided to test the Standard Gauge market dominated by Lionel and the fading Ives. Over the next three years he introduced three different locomotive designs, two sizes of passenger cars, and a complete line of freight cars that many collectors consider more handsome and better proportioned than any of Flyer's competitors were making (see Chapter 4). By 1928, when the Ives Corporation failed, American Flyer was solvent and its Standard Gauge trains were commercially successful.

In partnership with Lionel, Coleman's company operated the bankrupt Ives until some time in 1929, but this arrangement was not entirely satisfactory. Problems arose, possibly because of such factors as policy disagreements among the managers of the two parent companies, or logistical problems caused by the distances involved. Ives was in Connecticut, Lionel in New Jersey, and American Flyer in Chicago, and transportation and communication over so many miles was still relatively slow in 1929, lacking today's jet travel, direct distance dialing, faxes, and the Internet.

Lionel bought sole control of Ives in 1929 and set about devaluing and eventually dismantling the company over the next several years. At the dissolution of their management alliance, Lionel retained the Ives name, most of that firm's assets, and especially the rights to the superior Ives remote control reverse. American Flyer took away the magnificent Ives No. 1134 locomotive design and tooling.

At the time of the Ives takeover, Lionel had not produced a steam engine in Standard Gauge since 1926, and American Flyer had never produced any sort of steamer for its wide track line. The Ives No. 1134 was an outstanding design that captured the flavor of American-style steam locomotives more accurately than the later Lionel interpretations.[3] Lionel had already introduced its new steam-outline No. 390E in 1929, and its appearance was radically different from the Ives No. 1134. Lionel management must already have been working on subsequent locomotive designs that would bear a family resemblance to the No. 390E. It is likely that they considered the Ives design to be too foreign to the Lionel character, and thus passed it over to American Flyer when the two parted company.

American Flyer may have been working on an original steam locomotive design as early as 1928. The company was comfortable with cast iron technology, thanks to years of experience with the O Gauge clockwork and electric lines, and eventually sold a cast-iron Standard Gauge loco and tender under catalog No. 4672 in 1931 and 1932. This locomotive is somewhat reminiscent of the Ives cast-iron steamers sold from 1921 through 1928, but with a family resemblance to Flyer's O Gauge steamers. It was apparently not ready for production in time to compete with Lionel's new No. 390E in 1929, however. The sudden availability of the radically new and modern No. 1134 allowed American Flyer to produce a new steamer almost as quickly as Lionel did.

Regrettably, American Flyer did not retain the unique cab-mounted motor and drive train designed by Ives for its versions of No. 1134,[4] but installed a conventional electric motor between the wheels. Nevertheless, Flyer's version is almost as attractive and realistic as the earlier Ives model. The boiler and tender were both made using the zinc alloy casting technique pioneered by Dorfan a few years before. This production method resulted in smooth, well-detailed boilers and tender bodies that appeared almost indestructible when new, but fell victim to the same problem that was beginning to plague Dorfan in 1929.

Metallurgists had not yet managed to maintain purity in the molten zinc formula, and the castings began to expand and crack as they aged. As a result, examples of both Ives' No. 1134 and the Flyer versions (cataloged as Nos. 4664 and 4694) proved to be very fragile in the long run, and most require restoration when encountered by collectors today.

American Flyer used the Ives casting for just two years (1929-30), meanwhile completing work on the less expensive cast-iron No. 4672. At the same time, the company's engineers were adapting what they had learned from working with the Ives design to create a new cast zinc boiler, which appeared in the line under catalog No. 4675, in 1931. At 27", the new locomotive and tender were two inches longer than the Ives design they replaced, and the extra length made it perhaps the most graceful of all Standard Gauge locos of that time. The Ives influence is readily apparent, however, in the tapered boiler, North American-style domes, and typical boxy coal tender.

Flyer produced the new design for several years under five different catalog numbers and in varying levels of trim, the most elaborate (Nos. 4681 and 4696) having copious quantities of brass tubing under the running boards (the so-called "brass piper" models, which are much sought after by collectors). Two different tenders were offered: the coal style and a heavy Vanderbilt oil-carrying type. The last of these handsome models were made in 1934 or early 1935.

Improvements in casting techniques during the early 1930s meant that the later Flyer locomotives were somewhat more durable than the early ones, but problems continued to bedevil manufacturers for several years. Lionel first employed the die casting process to make frames for its No. 390E in 1929, and these are now usually found warped or broken. The same is true of some later Lionel loco frames. It was not until around 1937, when Lionel's No. 700E scale Hudson first appeared, that engineers were becoming more confident of the level of durability that Dorfan had bravely predicted with its "unbreakable" locomotives in 1924. Nevertheless, some zinc-cast models from the late 1930s, notably Lionel's semi-scale No. 763E Hudson, continued to suffer some degree of deterioration.

William Coleman's company met the problems caused by the Depression in much the same way as Lionel, concentrating on low-priced, high volume sets in O Gauge. Just as Lionel created the Lionel-Ives and Winner lines, Flyer marketed sets of tiny O Gauge trains under the "Champion" trademark. The Standard Gauge line proved too expensive to maintain, and was discontinued completely after 1936. By that time, many of the more elaborate items were no longer in production, such as the largest (19") passenger coaches, made only through 1934, and most of the box cab electric locos. It is probable that most of the items sold in 1935 and 1936 were inventory left over from previous years. While Lionel managed to keep its largest trains afloat a few years longer than did American Flyer, the best years of Standard Gauge were definitely past.

The American Flyer Alternative

The most desirable Standard Gauge sets in the 1920s and 1930s were the huge passenger sets made by Lionel (top two shelves), Ives (bottom two shelves) and American Flyer, such as this "President's Special" on the middle shelf. (Carail Museum Collection)

Nevertheless, there were some very good years for Lionel's Chicago competitor. Unlike Dorfan and Ives, whose adventurous use of the new die-casting technology resulted in nicely detailed but ultimately somewhat fragile locomotives, American Flyer employed the time-tested technique of stamped-steel production. To distinguish its products, the firm's designers incorporated abundant amounts of brass trim. While not necessarily realistic, all that shiny metal made the toys very attractive on the retail shelves. Even the lowest priced New Haven locomotive was fitted with brass overlays on the pilots, and the St. Paul design was generously provided with brass handrails, ladders, bells, pantographs, doors, window frames, and identification plates.

On the freight cars, the trim was somewhat more restrained, although most of them carried two, or more often three, large brass plates per side. One identified the brand name, one the catalog number, and the third proclaimed the company's success: "OVER 6 MILLION HAPPY OWNERS." (As the years passed, the figure on these plates was raised first to seven and then to eight million.) Two cars received extra attention in the trim department. Premium versions of the caboose had ladders, steps and handrails galore, plus twelve individual window frames and a shiny brass smoke stack. And the tank car body was brightly girded with four brass straps, encircling handrails, and a tall ladder on each side.

In the latter 1920s through the early 1930s, William Coleman's company produced magnificent train sets that differed in style from Lionel's great "Blue Comet" and "State" sets, and which attracted a lot of attention in the premium-price market. The "President's Special" passenger trains enjoyed a prominent place in the catalogs, and the

Three American Flyer trackside accessories are visible here, mixed in with Lionel items: 4218 Block Signal (left foreground, restored in custom colors), 4206 Flashing Highway Signal (seen from the back, center), and 4116 Bell Ringing Signal (orange pole with white crossing sign, right of center in the background). These accessories were stamped with different catalog numbers, depending upon whether they were intended for Standard or O Gauge trains. For example, the 4218 Block Signal was stamped "2218" instead when it was sold for O Gauge use.

later versions were elaborately trimmed, even including a large brass American eagle ornament on the locomotive pilot. Most lavishly decorated of all were the 19" enameled passenger coaches. Whereas the earlier lithographed cars had their contrasting window frames and other details printed on the sides, the painted cars were fitted with a multitude of brass: handrails, doors, steps, diaphragms, up to eight identification plates, and as many as thirty-six separate window frames per car.

Even though Flyer had fewer sizes of passenger cars than Lionel (two vs. five, respectively), the Flyer cars within a given set often differed significantly from each other in appearance. In a Lionel four-car "State" set, for example, there were three identical Pullman cars, distinguished only by name and number. The windows and doors on the observation cars were the same as on the Pullman cars, the only difference being the addition of a brass observation platform on one end.

By contrast, an American Flyer "President's Special" set contained four entirely distinctive coaches. First came the No. 4390 Club Car, a combine with baggage doors at one end and fourteen tall and narrow windows on each side. The No. 4391 Pullman featured eighteen similar windows per side, but the No. 4393 Diner was radically different. Instead of using the Pullman car's design for a diner, the way Lionel did in some sets, Flyer punched-out each diner car side to receive two narrow and eight wide windows, giv-

ing it a highly individual look. Finally, the No. 4392 Observation combined the two concepts, with nine of the tall windows at the forward end, and four of the wide windows back toward the rear deck. Having four different car designs increased Flyer's tooling and production costs, but these cars surpassed Lionel's by more closely duplicating the window arrangements of real trains.[5]

Most impressive of all the sets was a brass and chrome-colored masterpiece called the "Mayflower." To create this unusual and costly toy, American Flyer chrome-plated the bodies of the locomotive and passenger cars from the "President's Special" set, then fitted them with the usual array of brass. Although unlike anything then traveling on the nation's railroads (the era of stainless steel streamliners was still years in the future), the "Mayflower" helped to establish a reputation of high quality for the company. Few were sold, but these beautiful sets undoubtedly helped Flyer bring its lower-priced sets to the attention of customers who might otherwise have bought trains from Lionel.

American Flyer manufactured a complete line of accessories, second only to Lionel in variety. The company made many appealing signals, lampposts, bridges, and tunnels, and an especially attractive two-story switch tower. Although lacking houses for the imaginary residents of Flyertown, the line did feature handsome lithographed freight and passenger stations, as well as water towers, derricks, and several small train-related buildings.

While not as innovative as its competitors, American Flyer succeeded by making substantial and durable toys which were both attractive and well engineered, and the company thrived until faced with the shrinking markets of the Depression years. Despite continued efforts to introduce new and more modern designs, Coleman's trains could not generate the profits needed for head-to-head competition with Lionel. By 1937, management was actively seeking a buyer for the firm, and A. C. Gilbert, whose company marketed the famous Erector line of construction toys, acquired American Flyer in 1938. Eventually the operation was moved to New Haven, Connecticut.

By that time, the only Standard Gauge trains still on the market came from Lionel, and most of these consisted of inventory from past years. The O Gauge market had proven to be most profitable, with Lionel dominating the middle and upper price brackets and the company headed by Louis J. Marx successfully entrenched in the lowest price field. Gilbert wisely chose to create a new and different market for American Flyer. For 1939 production, he introduced a new series of smaller die-cast locomotives, built to 3/16" scale as opposed to approximately 1/4" to the foot for O Gauge. Although initially the new line was made to run on O Gauge track, Gilbert converted them to narrower two rail S Gauge (7/8" between the running rails) after World War II, and his company again established the American Flyer trademark as Lionel's principal competitor.

With the departure of Ives, the failure of Dorfan and A. C. Gilbert's new approach to American Flyer production, it seemed that the market for large scale trains was forever gone. Lionel sold off its remaining inventory as the war years approached and emerged in 1945 with just one track gauge, the familiar three-rail O Gauge.[6] American Flyer began touting the realism of its somewhat narrower and definitely more authentic two-rail system and promoted it both as toys and for the scale model enthusiast. The trend among many hobbyists, however, seemed to be moving toward even smaller trains, those produced in HO scale and running on track little more than half as wide as O Gauge.

Neither company would have predicted a resurrection of Standard Gauge trains in years to come, and in fact this rebirth was slow to develop. It probably began with the writings of the late Louis J. Hertz, whose numerous books (most notably *Riding The Tinplate Rails* in 1944, and *Messrs. Ives of Bridgeport* in 1950) stimulated curiosity about antique trains among adult hobbyists and collectors. With the organization of the Train Collectors Association in 1954, interest developed quickly, and attics all over North America began to give up their hidden treasures. Over the next few decades, the hobby grew to the point where dedicated craftsmen turned their attention to the commercial manufacture of Standard Gauge trains once again.

chapter 7 # Notes chapter 7

(1) William Hafner was not so tempted. His company manufactured only clockwork trains throughout its long history, which finally ended in 1951 with the sale of assets to the All Metal Products Company of Michigan.

(2) Steven H. Kimball, *Greenberg's Guide To American Flyer O Gauge*, pp. 27-54.

(3) Ron Hollander in *All Aboard*, (p. 96) suggests that the influence of Lionel's Italy-based design staff resulted in anomalous features on some Lionel locomotives, such as the European-style boiler bands on the Nos. 392E and 492E.

(4) See Chapter 6 for a description of this drive system.

(5) Preference for either of these two interpretations is a matter of taste. Some hobbyists like the more realistic variety of window treatments in the Flyer sets, while others favor the unified look of a Lionel passenger train.

(6) The O Gauge track supplied with Lionel's more expensive trains was substantially made from heavy steel. Lighter in weight was the O27 track supplied with more economical sets. Although the diameter of an O27 circle was several inches smaller that a regular O Gauge circle, the distance between the rails was the same for both types. All but the largest locomotives could be run successfully on either size.

Reproduction toy trains and accessories have made it possible for operators to capture a vintage layout appearance with pristine equipment, and at much lower cost than using original antique models. Some newer items, such as the Lionel Trains, Inc. copy of a classic 384 steam locomotive and tender (center), wear attractive new color schemes that were never offered between the World Wars. (Carail Museum Collection)

8

THE RESURRECTION

---

of Standard Gauge

The toy train industry rebounded with startling speed and energy after the close of World War II. Lionel rushed a single O Gauge train set into production in time for Christmas of 1945, and even managed to include one of many innovations to come: the first realistic operating knuckle coupler. In 1946, both Lionel and American Flyer produced a full line of products—the latter in a completely new format (S Gauge, scaled at 3/16" to the foot) that emphasized two-rail track and locomotives that puffed artificial smoke. Lionel's steamers were similarly smoke-equipped.

Although heavily committed to wartime contracts from 1942 through early 1945, the toy train divisions of these two corporations had not been idle. It is evident from the quantity of new products and features that designers and engineers had been busy making plans for the expected postwar demand. After years of deprivation during the Depression, and strict rationing during the war, the public was hungry for just about any type of consumer goods. Auto makers could sell almost anything with four wheels and an engine, and in fact the early postwar cars were barely disguised reissues of late-1930s designs.

Planning for the conversion from wartime to peacetime production began at Lionel in December 1942, and probably also at American Flyer well before the war ended. With the defeat of Germany, it must have seemed inevitable that Japan's aggression could not long continue in the Pacific theater, and contracts for navigational equipment (a specialty of Lionel) were not being renewed. The government permitted Lionel to begin tooling for toy production in May 1945.[1] As thousands of military personnel returned home, a great economic upheaval occurred.

During the early 1940s, hundreds of thousands of women found employment in factories and service industries that supported the war effort. With the return of the fighting forces, these jobs reverted for the most part to men re-entering the work force, and many women, in turn, went back to more domestic endeavors. With the male/female population balance somewhat restored, many ex-factory workers and ex-servicemen married and began new families (the so-called "baby boom"), creating a demand for jobs, housing, automobiles, and an array of modern household appliances that benefited from war-inspired technological advances. Employment opportunities flourished.

Television rapidly evolved from curiosity to necessity, creating a whole new entertainment industry. By the early 1950s, the first wave of an expanding population entered the public schools, requiring much new construction.

A new concept in neighborhoods developed. Previously, the population had resided in cities, small towns, or on farms, but with the first mass-produced housing developments came a new concept: suburbia. These residential communities lacked the familiar town centers of the past, and influenced the beginning of a revolutionary pattern of commercial enterprise—the shopping mall—which got its start in the densely populated northeastern states of New Jersey, New York, and Connecticut.

As the entire structure of the Western economy realigned itself, the toy industry rode the crest of its prosperity. Less than a decade after the war, the baby boom fueled a tremendous demand for toys of all sorts, and especially those which could be seen to have educational value. Toy trains were seen as having diverse educational benefits, including safe experimentation with electricity, development of physical dexterity, and knowledge of the transportation industry as a whole. They were also widely touted in the 1950s as a pastime that fathers and sons could share together, an important bonus in those days when family values were strongly emphasized.

Young parents, concerned not only with entertaining their children but with giving them the "advantages" which they themselves had not enjoyed, bought chemistry sets and microscope sets and Erector sets, and especially toy trains, in unprecedented numbers. Although prices were high, just as they had been three decades earlier, disposable income was rising steadily, and families believed, correctly, that Lionel and American Flyer trains represented good value. With but a single slight relapse (the conflict in Korea), Lionel and American Flyer responded to consumer demand with ever-expanding production figures, culminating in peak sales in 1953 ($32,900,000 for Lionel alone)[2]

Yet another quiet revolution was in the making. The average work week had been shrinking since before the war, and now commonly stood at about forty hours in most industries and professions. The resulting increase in leisure time enlarged that adult segment of the toy market collectively described as "hobbies" as thousands of men (and a lesser but growing number of women) sought new creative outlets for their idle hours. Many turned from toy trains to scale model railroading, especially the smaller HO trains that were half the size and a quarter the bulk of Lionel's O Gauge.

As 1954 began, prospects seemed bright for continued growth and prosperity in the toy and hobby industries. And yet another influential event would soon occur; one that would see a tiny but stubborn resurgence of interest in the grand Standard Gauge trains that had been the hallmark of an affluent 1920s America.

Birth of the TCA

In the 1950s, the most popular hobbies were postage stamp and coin collecting—pursuits that retain a large following today. In fact, many hobbies are centered around acquisition and collection, and toy trains are no exception. This hobby enjoys the added dimensions, however, of layout-building and operation, borrowed from the scale modelers. No doubt nostalgia plays a major role, as many adult toy train enthusiasts admit to taking the most pleasure from recreating their childhood amusements.

Williams special reproduction of the Lionel 408E locomotive for the Train Collectors Association's twenty-fifth anniversary. (Carail Museum Collection)

There was some limited interest in collecting Standard Gauge trains prior to 1954, thanks in part to the influence of the writings of Louis H. Hertz and others. A Standard Gauge Association was formed in 1947, but by March 1953, fewer than 150 members had joined. Other than this group, the first sustained organized approach to the hobby began on June 20, 1954,[3] when a small number of like-minded collectors met at Alexander's Train Museum in Yardley, Pennsylvania, to discuss the formation of a new national association. A second meeting on October 17 resulted in the fledgling Train Collectors Association, which was destined to grow into the largest and most influential international organization devoted to the collection, history, and operation of toy trains.[4]

The mission statement of the TCA is "To preserve an important segment of history—Tinplate Toy Trains— through research, education, community outreach, fellowship and to promote the growth and enjoyment of the hobby."[5] The success of this enterprise and of its research publication, the *TCA Quarterly*, have resulted in many thousands of members in the decades since 1954, and in the formation of other similar clubs.

These sister organizations often emphasize specific and complementary aspects of the hobby. For example, the Toy Train Operating Society (TTOS) caters its *Bulletin* especially to those who run their trains, and features technical articles and information. Others devote themselves to information about specific manufacturers, such as the American Flyer Collectors Club (AFCC) and the Lionel Collectors Club of America (LCCA). These and other groups also encourage international memberships, with the TCA being represented in at least fifteen foreign lands. There are also associations centered in other countries, such as the Lionel Collectors Association of Canada (LCAC).

Virtually every field of interest related to toy trains is represented within one or more of these organizations, and Standard Gauge trains attract a substantial share of attention. Their historical significance lures some aficionados, while others are most fascinated by seeing these huge toys in operation. Still others enjoy recreating the fantastic layouts envisioned in the Lionel catalogs of the 1920s and 1930s.

As the train collecting hobby grew after formation of the TCA, more and more old Standard Gauge trains were found packed away in attics all over the United States. Many were then preserved in the condition in which they were discovered, and maintaining old trains in original paint is still a highly significant aspect of the hobby. Those who wanted to run these toys soon found that they needed repair or even complete restoration. However, there was (and still is) some element of resistance to making them look and run like new, and some reluctance to removing the paint and lettering applied by the venerable manufacturers, no matter how damaged or timeworn.

In addition, as TCA and other club memberships grew, the finite nature of the supply of antique Standard Gauge became increasingly apparent. With more and more collectors pursuing fewer and fewer trains, these toys became more highly prized, and therefore more expensive. One by one a small but dedicated number of craftsmen re-entered the field to meet the growing demand by making reproductions of classic Lionel designs of the 1920s and 1930s. These re-creations were greeted with enthusiasm by collector/operators, encouraging further production and a diversification of the items available. Later, some original designs appeared. Some were toy-like interpretations of trains that had never been offered by the vintage makers. Other builders created Standard Gauge versions of toy trains that had previously been available only in O Gauge, such as Lionel's Milwaukee Hiawatha. Still others made modern designs.

In the latter quarter of the twentieth century, the popularity of large toy trains as playthings has returned, but primarily in the form of No. 1 Gauge offerings from such firms as LGB, Aristo-Craft, and USA Trains, and even Lionel itself, among others. These modern toys are made with contemporary technology, including the use of a high percentage of plastic parts. By contrast, Standard Gauge has continued to be a specialized area appealing mostly to collectors, although interest has been high enough to attract even modern Lionel to offer reproductions of their own antique classics. In general, construction follows the patterns established in the classic years, being of stamped steel and employing simple, basic, open-frame motors instead of today's electronic marvels.

While a few producers of postwar Standard Gauge trains enjoy widespread distribution, others have made and sold only a very small number of trains. While they may be little known outside of the hobby, their efforts have produced some beautiful and fascinating toys, earning them an important place in the history of Standard Gauge. Following are some of these manufacturers, large and small.

Classic Model Trains

Charles Wood is perhaps best known among those who repair and restore old toy trains for his extensive line of train enamel, carefully matched to reproduce the colors used by Lionel, Ives, and American Flyer. In 1977 he purchased the Classic Models Standard Gauge line from Fred Mill (see below; also Williams Reproductions Limited) and renamed the company Classic Model Trains.

In addition to locomotives and cars carried over from the original firm, Wood's company has added new designs to his inventory. Construction follows the techniques used by vintage manufacturers: stamped-steel bodies, cast-zinc driving wheels, and brass trim. Only the motors are a break with tradition, being a more modern, direct current design (made by Pittman, a company closely associated with HO Gauge modeling) instead of the open frame AC/DC type used in the 1920s and 1930s.

Like so many other small manufacturers, Classic Model Trains began as a hobby, making only a limited quantity of products for the relatively small Standard Gauge operator market. As its reputation spread, Wood developed decorative paint and lettering schemes with authentic looking heralds from many railroads, including Pennsylvania, Reading, Union Pacific, B&O, and Erie. Today he offers both steam and electric-style locomotives, plus a variety of freight cars and coaches. One of his most distinctive designs is a "Camelback" locomotive of the type operated on such eastern rail lines as the Reading. This design features a cab mounted above the center of the boiler, ahead of the firebox.

These products retain a definite toy-like appearance reminiscent of the very early years of Standard Gauge production. The thick-rim driving wheels resemble those from Lionel's Classic Period, while the open frame trucks suggest an arch bar design from the nineteenth century. The freight cars are relatively short, like the 1906-1926 Lionel designs, and are constructed from heavy-gauge sheet metal and attractively painted.

Passengers wait to board a Classic Model Trains coach on the author's layout. (Charles Wood Collection)

Charles Wood's observation car evokes the style of early Lionel coaches, with their arched windows, brass steps and railings, and open clerestory roofs. However, they are completely original in design. (Charles Wood Collection)

Classic Model Trains distinctive 4-6-0 Camelback locomotive and tender, seen here on the author's layout. (Charles Wood Collection)

Classic Model Trains boxcar, showing extensive lettering and a realistic Reading herald. (Photograph courtesy of Charles Wood)

The initials "SL" on this box cab locomotive identify it as a product of Fred Mill's Classic Models Corporation. Compare this design with the next photograph, showing production from the same tooling by Charles Wood. (Photograph courtesy of Charles Wood)

Classic Model Trains log car, preserving the manufacturer's family name. (Photograph courtesy of Charles Wood)

Classic Model Trains box cab electric locomotive, adapted by Charles Wood from patterns by Fred Mill (see previous photograph). (Photograph courtesy of Charles Wood)

Classic Model Trains Pennzoil tank car. (Photograph courtesy of Charles Wood)

In 1969, TCA members Fred Mill and Jerry Williams joined forces to create a company dedicated to the manufacture of newly-designed Standard Gauge trains. Their initial offerings were directed toward their fellow collectors, and included two locomotives (a diminutive steamer and a four-wheeled box cab electric), three freight cars, and a day coach.[6]

The partnership lasted less than two years. It soon became apparent that Mill and Williams entertained differing ambitions for their enterprise. Williams believed that collectors would be more interested in purchasing reproductions of original Lionel items than innovative designs. He relinquished his interest in Classic Models and established his own Williams Reproductions Limited (see below), while Mill continued to produce their original line. Mill advertised his products under the name Standard Lines Electric Trains. He sold the company to Charles Wood in the autumn of 1976 (see Classic Model Trains, above).

Classic Models' early 0-4-0 steam locomotive was available as an easily assembled kit. At first, it came equipped with a coal bunker and no tender, but Fred Mill later extended the design to create a 4-6-0 "ten-wheeler" with a conventional coal tender.[7] This same design was carried over into Charles Wood's Classic Model Trains line. Mill's imaginative approach to production resulted in one interesting conversion that helped keep the cost of his products at a reasonable level. He created his box cab electric locomotive out of the same body first used for a caboose, by simply changing the window treatment and adding appropriate trim.

Although not reproductions of Standard Gauge trains, Classic Models Corporation products exhibit the same characteristics as the early Ives and Lionel offerings: simple stamped-steel construction, minimal detailing, and foreshortened appearance. Note that both the locomotive and the caboose share the same side-body stampings. (Photograph by Ed Richter, Nelson G. Williams Collection)

Classic Models Corporation locomotive, tender, and coaches, sold in 1970. (Photograph by Ed Richter, Nelson G. Williams Collection)

Fred Mill's box cab electric locomotive and freight cars. The tooling was later sold to Charles Wood for his Classic Model Trains line. (Photograph by Ed Richter, Nelson G. Williams Collection)

James Cohen

James Cohen is best known for creating highly accurate reproductions of the earliest Lionel Trains, J. L. Cowen's 2-7/8" Gauge. In addition, he made tooling for Lionel's early Standard Gauge steamers and the earliest versions of Standard Gauge freight cars sold by Lionel between 1906 and 1910. He also made trolley and day coach reproductions in very limited numbers. Recently Cohen sold his designs and tooling to Joseph L. Mania (see below).

Duane Eberhart[8]

Following the death of Red Forney (see next entry), Duane Eberhart manufactured a dozen of the long Forney-designed hopper cars, as well as other Forney cars.

Forney mining train. (Photograph by Ed Richter, Nelson G. Williams Collection)

Forney GP-9 diesel locomotive and freight cars. The locomotive is powered by two motors. (Photograph by Ed Richter, Nelson G. Williams Collection)

Over the ten year period preceding his death in 1985, Willard L. "Red" Forney developed a modest line of Standard Gauge trains, first in partnership with Glenn Gerhard (see below) and later on his own in Carlisle, Pennsylvania. Their early efforts were made of sheet metal in the classic tinplate tradition, and the partners provided some rolling stock for the G Gauge line sold by Delton Locomotive Works.

By 1978, after Gerhard's move to Albany, New York, Forney was producing three sets of his own design: a U.S. Army train and two mining trains inspired by the pioneering Carlisle & Finch effort some eight decades earlier. The Army train was pulled by an unusual 4-4-4 diesel locomotive, and had two flatcars carrying military vehicle models, plus a boxcar, gondola, and caboose.

Other Forney trains include hopper cars, boxcars, flatcars, tankers, and a caboose. Some of his products bear a resemblance to those made by McCoy Manufacturing, since Forney spent a month in the Seattle area learning welding techniques from Margaret McCoy. Some of the freights were built in two sizes: shorter 14" versions that go well with the classic vintage designs, and huge 22" models that illustrate just how massive a scale-length car in Standard Gauge appears. Forney also made a GP-9 diesel and a Pennsylvania GG-1 electric locomotive. Forney trains were made in very limited numbers, and are therefore quite rare. Least common are several white boxcars—one of them adorned with lettering for the Three Mile Island atomic energy plant located just south of Harrisburg, Pennsylvania. Printed on this car is a date (3-28-79) commemorative of the control accident at that facility which drew public attention to the dangers of domestic nuclear power production.

In spite of the company's short life span, the Forney line is as varied as that of any other latter day manufacturer, excepting only the extensive McCoy output. At least eighteen different railroad and company names were used on the rolling stock.

Forney white boxcars; the Three Mile Island commemorative is at upper right. (Photograph by Ed Richter, Nelson G. Williams Collection)

Above: The very simple construction of Red Forney's freight cars, including hook couplers and rudimentary arch bar trucks, capture the flavor of Standard Gauge trains from the early part of the twentieth century. The car at upper left carries two plastic toy cranes of modern design. (Photograph by Ed Richter, Nelson G. Williams Collection)

Red Forney made this interurban car from two Lionel coach bodies, with trolley poles added. (Photograph by Ed Richter, Nelson G. Williams Collection)

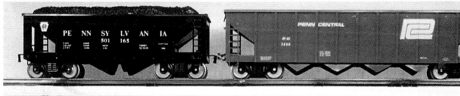

Red Forney built foreshortened 14" freight cars (left) with proportions similar to vintage Lionel and Ives trains, and much longer (22") close-to-scale freight cars (right). (Photograph by Ed Richter, Nelson G. Williams Collection)

Although built to run on Standard Gauge track, Glenn Toy Trains are closer to the size of the larger contemporary models of such manufacturers as LGB, at a scale of approximately 1:24. Unlike either the classic tinplate manufacturers (who built from stamped steel), or modern day makers of plastic trains, Glenn Gerhard cast his products from heavy-gauge aluminum, then assembled and painted them in his basement workshop over a ten year period, beginning in 1977.

Gerhard's first efforts in the field were in partnership with Willard L. Forney (see above), prior to his move from Pennsylvania to Albany, New York. Although lacking formal training as a machinist, he taught himself the necessary metal-working skills. In addition to his locomotives and rolling stock, he produced the first wide-radius Standard Gauge track switches since the demise of the Boucher line.

After studying the stamped-steel construction techniques used by McCoy Manufacturing, Gerhard determined that for his small-scale operation, the required tools and dies would be too expensive. He turned instead to the M. G. Carter Foundry[11] to make aluminum castings from his patterns.

Only modest numbers of locomotives were made during the ten years Gerhard built his trains. Most common is his model of an Alco F-unit diesel, with production figures of more than three hundred; steam locomotive production totaled only about twenty-five. The latter were patterned after a Pennsylvania 0-6-0 switch engine. As with most small manufacturers of toy trains, low volume made for a high per-unit cost, and Glenn Toy Trains were quite expensive. Even at the list price of $900 for the steamer, sales of so few engines could not have paid the original tooling costs, estimated at about $24,000. They were actually discounted to as low as $500. Lacking the income to keep his business going, Gerhard stopped making trains in the latter 1980s.

Glenn Toy Trains freight cars were made in several sizes, 14", 16", and 19". The smallest equaled both Dorfan and American Flyer models in length, and were larger than Lionel's 200 series. They were quite realistic. The two longer versions exceeded anything made by the vintage Standard Gauge manufacturers, being even better proportioned approximations of prototype cars. Eight types were sold: flatcars, hoppers, boxcars, tankers, gondolas, stock cars, refrigerator cars, and cabooses. There are variations of each type, such as bulkheads on some flatcars and car bodies made to look like either wood or metal. The cars featured prototype road names and heralds, and were well detailed with catwalks, ladders, and door latches.

Glenn Toy Trains freight cars. (Photograph by Ed Richter, Nelson G. Williams Collection)

Glenn Toy Trains 0-6-0 Pennsylvania switcher and Nickel Plate Road caboose. (Photograph by Ed Richter, Nelson G. Williams Collection)

Bob Hendrich ———————— John E. Harmon

Roberts Lines (see below) sold what is probably the largest model of a Pennsylvania GG-1 electric locomotive, measuring 29" long and weighing 26 pounds, made by Bob Hendrich of Glendora, California. Nelson G. Williams reports that fifty-eight of these locomotives were produced. Hendrich also modified some of the long Roberts Lines passenger coaches into dining and observation cars.

Roberts Lines GG-1 Box Cab Locomotive, built by Bob Hendrich. (Photograph by Brad Varney, Nelson G. Williams Collection)

During the late 1970s, John Harmon made twelve sets of reproduction Boucher freight cars, excluding only the caboose. In addition, he made two sets of these cars as they were made by Voltamp, using the earlier company's lettering and truck designs. Harmon followed the original designs closely, employing the same stamped-steel construction as was used to manufacture the originals.[12]

In addition to these sets, Harmon made about a half dozen extra tank cars, boxcars, and flatcars, as well as extra trucks, couplers, and decals. These parts were made available for restoration of original Boucher cars.

John A. Daniels of Pasadena, California, produced a small number of Standard Gauge locomotives based on the Pennsylvania GG-1 electric design.[13] JAD Railways, named for Daniels' initials, also produced a model of a streamlined steam train that was equally famous among both prototype rail fans and toy train operators.

While both Lionel and American Flyer built attractive and colorful versions of the Milwaukee Road "Hiawatha" stream-lined passenger train in O Gauge during the 1930s, no Standard Gauge editions were made at that time. Due to economic conditions during the Depression, it is unlikely that sales of a necessarily expensive "Hiawatha" in the large scale line would have been sufficient to guarantee a profit. JAD Railways proved how attractive a Standard Gauge "Hiawatha" could be by producing its massive set, closely resembling the Lionel model, several decades later.

Construction of the JAD "Hiawatha" followed traditional tinplate techniques, with stamped-steel bodies and a bright enamel finish. The colors chosen closely match those used by Lionel nearly half a century earlier. Comparison of

The JAD Railways "Hiawatha" combine is much shorter than scale length, to allow it to travel around sharp Standard Gauge curves. (Carail Museum Collection)

this model with the Lionel O Gauge version, however, reveals that the JAD version has much shorter coaches. The Lionel "Hiawatha" was designed to operate only on wide radius O Gauge track (6' diameter circles), whereas most Standard Gauge track has 42" diameter curves. A train twice the length of the O Gauge model would have been magnificent, but would have needed 12' diameter curves to run satisfactorily.

JAD Railways Standard Gauge interpretation of the Milwaukee Road "Hiawatha" streamlined loco-motive and passenger cars (top shelf). On the middle shelf is Lionel's O Gauge version of the same train, with American Flyer's O Gauge "Hiawatha" at the bottom. (Carail Museum Collection)

Liberty Lines 600E Hudson. (Harlen Creswell Photograph and Collection)

Some manufacturers of latter day Standard Gauge got their start making reproductions of original Lionel items before branching out into original designs. One Seattle, Washington, enthusiast set out to improve on a Lionel design, and in the process created his own workshop industry. Liberty Lines subsequently grew to encompass passenger and freight cars, signals, and even a giant electric locomotive that rivaled Lionel's No. 381E.

Harlen K. Creswell began collecting Standard Gauge trains in 1975, and within a few years his interest had grown to the point where he was making tenders to go with some of his Lionel and American Flyer locomotives. By 1978 he was ready to attempt a complete locomotive, and he took as his inspiration Lionel's largest, the No. 400E steamer with a 4-4-4 wheel arrangement.[14]

Although lacking the sophisticated tools and dies used for mass production by the commercial manufacturers, Creswell developed tooling to make a stretched version of the No. 400E boiler and frame. He then constructed a 4-6-4 drive train, resulting in a Hudson locomotive with a character nearly identical to the No. 400E but with much more realistic proportions. The addition of a New York Central-style coal tender produced an impressive steamer that stimulated substantial interest among collectors who examined it. Creswell decided that there might be a enough of a market for it among collectors and operators to justify production.

In a relatively short time he was building his Hudson, numbered 600E out of respect for its No. 400E heritage, in the traditional Lionel colors of black, gunmetal gray and "Blue Comet" blue, plus a special custom two-tone green. With a motor capable of moving a 30-pound train, and optional accessories such as smoke, chugger sounds and a whistle, the Liberty Lines Hudson was available only in limited numbers, due to the large amount of handwork required to build one.

Lionel's largest Standard Gauge engine was the No. 381E box cab electric design, modeled after the Milwaukee Road's bi-polar Olympian locomotive and used to pull the first version of the famous State set. This impressive model rode on a total of twelve wheels, but the prototype had more than twice that many—twenty-eight. Creswell turned his attention to making a bi-polar that more closely approximated the original. Again paying homage to Lionel, he numbered his Olympian 3281, gave it a complement of twenty wheels, and matched it with a car Lionel never made: a four-door baggage car to go with the State cars.[15]

Unlike Lionel's handsome but underpowered original, which was driven by just a single motor, Creswell geared six motors to the Liberty Lines Olympian's drive wheels. The baggage car was made with simulated rivets and a roof that closely matched that of Lionel's largest cars. As a bonus, the locomotive could be wired to accept power from overhead catenary lines.

Liberty Lines grew to include a Standard Gauge steam switcher, a trolley, three- and four-car passenger sets, and several freight car designs, certainly an extensive inventory for a home workshop industry. Although never available in large numbers, these impressive products played a significant role in the continuing revival of interest in Standard Gauge that occurred during the 1980s.

Since the dissolution of the original Lionel Corporation's toy train division in 1969, several different corporate entities have owned the rights to this famous name. Most of the products produced since 1970 have been in O Gauge, with low volume production in both large scale (No. 1 Gauge track), and S Gauge under the American Flyer trademark, owned by the Lionel Corporation and its successors since 1965.

Under the corporate title Lionel Trains, Inc., owned by Richard P. Kughn in the latter 1980s and early 1990s, the company revived interest in Standard Gauge by selling reproductions of some of its most famous classic era products, as well as such O Gauge tinplate treasures as the "Hiawatha" and the 800-series of large O Gauge freight cars. In Standard Gauge, the company offered several steam and electric-type locomotives, both passenger and freight cars, a few stations and accessories, and a magnificent chrome-plated copy of American Flyer's "Mayflower" set.

Lionel contracted for offshore production of these items by Samhongsa of Korea, under the supervision of Mike Wolf

(see Mike's Train House below), who had begun making copies of Lionel tinplate in 1983. This arrangement with Wolf was terminated after a few years, and since the sale of Lionel by Richard Kughn to the consortium now known as Lionel L.L.C., the Standard Gauge revival has been abandoned.

Lionel Trains, Inc. reproduction of American Flyer 4689 "Mayflower" locomotive, 4390 Club Car, and part of 4391 Pullman. (Carail Museum Collection)

Lionel Trains, Inc. reproduction of Lionel 400E locomotive in "Blue Comet" colors. (Carail Museum Collection)

The former James Cohen line of 2-7/8" Gauge Lionel reproductions was taken over by Joseph L. Mania of Freehold, New Jersey. As this is being written, Mania has introduced the first of a new series of models representing the earliest Lionel Standard Gauge production, including the Nos. 5, 6, and 7 steamers and the 10-series freight cars. Pre-production samples of the locomotives were first shown in 1997.

These No. 1050 2-7/8" Gauge passenger cars built by Joseph Mania faithfully reproduce the Lionel versions made in 1905. Other Mania reproductions appear in Chapter 1. (Photograph by Sean Smyth)

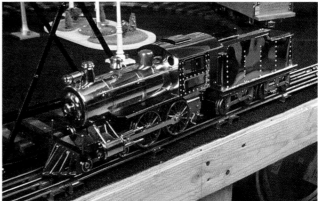

Lionel made premium brass and nickel versions of its No. 6 locomotive and tender under two catalog numbers: No. 6 Special and No. 7. These Joseph Mania reproductions are made with tooling first developed by James Cohen. (Photograph by Sean Smyth)

McCoy built this locomotive to commemorate the founding of the Train Collectors Association (TCA) in 1954. (Photograph by Ed Richter, Nelson G. Williams Collection)

Bob McCoy's interest in Standard Gauge trains began in the 1950s, before collecting these toys became an organized, widespread hobby. Since most Lionel and American Flyer Standard Gauge items were at least two decades old by that time, he found that many of them required repair or replacement parts. At the time, few hobby shops still carried original parts, and the main source for needed items was to take them from other old trains. Only a very few reproduction parts were being made in the 1950s, most with questionable accuracy. The greatest need was for drive wheels, since the zinc castings of the 1920s and 1930s were often cracked and swollen, making the motors inoperable.[16]

To satisfy his own needs, McCoy learned to cast exact duplicates of vintage toy locomotive wheels, and in order to make them available to fellow collectors, he opened the McCoy Manufacturing Company in 1958, just south of Seattle, Washington. For the first several years, this low-volume business was little more than an avocation, but as McCoy pursued his hobby of restoring the trains he collected, he developed the skills necessary for manufacturing entire locomotives and cars.

As other collectors became aware of his activities, they encouraged him to make additional parts, and even to make reproductions of early Lionel products. During the early 1960s McCoy made the dies to duplicate the old Standard Gauge No. 1911 loco. This effort was followed by copies of the Nos. 54 and 1912 box cabs and all three of Lionel's early steam locomotive designs, as well as Lionel's 2-7/8" Gauge models. The accuracy of these models made them difficult to tell from originals, a fact which caused collectors to protest, since they feared the value of their original items would be lessened by unidentifiable reproductions. As a

In a departure from the practice of recreating vintage Standard Gauge trains, McCoy expanded the list of available models with such products as this San Francisco cable car (right). The "Wapid Wabbit" is a whimsical variation on the railbus design usually referred to as a "Galloping Goose." (Photograph by Ed Richter, Nelson G. Williams Collection)

Colorful McCoy boxcars pulled by a special TCA locomotive that resembles the Ives 1764 built by Lionel in 1932. (Photograph by Ed Richter, Nelson G. Williams Collection)

result, McCoy turned his attention to making original designs in Standard Gauge.[17]

The first McCoy freight car appeared in 1964, and the company has since grown to be the largest contemporary producer of locomotives and cars in Standard Gauge. With few exceptions, the products are original designs, but are made in the style of original tinplate from the years between the World Wars. The freight and passenger cars are stamped from steel, then painted and decorated for a wide variety of railroads. The locomotives are similarly varied, ranging from simple four-wheeled box cab versions to eight-, twelve-, and sixteen-wheeled electric locomotives.

The first original McCoy steam locomotive was a model of a nineteenth century American 4-4-0 engine, joined later by a large 2-6-0 design. The company also made railbus, trolley, handcar, traction, and diesel switcher models in a wide assortment of road names. Among their most attractive offerings are an array of circus cars, including flatcars with animal cages, specialized box and stock cars, circus work cars, and performers' coaches. No other manufacturer produced so great a selection of circus-related railroad equipment in Standard Gauge. A favorite item of the McCoy family is the company's first accessory, an operating carousel, initially made in 1978.[18]

A significant portion of the McCoy output was devoted to creating special convention cars and locomotives for such organizations as the Train Collectors Association (TCA) and the Toy Train Operating Society (TTOS). For the former, they made a twelve-wheeled box cab locomotive similar to the very rare Ives No. 1764 in 1974. (This engine is decorated with appropriate TCA lettering, making it easy to distinguish from an original Ives piece.) For the TTOS in 1975 and 1976, McCoy made a steamer like Lionel's No. 5.[19] Unlike the early

reproductions, however, these convention specials are clearly marked as modern production, and are therefore not confused with original vintage toys.

Considerable numbers of McCoy freight and passenger cars were produced over the years for various regional divisions of both the TCA and the TTOS. For example, one of the most varied sets was made over a period of seven years for the TTOS Canadian Division. Pulled by a Canadian Pacific steam engine in authentic black, maroon, and gray colors, the six freight car designs carry heralds from such lesser known railroads as the Esquimalt & Nanaimo Railway and the Quebec, North Shore & Labrador Railway.[20] These and some other McCoy products were made in very limited numbers, and they attract considerable attention from collectors.

McCoy Manufacturing was always a family business. After Bob McCoy's death it was operated by his widow, Margaret, and his son, Bob, Jr. Sadly, McCoy Manufacturing ceased operations in June, 1998. McCoy reproduction parts are known to all who repair and restore vintage Standard Gauge, and the firm's original designs introduced many of today's toy train fans to the pleasures of collecting and operating these large-sized models.

Two very special McCoy boxcars: one commemorating the visit of Willard ("Red") and Janet Forney, when Forney was studying the McCoys' manufacturing techniques (left); and another honoring the company's founder, Bob McCoy, after his death in August 1995 (right). (Photograph by Ed Richter, Nelson G. Williams Collection)

MTH Electric Trains (Mike's Train House)

Mike Wolf produced very accurate copies of Lionel locomotives such as this 385E, both under his own brand name and for the Lionel Classic line sold by Lionel Trains, Inc. (Maurice Weisblum Photograph and Collection)

Mike Wolf began his career in toy trains by assembling Standard Gauge locomotives for Jerry Williams in 1973, at the age of twelve (see Williams Reproductions Ltd. below). He later established his own company, first as a distributor for Williams products and then as a manufacturer of toy trains under his own name. By 1983, Jerry Williams was concentrating on his new line of original O Gauge products and sold the tooling for his Lionel Standard Gauge locomotive reproductions to his young former employee.[21]

Wolf's first efforts, the Nos. 9, 381E, and 408E and the No. 94 high-tension tower from the former Williams line, appeared in early 1983, and were well received by collectors. He then arranged for copies of the Lionel 200-series freight cars and the No. 400E steam locomotive to be made by Samhongsa of Korea. In 1987, Lionel Trains, Inc. contracted with Wolf for the production of items for their Lionel Classic line, a business arrangement that lasted for several years and resulted in copies of a number of Standard Gauge trains and accessories under the larger company's trademark.

While working with Lionel, Wolf was also involved in the creation of some significant locomotives for the O Gauge line, also manufactured for Lionel by Samhongsa. When Lionel dissolved the partnership a few years later, Wolf reestablished his own company, and has since been producing a greatly expanded line of premium O Gauge trains, plus an economy O Gauge line (Rail King). Both categories include various steam and diesel locomotives, freight and passenger cars, and specialty items. Power supplies, track products, and accessories (some of them motorized) round out the line.

In spite of this concentration upon O Gauge, MTH Electric Trains (the most recent corporate name) still manufactures Standard Gauge items, including copies of Lionel's 200-series freight cars, the No. 400E locomotive and tender, the No. 9 box cab electric, and various accessories. These pieces are identified by MTH plates, however, instead of the Lionel plates that were affixed to them when Wolf was overseeing Standard Gauge production for Lionel Trains, Inc.

Harry A. Osisek

Between 1986 and 1991, the father and son partnership of Harry A. Osisek, Junior and Senior, reproduced rolling stock and miniature wagons of the distinctive Ives Circus Train. The three freight cars (192C Boxcar, 193C Stock Car and 196C Flatcar) were accurate recreations of the original Ives designs, decorated with circus train lettering and the special enamel colors originally used by Ives,

and fitted with trucks and couplers made by Rich-Art (see below).

The Osiseks also made copies of the Ives Circus Wagons—one an animal cage and the other a ticket wagon—to be carried on the flatcars. Rounding out the set was a performers' coach, patterned after the No. 184 Club Car, 185 Pullman, and 186 Observation car.

Pride Lines LTD.

This Lindenhurst, New York, firm headed by John Davanzo specializes in tinplate trains and toys, including reproductions and original designs. Among their best-known products are copies of the rare Ives glass-domed station platforms and Lionel trolleys.

A substantial part of their output consists of licensed toys which represent animated Walt Disney characters, including a reproduction of the Mickey Mouse Circus Train that Lionel made in 1935. Pride Lines also makes this Circus Train in Standard Gauge.

Pride Lines reproductions: Ives 121 Station Platform with glass roof, and Lionel 8 "Pay As You Enter" Trolley. (Maurice Weisblum Photograph and Collection)

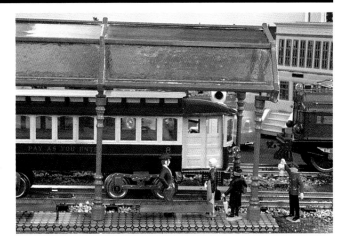

The Rich-Art Company

One of the most extensive lines of premium reproduction Standard Gauge trains available to date is manufactured by the Rich-Art Company of Escondido, California. Founded by Dick Mayer and Art Varney[22] in the mid-1960s, the firm specializes in reproductions of classic period Ives, Lionel, and American Flyer trains, but also produces original designs. The company's first model, released in 1970, was a copy of the Ives No. 3245 Olympian locomotive. Later products included a Standard Gauge version of the Milwaukee "Hiawatha" and copies of various Lionel products in O Gauge.[23]

The company's range of merchandise is very broad, with the greatest variety being available in Standard Gauge. These include the premium American Flyer sets ("President's Special," "Mayflower," "Flying Colonel") and the largest Flyer steam locomotive—the No. 4696 "brass piper" engine. A recent addition is the very scarce Flyer No. 4006 Hopper Car.

Ives copies in the Rich-Art line include the No. 1134 steamer (painted and copper-plated versions), and all of the locomotives with St. Paul-style cabs, including the long-cab version of the No. 3245. The passenger cars that go with these engines are the late transition items with American Flyer-style bodies.

Two innovative Rich-Art designs are available both in Standard Gauge and engineered to run on No. 1 Gauge track (compatible with contemporary LGB and similar products). These are models of the unusual McKeen motor car, used for a few years for interurban passenger service in the Los Angeles area; and the Milwaukee Road Cascade bi-polar electric locomotive, which served as the inspiration for the largest Lionel and Ives locomotives of the classic era. This impressive engine rides on a prototypical twenty-eight wheels.

Roberts Lines[24]

Under two different owners, Roberts Lines offered a diverse selection of Standard Gauge trains, ranging from diminutive four-wheeled novelties to very large steam locomotives in both finished and kit form. The former were first made by the marque's founder, Russell Roberts, and the latter are the work of his successor, Bob Thon. Thon carried on the four-wheel tradition by making a few gondolas and refrigerator cars, some now in the collection of Nelson G. Williams, and others presented to former officers of the Toy Train Operating Society. His most successful product was a whimsical outhouse-on-wheels called "Johnny On The Spot."

The larger Roberts freight cars have 14" frames mounted on reproductions of early Lionel trucks. His company also sold gondola and hopper cars made by Duane Eberhart (see above), using bodies from the Forney line, and a gigantic Pennsylvania GG-1 locomotive made by Bob Hendrich (see above) of Glendora, California. Other Roberts Lines products produced by Bob Thon include cast-aluminum passenger cars in both 21" and 24" versions, and twenty trolley sets.

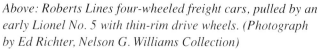

Above: Roberts Lines four-wheeled freight cars, pulled by an early Lionel No. 5 with thin-rim drive wheels. (Photograph by Ed Richter, Nelson G. Williams Collection)

Above, right: Roberts Lines freight cars.

Right: Roberts Lines trolley car set, number 19 out of a total production of 20. (Photograph by Ed Richter, Nelson G. Williams Collection)

Sirus & Varney

After launching the Rich-Art Company with Dick Mayer, Art Varney left that firm for a brief period in the early 1970s. Working with George Sirus, Art made and sold copies of the Ives No. 3245 Olympian locomotive and the American Flyer "President's Special" in limited numbers. He then returned to Escondido and resumed his association with Rich-Art (see above).

Smith Metal Works

Wayne Smith designed and marketed a Standard Gauge engine house large enough, at 24" long, to hold Lionel's biggest classic period locomotives. This product and similar three- and five-stall roundhouse buildings were designed as kits, to be assembled by the purchaser, using a screwdriver.[25]

Standard Lines

See Classic Models Corporation.

Tintown

The company Clarke Spares & Restorations makes accessories under the brand name Tintown that are compatible with Classic Period Standard Gauge trains in visual style and in their stamped-steel method of construction. The elaborate covered station platform is lighted by six bulbs suspended beneath the roof. A smaller version suitable for O and S Gauge is also available. A simple but attractive girder bridge accommodates trains in Standard Gauge, as well as smaller sized models.

Tintown Standard Gauge station platform. (Photograph courtesy of Clarke Spares & Restorations)

T-Reproductions

Norman Thomas, Jr. reproduced several of Lionel's most famous Standard Gauge accessories during the 1980s. His products included the No. 116 Station, No. 840 Power Station, No. 444 Roundhouse and No. 300 Hellgate Bridge. Thomas also made an enlarged version of the No. 128 Terrace to hold the large station; Lionel's terrace was sized for the smaller Nos. 122 and 115 Station designs.[26] T-

Reproductions later encountered legal difficulties over the use of copyrighted Lionel designs, and subsequently stopped producing these desirable items. The company has since manufactured licensed duplicates of the much larger Buddy L line of trains.

T-Reproduction copies: Lionel 112 Station mounted on 129 Terrace, which was enlarged to accommodate Lionel's largest station. The original 129 Terrace was wide enough only for the 124 and similar stations. (Maurice Weisblum Photograph and Collection)

Reproductions blend well with original Lionel pieces on M. Weisblum's Standard Gauge layout. Left to right are a Lionel Trains, Inc. 113 Station behind a restored original Lionel 83 Traffic Signal; original Lionel 155 Freight Platform; Mike's Train House (Lionel) 840 Power Station; and Williams (Lionel) 408E Locomotive. (Maurice Weisblum Photograph and Collection)

Williams reproduction of Lionel 381E St. Paul Olympian Locomotive. (Maurice Weisblum Photograph and Collection)

Jerome M. (Jerry) Williams first became involved in the commercial manufacture of toy trains in 1969, in a short-lived partnership with Fred Mill under the name Classic Models Corporation (see above). The two men soon found they had divergent interests. Mill preferred to build Standard Gauge trains of original design, while Williams wanted to reproduce classic Lionel models. As a result, Jerry Williams relinquished his interest in the company and established Williams Reproductions Ltd. in 1971.

To launch his new enterprise, Williams chose perhaps the scarcest O Gauge locomotive of the 1930s: the Ives No. 1694E New Haven-type built by Lionel shortly before dissolving its subsidiary Ives Corporation.[28] With so few originals available to collectors, the No. 1694E was immediately successful and was later joined by a set of reproduction passenger cars (Ives Nos. 1685, 1686 and 1687).[29]

Having proven that the market for reproductions of rare items could be profitable, Williams next turned to Standard Gauge, and produced a copy of Lionel's least common model from the classic years: the No. 9E New York Central-type box cab. These locomotives were assembled by part time workers, some recruited from among neighborhood teenagers. The most notable of these was twelve-year-old Mike Wolf, who later went on to create Mike's Train House (see above).

The success of Williams Reproductions Ltd. owed much to an intelligent choice of items to be added to the line. Rather than making trains and accessories that collectors could readily acquire at reasonable cost, Williams chose such pieces as the No. 94 High-Tension tower. Although not really scarce, this accessory was fairly expensive at train meets. A collector might own one or two, but they looked best on a layout in larger numbers. The relatively economical Williams versions made owning numerous copies more practical.

Another Lionel locomotive that commanded high prices was the No. 381E Olympian, and the Williams reproduction proved very popular with collectors. It was followed by the No. 408E and the No. 8 Trolley. Nor was the O Gauge line neglected; Williams also manufactured copies of postwar Lionel passenger cars in that size. By 1976, the company was so successful that Williams left his position as computer systems analyst with the Mitre Corporation and devoted all his energies to making trains.[30]

Passenger cars soon joined the line; first came copies of the No. 418 size, and later the larger Lionel State cars. By 1977, Williams was more actively exploring the market among O Gauge collectors. In addition to copies of Lionel Trains, he introduced the first of his company's original designs: the General Electric E-60 locomotive familiar to riders of Amtrak.

The company had so far limited itself to manufacturing just the bodies, frames, and dummy trucks for its reproduction locomotives. Many purchasers bought the trains primarily for display, and those who wished to run them normally acquired used Lionel motors.[31] The lack of trucks and a motor for the new O Gauge E-60 might have seemed an impediment to sales, but buyers adapted running gear from such Lionel locomotives as the GP-7 series, and the new E-60 locomotive was a success.

Since then, Jerry Williams has devoted himself primarily to O Gauge production, making a complete line of freight and passenger cars in a wide variety of road names, as well as many different steam, diesel, and electric locomotives in both premium and economy categories, under the corporate name Williams Electric Trains.

Williams reproduction of Lionel 408E locomotive. (Maurice Weisblum Photograph and Collection)

Williams special reproduction of Lionel's 418 Pullman made for the Train Collectors Association's twenty-fifth anniversary. (Carail Museum Collection)

chapter 8 Notes chapter 8

(1) Bruce C. Greenberg, *Greenberg's Guide To Lionel Trains, 1945-1969*, Vol. II, 1991, p. 52.

(2) Ron Hollander, *All Aboard*, p. 214.

(3) Louis Hertz was instrumental in forming a short-lived club dedicated to collecting Standard Gauge trains, some years before the TCA was born. However, its membership was small and its influence extremely limited.

(4) *Train Collectors Association Directory of Information*, Vol. 43, No. 2A, p. 4.

(5) *Ibid.*, p. 1.

(6) John Hubbard, *The Story Of Williams Electric Trains*, p. 6.

(7) Information provided by Nelson G. Williams.

(8) *Ibid.*

(9) *Ibid.*

(10) Nelson G. Williams, "Glenn Gerhard and the Trains He Built," *The New Century Limited*, Fall/Winter, 1996, pp. 5-9.

(11) This firm bought the Glenn Toy Trains assets when Gerhard ceased his operation, and produced them for a short time with running gear for G Gauge (the same measurement as No. 1 Gauge). The line was not commercially successful.

(12) Mr. Harmon reports that copies of the caboose were made by another hobbyist at about the same time, but that these models varied somewhat from the original design by having aluminum parts.

(13) *Ibid.*

(14) H. K. Creswell, "600E Standard Gauge Hudson," *TTOS Bulletin*, July, 1980, p. 4.

(15) Harlen Creswell, "Completing the State Set!", *TTOS Bulletin*, November, 1981, pp. 4-5, 12.

(16) Mark Horne, *The McCoy Story*, p. 1.

(17) Margaret McCoy, "McCoy Manufacturing," *The Train Collectors Quarterly*, Summer, 1979, p. 3.

(18) McCoy, *op. cit.*, p. 4.

(19) Horne, *op. cit.*, p. 47.

(20) *Ibid.*, pp. 54-56.

(21) "CTT Visits Mike's Train House," *Classic Toy Trains*, March, 1994.

(22) Varney left the firm in the early 1980s, but his first name remains as part of the company's title.

(23) George Hall, "CTT Visits The Rich-Art Company," *Classic Toy Trains*, March, 1997, pp. 92-93.

(24) Information provided by Nelson G. Williams.

(25) Bob Thon, "Making 'Em Like They Used To," *Classic Toy Trains*, Fall, 1987, p. 42.

(26) *Ibid.*

(27) Hubbard, *op cit.*

(28) Fewer than a thousand examples are known to exist. It has been reported that, after experiencing poor sales of the No. 1694E domestically, Lionel exported left-over stock to Canada and overseas. However, this has not been confirmed, and there is little evidence to date of more than a few being found outside the United States.

(29) These cars are much more readily available than the locomotive, as Lionel continued to produce them, although with Lionel Lines instead of Ives lettering, for several years after the demise of Ives.

(30) Hubbard, *op. cit.*, p. 9. Williams' formal academic training was in the field of mathematics.

(31) McCoy Manufacturing Company made motors to fit many of these locomotives.

PHOTO A: While old toy trains look good on a shelf, they're at their best when running on a vintage layout, such as these restored Lionel treasures from before the First World War (foreground). These models (33 locomotive, and 35 and 36 Coaches) were made in great numbers, and can generally be found today at a reasonable cost.

9

BUILDING A STANDARD GAUGE LAYOUT

There are many different reasons for collecting Standard Gauge trains: investment, display, nostalgia, and fellowship with other collectors are among the most common. One of the most rewarding reasons, however, is to put these toys to the use for which they were sold: operation.

The fact that model railroading is so widely popular is due in part to the many different facets of the hobby that one can enjoy. Building and detailing locomotives or rolling stock satisfies the creative impulse, and making buildings and scenery is an artistic endeavor as well. Those interested in electronics will find a vast array of interesting gadgets that make miniature trains operate realistically and reliably. Many hobbyists derive great pleasure from designing track plans, or from the carpentry involved in building sturdy layout benchwork.

Building a railroad can be as complex or as simple as one desires. Achieving accurate scale models, for example, requires hours of painstaking work. A single locomotive, properly outfitted with all the details necessary to represent the prototype precisely, may require hundreds or even thousands of hours of effort. Some modelers may, therefore, have only a very few trains, but derive great satisfaction from the process of achieving an almost perfectly accurate miniature of a real locomotive. Some others may have only a limited amount of track—perhaps only a loop with a siding or two—preferring to spend their time constructing realistic countryside or complex diminutive urban areas for the trains to pass through. Still others don't bother with scenery at all, but delight in operating their locomotives and rolling stock over complex labyrinths of trackwork.

Those who operate toy trains (and almost all Standard Gauge models fall into the toy category) are usually not too concerned with achieving realism or prototype accuracy. Part of the charm of these models is their heritage as playthings, and the fact that they were meant primarily for children. A Standard Gauge layout, therefore, is more likely to be a caricature than a scale representation. The trains themselves, especially those built in the 1920s and 1930s, are substantially foreshortened in order to run on the tight radius curves of sectional track. While they represent the general appearance of real trains quite well, their proportions are often inaccurate, and they lack the complex detail of scale models. To many observers, they look best when surrounded by other toys: scenery, buildings, and miniature figures that evoke the era when they were built.

This philosophy governed the planning and execution of the layout featured in this chapter. It is a toy train layout, not a model railroad, and the components are either authen-

PHOTO B: A Lionel St. Paul locomotive (No. 10) pulls its three-car passenger train around a curve behind vintage cardboard Skyline houses, sold as kits in the late 1930s and early 1940s.

PHOTO C: Despite the large size of Standard Gauge trains, the track on which they run has relatively small-diameter curves—as little as 42". This view of about one-third of the author's layout shows how much can be done with a room-sized layout.

tic or reproduction toys of sixty-five or more years ago. The building techniques are simple and straightforward, and well within the capability of anyone who has a moderate amount of experience with such tools as a screwdriver, power drill, and handsaw. The end result offers many satis-

factions, such as pride of accomplishment and the preservation of historic traditions. But, most important, it's fun: fun to see, fun to operate, and fun to share with kids of all ages, from toddlers to seniors.

Getting started is easy. First, you need a table large and sturdy enough to support these big toys. However, you don't need a huge amount of space in order to enjoy Standard Gauge trains. A basic circle of track is only 42" in diameter. A satisfying layout, such as the one shown here, can fit into the corner of a basement or attic, or even into a spare room. Overall dimensions are just 6'8" x 13'0", and by eliminating the river, you can reduce the length to 12'.

These dimensions were not selected arbitrarily. They are the result of choosing a ready-made source for the table top, thus saving many hours of carpentry. This layout rests atop four interior hollow-core doors. Building supply stores stock these doors in a variety of widths, at a standard length of 6'8". This is an ideal dimension for a train layout. The 80" length is large enough for even wide-radius Standard Gauge track, which has circles measuring 72" in diameter. By placing the tables side by side, any size layout can be achieved. Our project layout has four, three-foot-wide doors with a one-foot gap in the center for a river, giving an overall length of thirteen feet (and no, I'm not superstitious).

Once you have decided on the overall size, you will need a strong, but simple, supporting structure. You could build four legs for each of the separate tables, but there is an easier and more economical way (Figure One). Using 1' x 3' spruce lumber, construct a rectangle about two feet shorter in length and width than the table. This will give a one-foot overhang around all sides. Using eight, 38" lengths of lumber, construct four L-shaped legs and attach them with screws inside each corner joint, perpendicular to the main rectangle.

When the table tops are in place, the overall layout will be just slightly less than 40" off the floor, a good height for viewing, and tall enough to afford room to work on the wiring underneath in relative comfort. (If you expect small children as frequent visitors, a lower layout height might be considered, but I prefer to provide stools to elevate young observers instead. This has the added advantage of keeping small ones firmly anchored in one place, preventing inquisitive fingers from exploring the trains or scenery.)

Next, brace each of these corner legs with a length of lumber at a 45-degree angle, one on each side of the leg. Before screwing them in place, use a square to be sure the

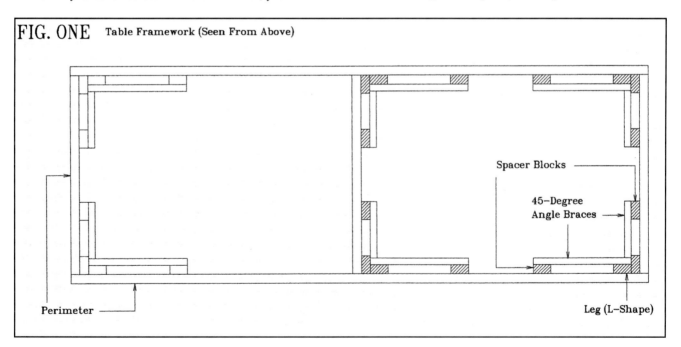

FIG. ONE   Table Framework (Seen From Above)

Spacer Blocks

45-Degree Angle Braces

Perimeter

Leg (L-Shape)

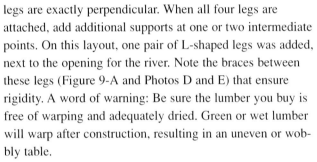

PHOTO D: A sturdy leg can be made very simply with two 1' x 3' boards in an L-shaped configuration. Screw them into each corner, and brace them with a pair of supports at an angle of 45-degrees, as shown. These supports will keep the leg perpendicular to the layout frame.

PHOTO E: Seen from inside the perimeter of the table frame, this leg is shown braced by two angled supports. Use screws rather than nails; they will not loosen under the stress of vibration from the trains.

legs are exactly perpendicular. When all four legs are attached, add additional supports at one or two intermediate points. On this layout, one pair of L-shaped legs was added, next to the opening for the river. Note the braces between these legs (Figure 9-A and Photos D and E) that ensure rigidity. A word of warning: Be sure the lumber you buy is free of warping and adequately dried. Green or wet lumber will warp after construction, resulting in an uneven or wobbly table.

When installing the legs, check the structure frequently on all sides with a long carpenter's level, especially if the layout is located on a concrete basement floor. Such floors are often quite uneven, and you may have to adjust the length of one or more of the legs to compensate. The easy way to do this is to install each leg temporarily with just one or two screws, with the top of each leg slightly below the top of the perimeter framework. Then, if you need to lengthen or shorten a leg, it can be removed and reattached at the proper level without having to saw it off (or worse, adding an unsightly extension to make it longer).

Now install the hollow-core doors. Measure carefully to preserve the one-foot overhang on all sides (Photo F), and leave a one-foot space in the center if you are planning on a river. The easiest way is to use small steel angles, available from any hard-

ware or building supply house, as shown in Photo G. Remember that except for the edges, these doors are hollow, and screws will not hold in their thin veneer sides. Therefore, the angles must be installed at points where the edges of the doors meet the supporting framework. You won't need very many; two to four angles per door are sufficient to hold them in alignment, and the weight of the doors, track, scenery, and trains will ensure that everything stays in place.

The edges of the table may simply be left bare, but it's best to add a strip of molding around the perimeter to provide both protection and a finished look. Molding can be purchased from any lumber yard or building supply store in a variety of styles and widths. (I used one-inch outside corner molding, visible in the upper right corner of Photo L.) Bevel the ends at the corners, and attach the molding with small finishing nails (wire brads). Countersink the nails, and cover the heads with wood filler for a finished appearance. Finally, paint the molding with a tough enamel. The edges of the table will be subject to some wear during the building process and when guests visit, so a tough coat of paint is advisable. If you elect to omit the molding, paint the table edges themselves. Save some paint for later touch-ups.

PHOTO F: The hollow-core doors are rigid and self support-ing, and do not need any bracing other than the rails of the framework. Note the use of a carpenter's level to assure that the table top does not tilt.

PHOTO G: These small steel angles are more than adequate to fasten the hollow-core doors firmly to the framework.

Developing A Track Plan

Once the basic table is built, the fun begins. Get out your track and experiment with some layout designs, directly on the table top. You may want to draw some designs first, but never decide on a finished track plan based on a paper design alone. Experiment with the track itself. This will give you an idea of how much room will be left over for accessories, and whether the track is a safe distance from the table edge. (Believe me, the saddest sound in all the world is the crunch of a Standard Gauge treasure hitting the concrete after jumping the track on a curve that is too near a table edge.) Test run some trains to be sure the plan is both workable and interesting. Try to achieve a design where the trains will do more than just run around in circles.

Many toy train operators prefer to use authentic antique track, and it isn't hard to find. In fact, any hobbyist with a moderately large collection has most likely acquired more track than could ever be put to use, and will probably part with it for a very reasonable sum. (The only exception is switches, which are a little hard to come by in good operat-ing condition.) Alternatively, you may wish to purchase reproduction toy train track, such as that sold by Antique Trains, MTH Electric Trains, or Rydin Industries (addresses in the Appendix). Rydin also makes regular and wide gauge switches, and will custom-build trackwork to your specifica-tions. (If you want a more modern appearance, the Gargraves Trackage Corporation makes flexible track with closely spaced wooden ties.) On the layout shown here, modern reproductions of antique track were mixed with original Lionel and American Flyer switches.

Place your accessories on the layout to test both appearance and clearance (Photos I and J). Remember that these big toys have a lot of overhang, especially on curves, and such things as buildings, telegraph poles, and crossing gates must not be too near the track. Check the spacing with the largest piece of equipment you have. Step back from the table and examine the overall effect. Is the scene balanced, without undue crowding or tall structures placed where they block the view? Have you left room for roads and bridges? Is there space for a few trees? Now is the time to make changes; it's much harder to move track or relocate build-ings once the scenery has been installed.

When you have decided on a final track plan, make a detailed drawing of every piece of track and each accessory. You won't remember where they go later. If you are using two different radii curves, as this layout did, identify them carefully and accurately. Then, take up all the track and other items and put them aside. Figure Two illustrates the track plan finally chosen for the project layout for this book.

45	Lionel animated gateman	152	Lionel automatic crossing gate
53	Lionel lamppost	200	Lionel turntable
57	Lionel " Broadway" and " Main Street" lamppost	280	Lionel bridge
58	Lionel lamppost	436	Lionel power station
60	Lionel telegraph post	437	Lionel switch tower
068	Lionel warning signal post *(this version made for Hafner)*	440	Lionel twin light signal bridge
77	Lionel automatic crossing gate	601	Ives double lamppost
78	Lionel train control block signal	2116	American Flyer warning light and bell signal
79	Lionel flashing highway signal	2206	American Flyer flashing highway signal
80	Lionel manual train control semaphore	2218	American Flyer block signal
83	Lionel traffic signal	Eur.	European flashing highway signal with warning buzzer
91	Lionel circuit breaker	H	Skyline house kit
92	Lionel floodlight tower	L	Lamppost, manufacturer undetermined
100	Lionel bridge approach ramp	M56	Reproduction Lionel 56 Lamppost, by Mike's Train House
104	Lionel bridge	M59	Reproduction Lionel 59 Lamppost, by Mike's Train House
107	Ives twin arm semaphore		
119	Lionel tunnel	Park	Reproduction of Lionel scenic plot, by Ron Morris
126	Lionel station	S	Pioneer Valley Models store kit
129	Lionel combination 124 Station and 128 Terrace	X	Marx "Main Street" lamppost

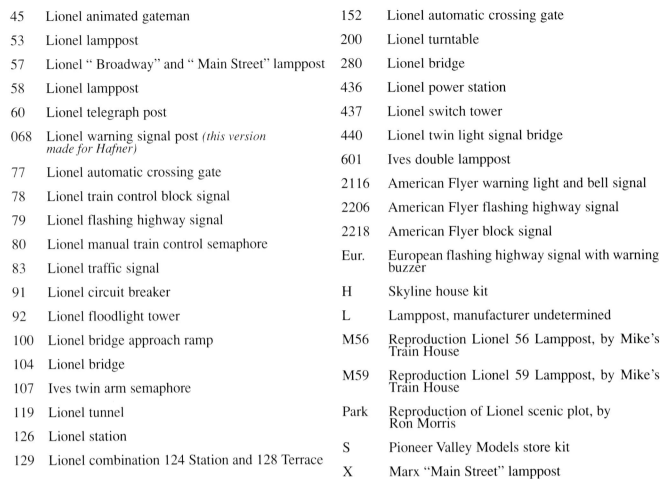
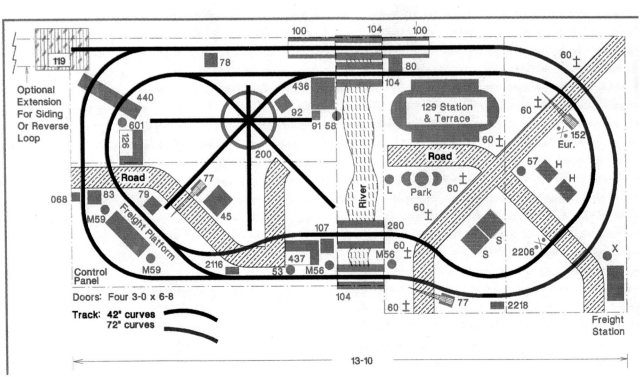

FIG. TWO

PHOTO H: Lay out the track in a variety of patterns, and test run the trains. Keep making changes until you are satisfied that you have a plan that will afford interesting movement, plus provide room for accessories and attractive scenery. Try to develop a track plan that will hold your interest after the layout is built.

PHOTO I: In this view, nothing is installed permanently. The final track plan has been chosen, and the accessories are in trial locations. Note that the station in the foreground (a Lionel model 126) is in a different location in later photos. In fact, it was tried in half a dozen spots before the best choice was determined.

If you have included a river, install the banks now. I used an ordinary dense-foam insulation sheet (again, the building supply store has these). Glue a strip along each side of the river opening (Photos K and L). Let it dry for a couple of days; the foam keeps air from reaching the glue, and it may take a long time to cure. Then, carve it to shape as shown in the photo, and sand it smooth. Paint it in a color appropriate to a river bank; information about painting may be found in succeeding paragraphs. The "water" is a plastic fluorescent light cover. These come in 2' x 4' sheets, in a variety of surface textures. The pebbled variety very closely resembles the surface of a slightly wind-blown river. These panels are easily cut to size with metal shears; proceed slowly, so that the edges will not develop radial cracks.

Put a wooden support (quarter-inch plywood works well) beneath the river banks, allowing about an eighth inch clearance for the "water" sheet to be slid into place. Figure Three is an end view of the river, showing the position of the support, the "water," and the foam banks. Photo L shows the river bank with a base coat of paint and the plastic "water" in place. You can alter the color of the water by painting the support beneath it. If the water is supposed to be shallow, gray is a good choice. Deeper water might be closer to blue. You can even shade it, with a darker shade in the center of the river than along the edges to simulate different depths.

This method of river construction is, like the rest of this toy-like layout, an approximation of the real thing, and is

PHOTO J: Although the river bed is not yet in place, bridges have been test fit to be sure that there will be adequate clearance for them. The roads (from Moondog Express) are temporarily in place, giving a general idea of how the final layout will look.

not meant to be painstakingly realistic. By contrast, scale modelers often spend a great deal of time and effort creating scenery that is as realistic as possible, and there are many techniques for achieving this. If you are inclined toward this type of realism, I recommend a trip to a hobby shop, where several books on the subject are available. If you want a toy train appearance like the one portrayed here, however, it's easy to achieve with relatively little effort and no special experience.

Scale modelers usually use elevated roadbed for the track, and ballast the ties with scale-sized gravel. It looks great! However, for a toy layout, I elected to simulate ballast with paint instead. It creates the desired impression, but with much less mess and in far less time. First, select a base color, and paint the entire layout with three coats. (Two coats would probably be adequate, but the doors will soak up a lot of paint, and three provides a smoother, more uniform surface.) I chose a light tan color that simulates the ballast on the Nova Scotia railroads near my home. Don't be tempted to paint just the areas where the track will be. No matter how well you plan, you may want to make changes later, and find you have failed to paint an area where track will cross.

Next spray the entire surface with speckle stone paint in a color close to the base coat (Photo L). Most paint and hardware stores carry this product. It goes on with a rough texture that gives the general appearance of gravel when the track is in place. Again, spray the entire table. You may want to have some dirt roads, paths, or parking lots, and by spraying everywhere, they will be ready-made wherever you need them.

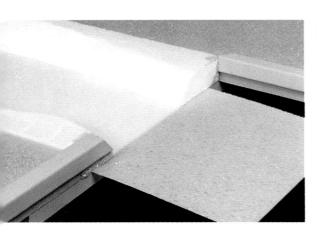

FIG. THREE

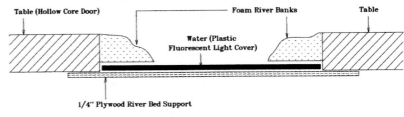

Table (Hollow Core Door) — Foam River Banks — Table
Water (Plastic Fluorescent Light Cover)
1/4" Plywood River Bed Support

PHOTO K: The river banks are roughly cut from foam insulation. The river itself—a plastic fluorescent light cover—is shown partially inserted between the river banks and the support underneath. It stays in place by friction, but can be removed during the painting of the banks to avoid getting excess paint on the plastic.

Right: PHOTO L: With paint applied, there is strong contrast between the river bank and the simulated water. The base coat is oversprayed with speckle-stone paint to imitate dirt and gravel, similar to the simulated ballast that surrounds the track.

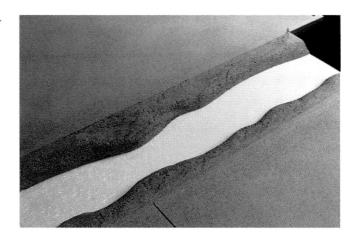

FIG. FOUR

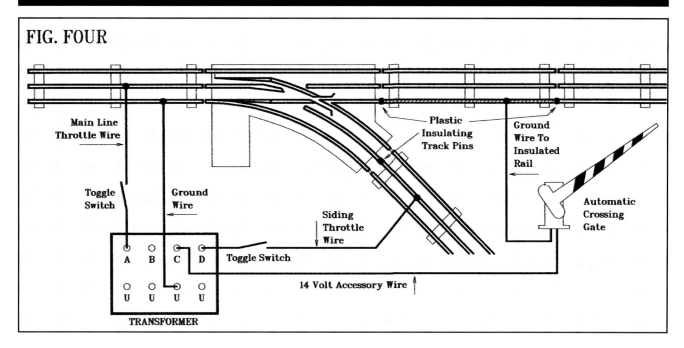

Main Line Throttle Wire

Plastic Insulating Track Pins

Ground Wire To Insulated Rail

Toggle Switch

Ground Wire

Automatic Crossing Gate

Siding Throttle Wire

Toggle Switch

| A | B | C | D |

14 Volt Accessory Wire

| U | U | U | U |

TRANSFORMER

When the paint is dry, it's time to lay out the track, but first work out your wiring plan. A small Standard Gauge layout need not have complex wiring, but some basic principles should be observed. First, you will need a transformer capable of handling the large motors these trains contain. Among the antiques, Ives and American Flyer locomotives draw less current than the larger ones made by Lionel, but in general all Standard Gauge locos require more transformer capacity than the smaller O Gauge trains.

The larger Lionel transformers from the late 1930s through 1969 are the best choice for Standard Gauge. Models V, Z, VW, ZW and KW all have sufficient wattage and are variously rated to produce up to 20 to 25 volts of alternating current. Other transformers have a similar voltage range, such as the pre-World War II Model R, and can be used for Standard Gauge, but with their lower wattage, they don't have much reserve for accessories or lights. (Also, the ground and throttle posts on these smaller transformers are labeled differently. The correct posts to use for track connections are printed on the faceplate, around the throttle dials.) If you choose one of these smaller types, get a second transformer for accessories. Postwar transformers such as Lionel's 1033 and most American Flyer models will work fine for accessories, but are too limited in voltage to run these big trains satisfactorily.

The finer points of wiring are beyond the scope of this book, and you may wish to consult one of the books on this subject that are listed in the Appendix. However, just a few

simple connections will get the trains running. The big transformers listed above (V, Z, VW, ZW and KW) have a variety of binding posts with hand-tightened nuts for attaching wires. The posts labeled "U" are a common ground. Connect this post to the outside rails of the track. The throttle posts are variously labeled "A", "B", "C" or "D", depending upon which model you are using. They are controlled by the dials or handles on the transformer that let you vary the speed of the trains. Connect one of them to the middle rail of the track (Figure Four). That's all there is to it!

The easiest way to connect wires to the track is by using a "Lockon"—a mechanical device that attaches to the middle and outer rails. On these devices, the wire clip labeled "1" is for the middle rail (throttle post A, B, C, or D); "2" is for the outer rails (ground post U). Lockons are unsightly, however, and it's almost as easy to hide the wiring completely on a permanent layout. When you turn a section of track over, you will see that the bottom of each rail has a slot running up the middle. You can spread the sides of the rail slightly with a screwdriver and force a wire into this slot. For an absolutely secure connection, solder the wire in place. When you install the track on the layout, drill a hole through the table and thread the wire through.

If you have more than one locomotive, you may want to store one on a siding while another one is running. If so, isolate the siding by using a plastic track pin in the middle rail at the beginning of the siding. (These pins are the same as O Gauge insulating pins, and are available at almost any shop

PHOTO M: Lionel's early operating accessories, such as this 77 Crossing Gate, came packed with a section of special track. In addition to the insulated middle rail, which provided power to a locomotive's motor, one of the outside rails was insulated. The short strips of gray insulation can be seen between the black metal ties and the rails. Plastic track pins in both ends of the rail insulate it from adjacent sections. Each accessory of this type is connected by two wires, one to the transformer and one to the insulated rail. When the train's wheels touch this rail, they complete the ground connection and activate the accessory.

that sells Lionel trains.) Then wire the middle rail of the siding to the other throttle binding post of the transformer. This gives you a separate speed control for the siding, as well as the ability to turn it off completely. Alternatively, you can wire it to the same throttle as the main line, but put an on-off toggle switch in the wire between the track and the transformer. Both of these options are shown in Figure Four.

Automatic accessories may be connected in a variety of ways. In the late 1930s, Lionel introduced an under-the-tie pressure switch (called a "contactor") that responds to the weight of a passing train. This method is not satisfactory for a permanent layout because the track is fastened securely and cannot move up and down to press on the contactor. Lionel's earlier method works best: the insulated running rail approach. If you can't find any original Lionel track with this feature, it's easy to make. On the metal ties of the track, there are little fingers that hold the rails in place. Pry up these fingers just enough to release one of the outside running rails. Using thin cardboard, automotive gasket material or two or three layers of electrician's tape, make insulators to fit between the rail and the tie (Photo M). Then replace the rail and bend the fingers down again, tight enough to hold the rail in place, but not so hard as to puncture the insulators. Finally, put a plastic track pin in both ends of the rail to isolate it electrically from adjacent track sections.

You can wire a crossing gate or model 45 Gateman to this section as shown in Figure Four. Connect one accessory wire to the insulated rail, and the other one to one of the accessory posts, such as C or D on a model ZW transformer. The amount of voltage for these posts can be adjusted by a dial (like the throttle control) to make the accessory operate at a realistic speed. About 14 volts is usually right; adjust as necessary. If the insulated rail has been installed correctly, the accessory will not operate unless a train passes over that section of track. However, when a train's wheels are present, they form a ground connection between the insulated rail and the opposite outside running rail. This completes the circuit, and the gate goes down, or the gateman comes out. (Some accessories, such as block signals or lighted semaphores, require slightly more complex wiring and are explained in the instruction sheets packed with them by the manufacturer, or in the books about wiring listed in the Appendix.)

If your layout is fairly small, use at least #18 gauge wire for all connections. This can be obtained in electronics or automotive supply stores. However, the larger the layout, the larger the wire you should use. Long stretches of small diameter wire will allow voltage drop to occur at distant points, making the trains slow down. Using #16 or even #14 gauge wire will prevent this problem. (Note that lower gauge numbers signify larger wire.) The best type of wire for toy train use is the stranded variety, which is made up of many small wires wrapped together inside an insulating outer sheath. Solid core wire is also available and is slightly less expensive, but it is also less flexible and breaks more easily if bent too often.

The transformers should be located so that the operator can view the entire layout when running the trains. On the

PHOTO N: This Lionel transformer, a model R from the late 1930s, has two separate throttles, allowing operation of two trains on different parts of the layout at one time. Next to the transformer is a 439 Panel Board, with switches that are wired between the transformer and various areas of track.

PHOTO O: The back of Lionel's 437 Switch Tower, made between 1926 and 1937, is fitted with six knife switches—the ideal functional control panel for toy train operation.

project layout, a corner location was chosen (Figure Two, p. 112). A Lionel model R transformer powers the trains (Photo N). This model has two throttles, and one was wired to the outside loop of track, while the second throttle powers the inside loop. This allows two trains to be run continuously. Next to the transformer is one of Lionel's 439 panel boards, marketed between 1928 and 1942. This clever accessory contains six knife switches which can be wired to control power going to various sections of track. In the photo,

all of these switches are "on" (in the upright position); pulling down any one of the knife switch handles disconnects power from whatever area of track it is hooked up to. At lower left on the panel board is a controller for one of Lionel's automatic track switches, and at lower right is a more modern knife switch (not an original Lionel product). The two circular dials near the top of the board are imitation volt and ampere meters, and at top center is a bulb that illuminates the panel.

Lionel made other accessories with functional knife switches that could be used to turn power on and off to the track. Some versions of the small 438 Switch Tower have two such switches, and the larger 437 Switch Tower (Photo O) has six. The large No. 840 Power Station also has a bank of switches. On the project layout, these knife switches are used to turn power on and off for the various tracks that surround the turntable.

With two Standard Gauge trains running, the model R transformer is taxed almost to its 110-watt limit, especially when one of the trains is pulling lighted passenger cars. Therefore, a second transformer, a model B of 75-watt capacity (Photo P), is connected to the lampposts, floodlight tower, building lights, and some of the signals. Alternatively, you can choose a larger transformer (such as the 250-watt model Z) to handle all of these chores, but these are relatively expensive. I used the R and B models because I had them on hand, and they do the job quite well.

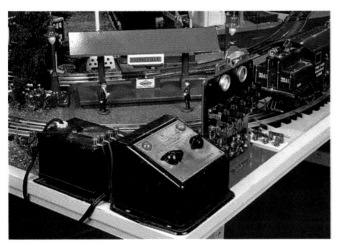

PHOTO P: Lionel Standard Gauge locomotives require higher voltage than comparable models made by either Ives or American Flyer. These relatively small models (R at right and the older B at left) produce up to 24 volts. Model R has two continuous rheostats for uninterrupted speed control. The older Model B is used for the lighting circuits, not for running the trains. It has a movable contact arm that slides over several brass studs, with an interruption in current between each step. Locomotives with remote control reverse units require either a transformer with a rheostat, or a separate rheostat connected between a step type transformer and the track. Despite its age, this vintage power unit still functions perfectly. Visible at right is a Lionel 439 Panel Board, and the station platform in the center is of unknown manufacture (probably European).

PHOTO Q: All of the tracks surrounding Lionel's 200 Turntable need connections to the power supply, but it must be possible to turn each of them off individually, so that just one locomotive at a time can be run. The knife switches on Lionel's accessories (437 and 438 Switch Towers and 840 Power Station) fulfill this function.

Installing The Track

If you are hiding the track wiring in the slots on the bottom of the rails, you will need to plan carefully where to drill the holes in the table. Since it's hard to be sure exactly where the track will go until all of it is in place, install short lengths of wire at this time, about 4" long, in the middle rail and one of the outside rails of five or six sections of track, which will be spaced randomly around the layout. Use a different color wire for each rail so you can tell the difference later. I use red for the middle rail and black for the outside ground rail. For now, bend these short lengths so they lie out of the way along the rails.

When all of the track has been located, you can drill the holes accurately in the table at the points where the wires emerge from the rails. Remember that in addition to the main track wiring, you will need a separate wire to the middle rail of each siding; you might want to use blue wire to help you identify these sidings when you are working under the table. Also install a wire on each insulated outer rail that will be used for an accessory. Use a different color (such as green) for the insulated tracks.

Consult your track plan and assemble the track (Photo R). Be sure to locate the insulated sections where you want the accessories to be. Before you fasten anything down, run temporary wires from the transformer to the track and test it with a locomotive and a few cars. It's much easier to eliminate gremlins (short circuits, improperly aligned curves, etc.) at this early stage. When everything works properly, and when you have the track exactly lined up where it will go, mark the spots where the wiring holes will be, drill them through the table top, and feed the wires through to the

underside of the table. (The doors that make up the table are hollow, and it can be tricky to get the wires to go through both surfaces. If you have a problem seeing the exit hole, put a strong light on the underside of the table to shine through it.)

Most toy train track has just three metal ties per section. You may wish to add extra ties to make the track look more realistic, as seen in Photo R and subsequent pictures. They can be made from any suitably sized strips of wood, painted brown to simulate real ties or black to match the metal Lionel ties. Self-tapping sheet metal screws (#6 x 1/2") are best for fastening the track down; drive them through the holes in the metal ties and into the table top. It's a good idea to drill pilot holes in the table before inserting the screws, to prevent the wood from splitting. Two screws per track section (one at either end) are sufficient. Don't fasten them too tightly; if you do, they will chew up the thin veneer of the table and will not hold well. If your layout has a river, don't forget to install the bridges before the track is fastened down.

The underside of the table will now have red, black, blue and green wires protruding a few inches down. Connect all the black ones to a ground wire from the transformer. Plan the route for this wire to keep it as short as possible, which minimizes voltage drop. Next, connect a wire from the throttle post to all the main line connections (red, on this layout). Connect each siding wire (blue) to a throttle post; don't forget a toggle switch for each one, located near the transformer (or use the knife switches on a Lionel 439 Panel Board or 437 or 438 Switch Tower, as on this project layout). Now, test the whole setup with a train, preferably the largest equipment you own.

PHOTO R: All of the track should be assembled and thoroughly tested before it is screwed down. When you are sure it all works, drill holes for the wiring, add extra ties if desired, and fasten everything in place.

Accessories and Scenery

While the test train is on the track, place all your accessories where you want them, and run the train again—to be sure there is adequate clearance for everything. Large Standard Gauge cars have a lot of overhang at the ends, and on curves they are likely to bump into anything located too close to the track. In Photo S, the station platform looks as if it is far enough away from the track for adequate clearance. However, this long Ives coach is about to scrape the edge of the station roof, which will gouge the paint.

Before you install the buildings and accessories, such as stations, lampposts, and crossing gates, you first must decide what type of scenery you want to build. It's possible to paint all your scenery directly on the table, but I prefer to make individual scenic plots, just as Lionel sold in the 1920s and 1930s. This permits you to construct a scenic area at the workbench, rather than directly on the layout, and also makes it easier to make changes, if you want to add any new items to the layout at a later date.

Quarter-inch poplar plywood underlay makes good scenic panels. This product is sold in 4' x 4' and 4' x 8' sheets and is originally intended as sub-flooring material for the building trade. It can be cut quickly to almost any shape with a hand or small power saw. It is light in weight and sands easily to a fairly smooth finish. Photo T shows such a panel, cut to fit into an area between some tracks. Note that the ends are beveled at a 45-degree angle, simulating a sloped lawn or the edges of a ditch next to the tracks. The cut-out area in the center is sized to receive a station platform. To determine the dimensions of these panels, make patterns from heavy wrapping paper, and trace their outlines on the wood as a guide for the saw.

Install your scenery on the panel. Paint the panel with a base color, according to the type of scenery it represents: gray for roads, brown for dirt, green for grass, etc. By using masking tape, you can paint different parts of the panel for different effects. In an area where there will be sidewalks next to lawns, for example, paint the entire panel a light

119

PHOTO S: Long cars operating on sharp curves require extra clearance for trackside buildings, lampposts, and accessories.

PHOTO T: This scenic panel is cut to fit between the tracks on one corner of the layout. The center area is cut out for a station platform, and the area surrounding it is spray painted to simulate concrete. The outer ends were painted green, and green sawdust was sprinkled on the wet paint to simulate grass.

gray for the concrete sidewalks first. When it is completely dry, mask the sidewalks with tape, and paint over the panel with green. Put on a thick second coat and immediately sprinkle grass over the wet paint. Model grass is available from hobby stores, or from specialty supply houses such as Scenic Express (address in the Appendix). You can also make your own, by dyeing sawdust. When it dries, peel up the masking tape to expose the gray paint beneath, and you'll have a sidewalk between the grass areas. Roads can be painted on, or you can use a commercial imitation asphalt road system, such as that sold by Moondog Express (listed in the Appendix). These roads are intended for O Gauge layouts, but they seem to look okay on a small Standard Gauge layout as well, as this project layout attests.

When painting and detailing the scenic panels, plan ahead for buildings, lampposts, and other accessories. Put the panels on the layout, and screw them down; flat head #4 x 1/2" self-tapping screws work well. Screw them firmly into the wood, then put a dab of paint on the screw heads to hide them. If the screws are in a grassy area, sprinkle a little grass over the wet paint on the screw head. Finally, drill holes for any necessary wiring and install the accessories (Photo U).

The next step is to install trees, people, fire hydrants, mail boxes, or anything else you wish, in order to make the layout come alive. In Photo V, hedges and shrubs have been added to the grassy areas at either end of the station platform. Several trees are visible in the background, and people wait for trains in front of the platform. A conductor stands next to a mailbox outside the Lionel 126 Station (behind the locomotive), and a baggage cart can be partially seen in the same area. Note also

that black bristol board has been fitted between the rails where the road crosses the tracks, to provide a smooth crossing for car tires.

In addition to railroad-related accessories, such as stations and switch towers, you may want to add houses or stores. On this layout, there are two private homes which were built from Skyline kits over fifty years old. Two cardstock stores (made by Pioneer Valley Models, listed in the Appendix) are also visible at the far end of the layout in Photo W. All of these buildings are scaled for O Gauge trains, and are therefore little more than about half size for Standard Gauge. But by putting them at a point farthest from the viewer, their smaller size increases the illusion of depth and makes the layout look larger.

Lionel made even smaller houses in the years between the two World Wars. These tiny bungalows and villas, pictured elsewhere in this book, are actually about half size for O Gauge trains and only quarter size for Standard Gauge. The company sold many thousands of them for use with these large trains, however, and customers didn't seem to mind. In the toy train world, matters of scale are highly flexible, and are easily compensated for by the imagination.

And speaking of imagination, that is your only limit when planning the scenery for your layout. Well-stocked hobby shops, especially those that sell large scale trains such as LGB, have a wide variety of items that look good with Standard Gauge trains: trees, hedges, fences, fire plugs, figures, and vehicles, to name but a few. There are even homes and other buildings that are the right size for Standard Gauge, but since they take up a lot of room, you won't be able to fit very many on a modest layout.

PHOTO U: The scenic panel is screwed in place between the tracks, the station is inserted into the space provided, and lampposts have been installed at either end of the platform.

PHOTO V: An Ives 1134 steamer pulls its string of coaches into the station area, where passengers wait to board. A toy train layout needs many small details if it is to be a convincing portrayal of the world in miniature.

PHOTO W: The smaller stores and houses in the background create the illusion of a large layout through perspective, and the many accessories, trees and smaller details help create a surprising amount of realism in this toy train world. This project layout was built in spare time over a period of less than a month.

Remember, also, that the best toy train layouts are never really finished. Much enjoyment results from adding new items to the scene, and from acquiring new trains to run. Photo W shows the project layout just after completion, in December 1996, but in other photos in this book, taken at later dates, you will see changes and additions that occurred over the following few months. Running the trains is fun, but often the greatest pleasure comes from adding to, and refining, the layout as you acquire new accessories and learn new techniques.

Why not try building your own antique Standard Gauge layout? If you start modestly, it need not be too expensive. For example, the train set shown in Photo X, a common American Flyer set from the 1920s, was purchased at an auction for just $200. Although somewhat shabby, some gentle cleaning made it look quite acceptable, and the rugged motor in the locomotive still runs well after many

decades. (Use caution and mild soap when cleaning old tinplate trains, however. Regular detergents will soften and remove the old paint.)

Many operators enjoy the age-worn look of old toys, and operate them in original condition. With a little more effort, these old toys can be made to look like new, although valuable pieces, especially those in scarce colors, cannot be repainted without causing a sharp reduction in value. Common models like the ones shown here are good candidates for restoration, however. John Hubbard's book on repairing prewar trains (see Appendix) will guide you step-by-step in learning how to do it.

Creating a Standard Gauge railroad is challenging and satisfying, and will make you very popular, both with the younger toy-loving members of your household, and with those older folks who may remember having these trains when they were young.

PHOTO X: Even after decades of use, these sturdy American Flyer trains see regular active duty on the author's layout.

Lionel, Ives and American Flyer Standard Gauge locomotives surround a Lionel 200 Turntable on the author's layout.

10

INFORMATION FOR COLLECTORS

There is no substitute for knowledge and experience when buying any product, and this is especially true in the case of antiques. The value of an old toy train depends on a variety of factors, each of which should be considered when making a purchase. The beginning collector is advised, first, to join one of the collector societies, such as the Train Collectors Association (TCA), which has the largest membership among such groups. In its long history, the TCA has assembled a comprehensive collection and library covering virtually all foreign and domestic toy train manufacturers.

Other associations tend to specialize in certain aspects of the hobby, although their membership may comprise individuals with a broad range of interests. The Toy Train Operating Society (TTOS) and the Lionel Operating Train Society (LOTS) emphasize running the trains, while others are devoted to one manufacturer, such as the Lionel Collectors Club of America (LCCA) and the American Flyer Collectors Club (AFCC). These organizations welcome international members, but there are also clubs in countries outside the United States, such as the Lionel Collectors Association of Canada (LCAC).

There are several advantages inherent in club membership, including interesting and informative publications that report the results of historical research and provide operating tips, layout building techniques, product reviews, and many other aspects of toy train lore. The TCA also maintains an extensive library for its members, located at the National Toy Train Museum in Strasburg, Pennsylvania. Most clubs sponsor train "meets," which are gatherings of members who come together to buy, sell, and trade their treasures, exchange knowledge and ideas, and engage in good fellowship. They also publish lists of trains for trade or sale, and circulate them among members.

Any novice collector should seek the advice of seasoned hobbyists, especially when considering the purchase of high-priced items. In general, most train collectors are eager to share their knowledge and expertise, and welcome the opportunity to help newcomers to become established in the hobby. Their assistance is invaluable in helping beginners to avoid costly mistakes.

The worth of any collector's item is determined by a complex interaction of factors, including inherent value (quality), aesthetic appeal, demand, scarcity, and condition. While any one of these factors may be enough to attract a buyer to a specific item, it is usually a combination of these elements that makes a particular toy train attractive to a greater number of collectors.

A. INHERENT VALUE

It is no accident that Lionel Trains are among the most sought-after toys in the world. During the first half of the twentieth century, that company established and maintained a reputation for high-quality products in every price range. With relatively few exceptions, Lionel Trains manufactured through the mid-1950s were well designed and substantially built, and have exhibited amazing durability. In fact, it is less common to encounter an old Lionel that does *not* work than one that does, and even mistreated Lionels are usually worth repairing.

Beginning around 1955, the quality of some Lionel products declined, as economic and social conditions began to erode the company's predominant position in the toy marketplace. While many excellent trains were made right up until the original company folded in 1969, a significant percentage of Lionel products were cheaply made and more easily broken than was the case during the years before and immediately after World War II. Nevertheless, the reputation of the company remained very positive, and even after sales declined to the point of bankruptcy, it is reported that the Lionel trademark remained among the very highest in public recognition and assumption of quality.

Since 1970, Lionel trains have been manufactured under license by a succession of companies: General Mills (Fundimensions), Kenner-Parker, Lionel Trains Inc. (LTI), and currently by Lionel L.L.C. The product line has been expanded dramatically, and has included everything from simple sets for children to highly detailed, limited production models aimed specifically at collectors. Although there have been problems with design and production quality in some of the offerings of these firms, the perception of quality remains closely associated with the Lionel trademark, and most of their products deserve this reputation.

For these and other reasons described below, a Lionel train may command a higher price than a product made by another manufacturer, even if it is an item that is relatively common and easily available. The public perceives Lionel trains as quality products, possessing substantial inherent worth simply because of the long-standing reputation of this well-known trademark.

In fact, it is not uncommon for householders to discover a common Lionel set from the 1950s in the attic, and expect to receive thousands of dollars for it, simply because they have heard that Lionel trains are valuable. While it is true that some Lionel trains are indeed worth a fortune, and all Lionel trains in good condition are valuable to some degree, the common pieces were made in such huge numbers that other factors, principally demand, limit their worth. Nevertheless, the reputation of Lionel trains ensures that they will maintain their value, especially when compared with other makes.

B. AESTHETIC APPEAL

Some toy trains are especially attractive to collectors simply because of their beauty. Lionel's "Blue Comet" sets in both O and Standard Gauge, for example, were made in substantial numbers, and many survive. Their scarcity on the market is due partly to the fact that they are so attractive on a display shelf that collectors are reluctant to part with them. To some extent, this creates an artificial scarcity, so that the high value placed upon these items is partially a direct result of their artistic appeal.

Another example is the relatively high price commanded by the extremely common Lionel Santa Fe F3 diesels, sold for many years under a variety of catalog numbers, beginning in 1948. In its red and silver Warbonnet paint scheme, this locomotive is undeniably beautiful, but there are so many thousands of them available that if their value were based upon scarcity, they would likely be among the least expensive items for a collector to acquire. The prices asked at train meets, especially for examples in like-new to mint condition, are disproportionate to their availability, simply because they are so very attractive.

The definition of beauty, of course, varies greatly among collectors. The brightly colored paint schemes of toy diesel locomotives may be "prettier" than the rugged "machine" appearance of Standard Gauge trains built seven or eight decades ago, but there is considerable beauty in the functionality of the latter. Other trains are merely cute, especially the tiny clockwork Ives and American Flyer sets from 1910 through the 1920s, and their allure to a certain segment of collectors guarantees their continuing value.

C. DEMAND

The most attractive trains tend to have extra appeal and may command higher prices, just as a beautiful home may sell for more than an equally functional but less-handsome house. However, forces other than simple aesthetics influence a train collector's desire to acquire a specific item.

For example, the rarest trains will always be in demand by collectors who desire to own something that few others possess, regardless of their aesthetic properties. Exclusivity is a major driving force behind many collectors, and is especially evident in the high prices paid for one-of-a-kind items, such as paintings and some postage stamps. And yet, rarity is not the sole ingredient in measuring demand, for some trains made in very small numbers, by obscure manufacturers, are valued less highly than some mass-produced merchandise by Lionel and others.

The popularity of an item among collectors may also depend on the intangible element of nostalgia. Many of today's train collectors remember with pleasure the experience of owning Lionel or American Flyer trains when they were children in the 1940s and 1950s, and seek to recreate that enjoyment by acquiring duplicates today. The continuing popularity of steam locomotives is especially evident in the many new models shown in the catalogs of contemporary manufacturers each year. Yet, steam power virtually disappeared from North American railroads nearly half a century ago, and most of the population has never seen an operating steam locomotive outside of tourist operations. Nostalgia for years gone by keeps steam alive in toys.

Some toy trains are in demand simply because they perform so well. While many collections are static, relegated to the display shelves, an increasing number of enthusiasts derive the greatest pleasure from putting their antiques through their paces on the rails, just as their manufacturers intended them to be used. (A similar attitude exists among old car buffs, who take pleasure not just in owning a vintage Mustang, Corvette, or Duesenberg, but in driving them.) For this type of collector, smooth-running and well-engineered toy trains of any age are more desirable than scarce ones.

For example, virtually every model of Lionel locomotive from the period between 1925 and 1935 was made in far greater numbers than Dorfan locomotives from the same period. Since the Dorfans are much less common, one would expect them to command much higher prices, but for most Dorfan locos, excluding those few that are really rare, this is not the case. Despite Dorfan's ingenious and imaginative engineering ideas, their products suffered defects that greatly shortened their lives as toys, both functionally and cosmetically, while the better-made Lionels survive in vast quantities. Dorfan locomotives are not cheap, but they do not command the prices that their relative scarcity would suggest. This is at least partly due to the fact that so few of them can be made operational today.

D. SCARCITY

The most misused words among collectors are probably "unique" and "rare." These terms are often employed when "scarce" would be a much more accurate description. Very few truly unique (one-of-a-kind) toy trains are ever offered publicly, but are usually traded privately. Unique products from manufacturers, as opposed to individual modelers, include factory prototypes and a very few items with extremely small production numbers, of which only one example is known to survive. This level of rarity (only one known example) is difficult to price, and the value of such an object is measured by what a given individual is willing to pay for the distinction of owning something that no one else possesses.

Truly rare toy trains are those that exist in extremely small numbers. Opinions differ as to the numerical definition of "extremely" small, but there are some items that might qualify. There still exist just handfuls of some of the earliest Lionel products—the 2-7/8" Gauge models made between 1901 and 1905. As another example, Lionel made just a few samples of a blue-colored "Boy's Train" at about the same time as their relatively unsuccessful pink "Girl's Train" (1957), but never put it into regular production. These trains may be considered to be genuinely rare.

The pink "Girl's Train," however, is commonly called "rare" by collectors, while thousands were actually sold. It is true that they were made in far fewer numbers than, for example, a 2055 or 681 loco from the same era, and "Girl's Trains" are difficult or expensive to acquire today. Nevertheless, one can usually find one or more being offered at any large, well-attended train meet. They are definitely "scarce," but they are most certainly not "rare," except by the most generous definition of that word.

Scarcity of a particular train may be the result of low initial production figures, or it may be caused by excessive demand that has removed most examples from the marketplace. For example, there were quite a lot of Lionel "Blue Comet" sets made throughout most of the 1930s, but they remain firmly lodged in collections, and tend to be passed down in families rather than offered for sale. By contrast, the 1957 Canadian Pacific set was made for only one year, and is truly *scarce*. It is not *rare*, however, and several have been observed by the author to be for sale at each of the big semi-annual TCA train meets in York, Pennsylvania.

Scarcity alone is not a valid indicator of value. Several Lionel locomotives and sets of the late Depression years were made in very small numbers, such as the 289E Commodore Vanderbilt engine (basically a common low-priced 1689E loco with an O Gauge motor and different number plates on the cab). Few were made, and they are not often offered for sale. They are not cheap, but the price is much lower than the small production figures might warrant. When displayed on a shelf, the 289E draws almost no attention, except from knowledgeable observers who notice the number plates on the cab or the distinctive O Gauge drive wheels. The train is simply not attractive or different enough to interest the majority of collectors, and the element of pride of ownership is largely absent.

Great age is not a guarantee of rarity or scarcity either. One of the very earliest American toy trains was a live steam model called the Dart, made in the United States by the Weeden Company as early as 1888. Thousands were sold, and examples may be seen and even bought at larger train meets. One collector displayed quite a variety of these crude but interesting and popular toys at the York TCA meet in October of 1996.

Scarcity, or the perception of scarcity, often contributes to very high prices for certain toy trains. Lionel recently produced its Fairbanks-Morse Trainmaster locomotive in a special blue and white Wabash paint scheme and sold it only through the JC Penney Company. Like other special production items for that department store, the Wabash FM came with a hardwood and acrylic display case. Judging by the frequency with which this loco is offered for sale at train meets, there must have been a fairly large number produced, but it remains much in demand.

There are probably two reasons for the popularity of the JC Penney Wabash FM. First, it is a very attractive piece, similar in decoration to the postwar 2337 and 2339 GP-9 locomotives. The Wabash design looks especially good on the big rectangular Trainmaster body, and it makes a handsome display in its special case. Second, the public believes it to be hard to find, an idea which is reinforced by the price usually found on them at train meets (around $1100 in 1996).

Scarcity or rarity is often determined not only by total overall production, but by differences in finish or detail. Train manufacturers often decorated their products in more than one paint scheme, or added premium parts to a portion of the production for special sets or targeted markets. For example, some Lionel sets sold by Macy's Department Store, Sears and Roebuck, and other designated retailers carried color combinations or model numbers unique to those distributors. Because they were made in smaller numbers, they are less common and are therefore considered to be more valuable.

American Flyer and Hafner produced sets specifically for export to Canada with Canadian National and Canadian Pacific decoration. Since these were not sold in the United States, and fewer were made for the smaller Canadian market, they are much in demand today. Similarly, the Ives Corporation decorated its O Gauge boxcars for many different road names and companies, and production figures were sometimes small. In these two cases, the scarcity lies not in the construction, as all of the

Ives and American Flyer cars were built exactly the same as normal production. The value lies in the decoration.

The matter of paint color is a special consideration. A factory-applied paint job in an uncommon, or even unique, color makes a common piece much more valuable. For example, the Lionel 390E Standard Gauge locomotive and tender combination was normally painted black, and as such it is a desirable item. But, some of these locos were painted two-tone blue in 1929 for the first "Blue Comet" set, and command at least twice the price of a black one. A two-tone green version is even less common, and may bring four times the price of the black version.

Unfortunately, repaints have been applied to common examples of the 390E and other trains known to exist in scarce colors. These forgeries are often very cleverly aged, and it takes an expert's examination to determine the validity of an original piece. The Train Collectors Association offers such advice at its major train meets, as do other clubs. **Novice collectors should never pay premium prices for trains in scarce colors without first having them authenticated.**

The element of scarcity or rarity is most influential when combined with one or more of the other elements that contribute to value. As an example, Lionel designed and produced its 1764 Standard Gauge locomotives and accompanying 1766, 1767, and 1768 Passenger Cars for the Ives line in 1932. So few were made that they may be considered very scarce, and they were very poor sellers, thanks to a high price tag in those economically depressed times. However, the models were very attractive, sturdily constructed, and ran well, so today collectors seek them avidly. The extremely high prices they command at train meets reflect all of the foregoing elements of collector appeal: inherent value, aesthetic appeal, demand, and scarcity.

E. CONDITION

Each of these foregoing qualities is tempered to a great degree by this fifth factor. Collectors expect to pay a substantial premium for toy trains in superior condition. It is common for collectors of modern era trains to keep them unopened in their original packaging, and train sets in their factory-sealed boxes often change hands many times without ever being opened or examined. The pleasure from this type of ownership comes from the preservation of an absolutely mint toy and its perceived or real value, rather than from the enjoyment of the trains themselves.

Many such sealed sets built from the 1970s through today are plentiful and readily available at train meets. There is also a brisk trade (at very high prices) in sealed sets from the postwar years (1945-1969), but relatively few have survived from the pre-World War II era. For this reason,

Mint (absolutely unused) trains dating from before 1942 are normally sold for much, much more than similar items with even a very small amount of wear. The price of a Mint pre-war train can easily be double that of an Excellent or Like New example, and in the case of scarce items, the difference can be several hundred percent.

Because the emphasis upon condition is of vital concern to collectors, the various train associations have formulated a set of guidelines. Following are the various classifications and descriptions of condition levels (with their abbreviations) that have been generally accepted by the hobby. (These grades apply to cosmetic appearance only. Trains in any category may or may not be in operating condition, although Mint and New pieces may generally be assumed to operate properly, excepting only older pieces in which internal wiring may have deteriorated over time. Collectors who intend to operate their acquisitions should always test them before purchase.)

Mint (M): New in the original box, with all original packing material; absolutely unused and unblemished. Wheels and pickup rollers must show no sign of ever having been on the track.

New (N): Unused and unblemished. Wheels and pickup rollers must show no sign of ever having been on the track.

Like New (LN): Unblemished, with paint or lithography shiny and fresh; minor wear on moving parts, such as wheels and gears.

Excellent (EX): Exhibiting only minor imperfections, such as tiny nicks or scratches in the paint; no dents or rust.

Very Good (VG): Finish may be somewhat scratched or otherwise blemished, but still retains an overall accept-able appearance; no dents or rust. (This level is probably the average for all of the prewar Standard Gauge trains traded between collectors.)

Good (G): Scratched, and may have minor dents or a small amount of rust; detail parts, such as handrails, may be loose or bent.

Fair (F): Heavily scratched, and may be significantly dented or rusted; may be missing parts.

Poor (P): Heavily worn and/or damaged, rusted, and missing parts.

Restored: Repaired and repainted to professional stan-dards in authentic colors and using only original or properly reproduced replacement parts.

Unfortunately for collectors, many thousands of early toy trains were just that: toys! They were played with by children under a variety of conditions, and while some were well cared for and preserved, others were mishandled to varying degrees. Even the toughest of them may have been reduced to scrap by overzealous or careless young engineers. And, many literally became "scrap," being sacrificed to the drive for metals in support of the war effort in the early 1940s.

When considered along with the other factors that deter-mine value, condition exerts a disproportionate amount of influence, both positive and negative. This is especially true for the trains discussed in this book, most of which were manufactured before World War II. In the case of the most common pieces, Excellent to Mint pieces are considered the standard, while less perfect examples (Very Good) are gen-erally quite inexpensive and are collected only for operation or when a limited budget must be observed. Common pieces rated Good or Fair are usually acquired at very low prices only for restoration or parts.

In the case of less common, but not really scarce prewar trains, collectors most often seek out Very Good to Mint examples, and the price differential between categories is wider than for the most common pieces. Examples classified as Good are collected for operation, or because of a limited budget, and Fair items are used for restoration or parts.

Limited production items, or those in scarce colors or with uncommon decoration or detail characteristics, are con-sidered highly collectible in almost any condition. For exam-ple, American Flyer made many thousands of their tiny 1107 Passenger Car, all manufactured in the same basic way from the same materials. Most are available at low prices, but some were lithographed in particular names and colors intended for limited markets, such as the Dominion Flyer cars sold in Canada, and these are highly prized by collec-tors today. In such cases, collectors are reluctant to restore even Fair or Poor examples. If the value of a piece depends primarily upon its rare factory-applied paint or lithography, restoring it would effectively destroy its value.

Scarce (limited production) trains in any condition are considered to be desirable, and the price difference between average examples (Very Good) and lesser Good and Fair ones is likely to be less than in the case of common trains. When an item is scarce, even a rating of Poor is less of a deterrent to collectors who may have little hope of finding the piece in any better condition.

Similarly, the price spread between average (Very Good) examples and Excellent, Like New, and Mint exam-ples is much, much greater. Scarce pieces in premium condi-tion trade at very high prices, when they are available at all. Reproductions have been made of many of the more famous and desirable antique trains. Those made by reputable manu-facturers are usually marked prominently as copies, but there are some unmarked ones. In addition, some unscrupulous traders have attempted to disguise the reproduction identifiers on certain products and may attempt to pass them off as originals. **Novice collectors should obtain advice before buying items known to have been reproduced. Such models are listed in italics in succeeding chapters.**

Determining the value of restored toy trains is somewhat difficult. Operators may prefer properly restored trains that have been mechanically reconditioned. Some collectors prefer the appearance of professionally restored trains, rather than shabby examples in original factory finish, as display shelf items. In this author's opinion, a properly restored toy train is of greater value than one in Good condition or less, except for those trains for which the factor of scarcity depends upon the color or finish.

As an example, consider the Lionel 390E locomotive mentioned. In black, the most common color variation, it has a base value of perhaps $500 to $600 in less than average (Good) condition. In the same condition, but factory-painted blue, the value would be about double, and in green, quadruple the value of a black one. If one were to restore a black one, the value would probably be at least equal to, or somewhat more than, the Good example. However, if one were to restore a blue or green version, the value would be no more than a black one. This is because the value to a collector resides in the scarcity of the factory-applied finish. Restoring the piece obliterates the factory finish and thus compromises the factor of scarcity. Any restored toy train, no matter what color it is repainted, will not be more valuable than the most common version of that item. If, however, the scarcity factor of a train's value depends not upon its color, but upon its construction, a restored version may retain more of its worth.

Determining Condition

Collectors must make subjective decisions when examining trains that are offered for sale. One person's estimate of *Excellent* or *Very Good* may differ considerably from that of another. An individual's estimate of the condition of any given piece is a major factor in the price that may be offered.

The photo shows an Ives 194 hopper car (labeled a "Coal Car" in that company's catalogs), probably manufactured in 1926 or 1927, and in original, unaltered factory condition. At the time this photo was taken (late 1996), this toy had survived for about 70 years. Close examination of the entire car reveals the following information. The paint is bright and fresh, and all of the stamped lettering information is unfaded, unscratched, and clearly readable. The paint on the truck frames, underside and interior is similarly fresh, with no dents evident anywhere on the structure. All parts (brake wheel, dump lever mechanism, couplers, and wheels) are present, clean, and completely free from rust.

This car would qualify as *Like New*, except for the presence of a few small chips in the paint. These are visible along the lower edge of the body near the center, at the bottom of the slanted body part at left, and in the black trim. The paint on most Ives products is known to be subject to flaking, and rarely does one find a better finish than this on an Ives car, but the presence of these chips prevents a rating of *Like New*. Therefore, the author rates this piece as *Excellent*, a very desirable acquisition for most collectors.

Two other two cars shown here illustrate the difference between *Excellent* and *Very Good* ratings. The orange and green American Flyer machinery car has only a few small scratches in the paint. All of the bright metal parts (couplers, rivets, wheels, journal boxes, and brass identification plates) are shiny and untarnished. All original parts are present, including the gold-painted brake wheels. Although not quite

Ives 194 hopper, or "Coal" car.

as clean as the Ives coal car shown above, it still grades as *Excellent*.

By contrast, the Lionel 312 Observation Car in the same photo has quite a few scratches on the sides and roof, although the paint is still fairly bright. Some metal parts are somewhat tarnished, but there is no rust evident. The brass observation platform is very slightly bent. The rubber-stamped lettering on both sides is clear and bold, with only a couple of small scratches. The original celluloid window material (clear panes with mottled blue transoms) is present, but partially loose and easily repairable. There are no missing parts, and the car grades a strong *Very Good*.

Interestingly, the machinery car bears two different number plates, 4022 on one side (which is correct for this car) and 4020, which is a stock car plate. There is no evidence that either plate has ever been removed, and the error probably occurred during assembly at the factory. However, there is no premium for such errors, since these identification plates are easily switched.

Several defects prevent a *Very Good* rating for the American Flyer 4021 Caboose shown in the photo at right. While there are almost no scratches, the paint is dull and somewhat blotchy, and the roof is slightly bent where the cupola has been pushed downward. Some of the metal parts are untarnished and could be cleaned up easily, but there is a slight amount of rust on the couplers and end railings. The

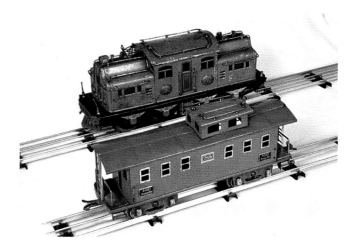

American Flyer 4021 Caboose and Lionel 408E locomotive.

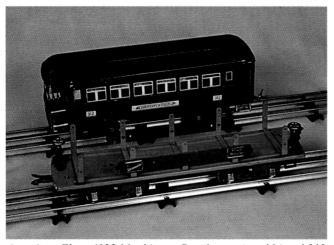

American Flyer 4022 Machinery Car (bottom) and Lionel 312 Observation Car.

brass ladders are bent, one handrail is missing, and there are a few dots of white paint and a small rust spot on the roof. As shown here, the car grades only *Good*, but it could be raised almost to *Very Good* by some careful straightening of the dents and polishing of the metal parts.

The Lionel 408E locomotive in the same photo is on the borderline between *Good* and *Fair*. The paint is scratched, but mostly still present, although it is dull. All of the bright metal trim is tarnished, although not really corroded. There are a few loose joints in the sheet metal body, but no dents. The wheel rims are rusted, and there is a little light rust on the motor side frames. Everything is dirty.

Several parts are broken. One pantograph is half gone, and the other is entirely missing. Only one cast headlight is still present, and both couplers are broken. This results in a *Fair* rating, although the missing and broken parts could be replaced with originals, in which case it might be considered *Good*. It is also common for collectors to replace the drive

wheels on these old locomotives, especially if they are to be operated. (After this photo was taken, the author completely restored this locomotive. It appears in photos elsewhere in this book.)

Sometimes, special circumstances exist which make it difficult or impossible to assign a strict grade according to the guidelines. In the accompanying photo, the black Lionel 1835E steam locomotive exhibits all the characteristics of *Excellent*: shiny unscratched paint, bright metal work, no dents, and no missing parts. However, it has a serious problem. The die-cast frame has been broken at a point just above the back edge of the cylinders. Broken die-cast parts are not uncommon in early toy trains, as the zinc alloy used in the casting process was often impure and tended to deteriorate over time.

Although the break in the frame is barely noticeable, and does not affect operation (thanks to Lionel's rigid design and construction), the locomotive cannot be graded as *Excellent*. Since toy train grading is primarily cosmetic—and this locomotive retains a truly excellent appearance—it would be reasonable to provide a conditional rating, such as "Broken frame, otherwise *Excellent*." In train club newsletters, one frequently encounters such listings where only one defect prevents a specific grade; they use the abbreviation "o/w" for "otherwise." Such an advertisement might read as follows: "212 caboose, orange and maroon, missing one coupler, o/w EX."

Of course, it would be possible to replace the broken frame on the 1835E, although finding an intact original frame for sale is not easy. Reproduction frames are available. It is also possible to repair a casting that has not deteriorated too badly at the break. Such replacement parts or repairs should always be disclosed when the pieces are sold or traded.

The second locomotive in the photo, an Ives 3237, presents a different problem. In terms of structure, this loco is *Excellent*. It has no dents, the trim parts are all present, bright,

Lionel 1835E (top) and Ives 3237 locomotives.

and undented, and there are no missing parts. The mechanical parts are similarly intact, clean, and only slightly worn. The body is tight and has no rust. However, as with many Ives products, most of the paint has flaked off. Ives was much less successful than Lionel in getting paint to stick to its shiny tin-plated steel.

The 3237, a fairly scarce locomotive, is much in demand by collectors and has been reproduced by the Rich-Art Company. Since so many original examples show some sign of paint deterioration, assigning a fair grade to this locomotive is especially difficult. Strictly speaking, it should be rated *Fair*, in recognition of its poor cosmetic appearance. However, this grade does not reflect its fine mechanical condition. In such cases, a conditional rating is appropriate, such as "Paint heavily flaked, o/w EX."

Some manufacturers of early toy trains employed the lithographic process to print highly detailed and realistic designs on their trains. While Lionel reserved this process for its low priced offerings, preferring paint for its regular and premium trains, Ives, American Flyer, and Dorfan produced many beautiful litho cars in both Standard and O gauges. (O Gauge rather than Standard Gauge cars have been used here to illustrate the grading of lithographed cars. The defects are easier to spot on the smaller cars.)

The principal advantage of lithography is the potential for complex and highly detailed designs, including road name heralds, rivets, simulated wood sheathing, and hinge details on doors. At its best, this process is a fine art. Unfortunately, the finish is highly susceptible to scratching or fading, and it cannot easily be restored. A conventional painted surface may be retouched or completely stripped and re-sprayed by any competent hobbyist, but duplicating a lithographed surface requires highly specialized techniques.

It is extremely rare to find a prewar litho car in *New* or *Like New* condition. Only trains that have not been played with, and that have been protected from the sun and humidity over the years, will maintain a truly fresh appearance. In the photo, the Marx 153 "Field" Coach is new production and exhibits the freshness of good lithography at its best, with a smooth, shiny

surface and clear, crisp lettering. The Ives 64387 Canadian Pacific Boxcar next to it is about 70 years older, and is almost as nice. The colors are bright, and the lettering and other details are dark and clear. Even the painted surfaces (roof, frame, and trucks) are remarkably sound, which is unusual for an Ives car. Only the tiniest flaws are visible: a nick in the finish above the "A" in "PACIFIC" and very light rubbed areas on the edge of the roof. It is definitely *Excellent* to a very high degree, and one is even tempted to label this car *Like New* in recognition of its fresh appearance.

The Dorfan 607 Caboose is similarly bright and clean looking, but its blemishes are a bit more obvious. The edges of the frame are nicked, as is the paint on the cupola roof. One very obvious scrape mars the litho next to the right hand window, and another smaller scrape is apparent above the "N" in "LINES". The bright work is beginning to tarnish, although there is no rust. This car is a strong *Very Good*.

The Ives 50 "Limited Vestibule Express" Baggage Car dates from about 1905 and is very well preserved. The lithography has quite a few nicks, but they are generally so small that they detract very little from its appearance. These cars were printed with a great many fine details, including railings, filigrees, and even tiny windows on the vestibules and red spring work above the wheels. Strictly speaking, this car grades *Very Good*, like the Dorfan caboose, but the higher standard of lithographic detail makes it much more attractive. It is uncommon to find lithographed trains of such great age in better condition than this.

The American Flyer 1105 Dominion Flyer car was made in small numbers for the Canadian market, and is a desirable collectors item, even at lower grades of condition. This example is rated *Good*. The colors are slightly faded and dull, and there are scratches and a couple of pinpoint rust spots on the sides. The roof is slightly rusted along the edge at one end, and the paint is dull. The back surface of the wheels are a bit rusty, and all bright work is somewhat tarnished. Nevertheless, the scarcity of the Canadian National lithograph design guarantees that this car will always be sought after.

The final car is an American Flyer product for its low-priced "Hummer" division—a 500 "Pennsylvania Lines" Coach folded from a single piece of lithographed steel. It has no floor, and the couplers are part of the steel stamping. Only the wheels and axles are separate parts. It has been well played with and has many scratches, but shows no dents in the metal. A little rust has begun to form in some of the scratches, and the finish is dull and faded. This level of preservation in a lithographed car is normally graded no better than *Good*, but this car is definitely worth collecting. Not many have survived in any condition. They were fairly flimsy, and because of their low original price, they were rarely as well cared for by their owners as more expensive toys might have been.

Back row, left to right: AF 500 Penna. Coach, AF 1105 Dominion Flyer Baggage Car, Ives 50 Baggage Car. Front row, left to right: Marx 153 Canadian Pacific Coach, Dorfan 607 Caboose, Ives 64387 Canadian Pacific Boxcar. The smaller O Gauge cars are shown instead of Standard Gauge models for ease of comparison.

Deciding On A Fair Price

As can be seen from the foregoing discussion, determining the worth of an antique toy train based on its condition is a highly subjective exercise. For this reason, any guide to values must be similarly subjective. In the next chapter, estimates of value are presented for most Standard Gauge trains and accessories built and sold in America between 1906, when Lionel introduced this size, and 1942, when the last of these large trains disappeared from the Lionel catalog. These values are based on the factors of inherent value (quality), aesthetic appeal, demand, and scarcity, as discussed earlier in this chapter.

No attempt has been made, however, to differentiate between levels of condition, because of the subjective nature of this component of overall worth. Instead, a single value is given for each item, assuming an average grade of *Very Good* ("finish may be somewhat scratched or otherwise blemished, but still retains an overall acceptable appearance; no dents or rust"). The collector may compare this standard against the actual condition of any toy train under consideration for purchase, deducting from the given value for a greater number of defects, or adding a premium for more well-preserved items. The presence of an original box also adds to the value, to a small degree for common items, and substantially for scarce trains. (It is not unusual for some uncommon boxes, especially those for the larger sets, to sell for many hundreds of dollars.)

Collecting Standard Gauge trains is a captivating hobby, and the hours spent seeking out and bargaining for new acquisitions is both fascinating and pleasurable. It need not be especially expensive. There are many vintage trains available, especially at the train meets sponsored by the various clubs and organizations listed in the Appendix. For example, Lionel made many, many thousands of smaller Standard Gauge electric-type locomotives (numbers 8 and 10), and examples in respectable condition can be readily found for as little as a couple of hundred dollars. And, if you take the time to learn repair techniques, you can find restorable trains for much less, and return them to pristine condition at great savings. Restoration is a fascinating hobby in itself.

An earlier warning is worth repeating: Until you have acquired a comprehensive knowledge of the field, be sure to seek out advice from seasoned collectors when contemplating large or expensive purchases.

Don't forget to bargain; most sellers are willing to accept reasonable offers. And most of all, have fun!

*Lionel's most elaborate electric-type locomotive was the
408, shown here pulling State Set passenger cars. This
popular locomotive has been reproduced by Williams
Reproductions Ltd. and Mike's Train House, as well as
by Lionel Trains, Inc., which made the units shown here.
(Carail Museum Collection)*

11

LOCOMOTIVES AND TROLLEYS

Value Guide

The power units listed in this chapter are arranged according to manufacturer, in alphabetical order. The entries are listed in the numerical order of their catalog numbers. Each entry contains the following information: catalog number; dates of manufacture; prototype design (if any); length in inches (minus couplers); brief description for identification, including wheel arrangement according to the Whyte system of classification (number of pilot wheels, number of drive wheels, number of trailing wheels, e.g. 2-4-2); color and/or significant variations (if any); and value in *Very Good* (VG) condition. Colors are listed in order from most to least common.

For an explanation of grading criteria and how to evaluate condition, see Chapter 10. Buyers should expect to pay a premium for items in better than *Very Good* condition, with the upward price differential being greater for scarce or expensive items. The values for items in less than *Very Good* condition are generally lower than those shown, with the downward price differential being greater for common or inexpensive items.

The value of restored pieces depends upon the quality of the restoration work, the scarcity of the item, and the use to which the piece will be put (operation or display; see Chapter 10). In general, the average value of restored items

is comparable to the most common version in *Very Good* condition.

Items which are known to have been reproduced are shown in italics. While most reproductions are so marked, there is always the possibility of unmarked or fraudulent items being presented as originals. Novices should obtain the advice of experienced collectors before purchasing high value toy trains. The catalog numbers for items which were advertised but not known to have been made are omitted from this chapter.

Items purchased in sets (locomotive plus cars, with or without track, transformer, and accessories), and those purchased with original boxes and/or original instruction books or other literature will command a premium, with the upward price differential depending upon scarcity. The premium for boxes depends upon condition (presence or absence of end flaps, tears in the cardboard, etc.) and scarcity of the set. Collectors place substantial value upon prewar boxes, especially set boxes, in *Very Good* or better condition.

Toy Standard Gauge locomotives of the prewar period are not scale models, but are designed to give the *impression* of specific prototypes. They vary from caricatures to reasonably realistic interpretations. Electric-type locomotives are generally patterned after prototype designs used by the New York Central (T-Class and S-Class, abbreviated NYC and NYC-S, respectively), New Haven (NH), Pennsylvania (PENN) and Chicago, Milwaukee, St. Paul & Pacific (St. Paul) Railroads. The latter exhibits a rounded cab structure, while the first three are more rectangular in appearance. Steam locomotives are generic designs, all with four driving wheels.

Note that the term "Standard Gauge" was exclusive to Lionel and Boucher, and that the products of other manufacturers are referred to as "Wide Gauge." The distance between the outer rails of the track, however, is the same (2-1/8") for all manufacturers. The term "Standard Gauge" is used in this book to describe all trains built to 2-1/8" Gauge.

American Flyer Wide (Standard) Gauge Locomotives

STEAM LOCOMOTIVES AND TENDERS

Following the bankruptcy of the Ives Company in 1928, American Flyer and Lionel assumed joint control and continued to produce trains out of the Ives factory in Bridgeport, Connecticut. Although Lionel was to assume sole control within a year, American Flyer retained the rights to manufacture the beautiful Ives 1134 Wide (Standard) Gauge locomotive and tender under its own brand name. The boiler and tender castings and mechanism were very sophisticated, with a realistic appearance, including a cab-mounted motor that allowed a prototypical amount of open space between the boiler and the drive wheels.

American Flyer used the Ives dies to make their first Standard Gauge steamers and sold them in 1929 and 1930. Unfortunately, like their Ives predecessors, these toys proved to be very fragile, due to impurities in the zinc alloy-based casting material, and most exhibit some degree of deterioration today, from pitting and breaks to major decomposition.

In 1931 American Flyer introduced two of its own steam engine and tender designs, one with a cast-iron boiler and the other using the zinc alloy casting technique. The smaller cast-iron model was carried for just two years, and was made with two different wheel arrangements, 2-4-2 and 4-4-2. The larger zinc alloy boiler was made with a 4-4-2 wheel arrangement only, in several different trim variations through 1935 and catalogued through 1936. Most versions, excepting only the earliest, were fitted with a red bulb under the cab to simulate a glowing firebox. Others included a bell-ringing mechanism and/or a remote control reverse.

There were two different Standard Gauge tenders made to accompany these engines. The smaller model, similar to the Ives design, had a rectangular body and a simulated coal pile. The larger tender represented the oil-carrying Vanderbilt style, with a rounded aft section.

ELECTRIC-TYPE LOCOMOTIVES

American Flyer built three different styles of electric locomotives. The earliest (1925) was a rectangular design patterned after the New York Central T-Class box cab prototype, and had three windows and simulated ventilators on each side, plus a raised central section on the roof. A brass handrail encircled the roof. Two windows and a door were stamped into each end of the cab. Trim variations included one or two die-cast headlights, one or two simple stamped-metal pantographs, and a bell. On some models the bell was connected by a rod to a cam on an internal bell-ringing mechanism. As the locomotive moved forward, the bell swung back and forth as the sound emerged from the cab.

Some early versions of this cab had double walls, with the window frames stamped into the inner wall. This system imitated Lionel's patented system of using metal inserts for door and window trim, and Flyer was forced to drop the feature to avoid legal action. Double-walled cabs are scarce and command a premium.

American Flyer (top) and Ives (center) locomotives are very similar, as they share a common heritage in the Ives 1134 design. Lionel locomotives such as this 1835E (bottom) are distinctive.

American Flyer electric locomotive designs: New York Central (top), New Haven (center), and St. Paul (bottom).

The NYC design was mounted on two different types of frame, a smaller version with an 0-4-0 wheel arrangement, and a larger 4-4-4 style with four wheel pilot trucks at each end. These premium locomotives pulled sets with Flyer's longest passenger cars and were fitted with larger, more detailed pantographs. Some sported a brass eagle on a pedestal on the lead truck.

The second design appeared in 1927 as a lower priced companion to the New York Central model and resembled locomotives of the New Haven Railroad. The cab was smaller, and the roof had overhanging extensions at each end and a raised center section, trimmed with less elaborate handrails than the NYC design. The window and door arrangement was the same, although on a smaller scale. Trim options included one or two die-cast headlights, a small stamped pantograph, and a stationary bell. The bell-ringing mechanism was not used on the New Haven models. The cabs were mounted on stamped-metal frames, each with an 0-4-0 wheel arrangement.

A year later Flyer introduced a third type, the St. Paul-style, and priced it between the New Haven and NYC models. The body was made in three sections. The almost square center cab had a rounded roof, three windows, and a door on each side, plus a ladder and two handrails. The two end hood sections were rounded across the top and were slightly lower than the cab. These hoods were trimmed with brass handrails, one or two die-cast headlights, one or two stamped pantographs, and a bell. Some models featured the ringing bell mechanism and a moving bell on top.

St. Paul locomotives came with two sizes of frame. On the longer version, the end sections of the body were also longer, and had three stamped ventilators on each side. The shorter versions had just two ventilators per side. All of these locomotives had an 0-4-0 mechanism.

A remote control reverse was offered on some models of both steam and box cab locomotives. All entries in the following listing have a manual reverse except as indicated.

4000 1925-27; NYC box cab; 14-1/2"; 0-4-0; green, dark green, red or orange with contrasting window frames and black frame; 25% premium for red or orange. **$200**

4019 1925-27; NYC box cab; 14-1/2"; 0-4-0; maroon with yellow windows and black frame; 150% premium for scarce early version with double cab walls. **$200**

4039 1926; NYC box cab; 15"; 0-4-0; tan with yellow windows and black frame. **$250**

4633 1930-31; St. Paul electric; 13-1/4"; 0-4-0; red with brass windows and gray frame; bell-ringing mechanism. **$250**

4635 1929-30; St. Paul electric; 13-1/4"; 0-4-0; red with brass windows and gray frame. **$200**

American Flyer 4635 St. Paul locomotive; compare the end hoods with the 4637 "Shasta" version. (below) (Carail Museum Collection)

4637 1928-33; St. Paul electric; 15"; 0-4-0; green with brass windows and tan frame; bell-ringing mechanism; remote control reverse. **$450**

4643 1927; NH box cab; 12"; 0-4-0; green with yellow windows and black frame. **$150**

4644 1928-1933; NH box cab; 12"; 0-4-0; green or red with gold colored windows and black (early) or gray (later) frame; 125% premium for brass plates inscribed "NATIONWIDE LINES"; 25% premium for remote control reverse mechanism. **$125**

American Flyer 4637 St. Paul "Shasta" locomotive; note the long end hoods, as compared with the short hood 4635 in the photo above. (Carail Museum Collection)

American Flyer 4678 locomotive; restored.

American Flyer's version of a New Haven box cab (bottom, 4644) included the characteristic overhang at each end of the roof. Ives New Haven locos (top, 3236) lack this feature.

4653 1927; NH box cab; 12"; 0-4-0; orange with dark orange windows and black frame. $200

4654 1928-31; NH box cab; 12"; 0-4-0; orange with blue windows and gray frame. $150

4660 Catalog number for the locomotive only, included in the 1930 No. 4664 and 1929-30 No. 4694 locomotive and tender set. $750

4664 1930; 4660 steamer (former Ives casting) and 4693 rounded Vanderbilt tender; 25"; 4-4-2; black. $800

4667 1927; NYC box cab; 15"; 0-4-0; red with yellow windows and black frame. $250

4670 Catalog number for the locomotive only, included in the No. 4672 locomotive and tender set. $575

4671 Catalog number for the coal-type tender included in various locomotive and tender sets. $85

4672 1931-32; 4670 cast-iron steamer and 4671 rectangular tender or 4693 rounded Vanderbilt tender; 23"; 2-4-2 (early) or 4-4-2; black with green stripe on loco frame; remote control reverse; 10% premium for Vanderbilt tender. $800

4675 *1931-32; die-cast zinc alloy 4692 steamer and 4671 rectangular tender or 4693 rounded Vanderbilt tender; 24-1/2" or 27"; 4-4-2; black with green stripe on loco frame; remote control or manual reverse; 10% premium for Vanderbilt tender; reproduced by Rich-Art.* *$700*

4677 1927; NYC box cab; 15"; 0-4-0; tan with yellow windows and black frame. $250

4678 1928-29; NYC box cab; 15"; 0-4-0; red with yellow windows and gray frame. $275

4680 Catalog number for the locomotive only, included in the No. 4682 locomotive and tender set. $675

4681 *1933-35; 4695 die-cast zinc alloy steamer and 4671 rectangular tender; 24-1/2"; 4-4-2; black with green stripe on loco frame, plus extra brass piping on sides; bell-ringing mechanism; remote control reverse; reproduced by Rich-Art.* *$1100*

4682 1933; 4680 die-cast zinc alloy steamer and 4671 rectangular tender; 24-1/2" or 27"; 4-4-2; black with green stripe on loco frame; remote control reverse. $850

4683 1930-31, 1933-34; St. Paul electric; 13-1/4"; 0-4-0; red with brass windows and gray frame; bell-ringing mechanism; remote control reverse. $275

4684 1928-31; NH box cab; 12"; 0-4-0; green or red with gold colored windows and black (early) or gray (later) frame, or orange with green windows and gray frame; remote control reverse mechanism. $150

4685 1929-30; St. Paul electric; 13-1/4"; 0-4-0; red with brass windows and gray frame; remote control reverse. $200

American Flyer 4687 "President's Special" locomotives, with 4090 Baggage Cars; note variations (painted and unpainted windows, brass and nickel trim). (Carail Museum Collection)

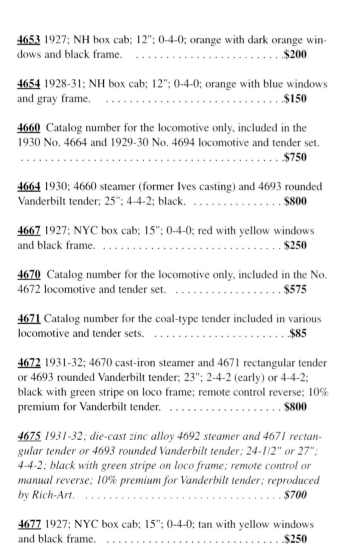

4686 1928-29; NYC box cab; 18-1/2"; 4-4-4 with swiveling pilot trucks; blue with brass windows and black frame; bell-ringing mechanism. **$800**

4687 1927; NYC box cab; 18-1/2"; 4-4-4 with swiveling pilot trucks; blue with gold colored windows and black frame. **$650**

4689 1928-34; NYC box cab; 18-1/2"; 4-4-4 with swiveling pilot trucks; blue with brass windows and black frame; brass pedestal with eagle on one pilot truck; bell-ringing mechanism. **$1,250**

American Flyer 4689 "President's Special" locomotive, and 4390 Club Car. (Carail Museum Collection)

4689 As above, except chrome plated instead of painted; reproduced by Rich-Art and Lionel Trains, Inc.; unmarked re-plated cabs have been reported. *$10,000*

4692 Catalog number for the locomotive only, included in various locomotive and tender sets; reproduced by Rich-Art. . . *$700*

4693 Catalog number for the Vanderbilt tender only, included in various locomotive and tender sets; reproduced by Rich-Art. *$150*

4694 1929-30; 4692 steamer (former Ives 1134 casting) and rectangular tender (former Ives casting) with brass "GOLDEN STATE" plates or 4693 rounded Vanderbilt tender; 23-1/2" or 26"; 4-4-2; black; 10% premium for Vanderbilt tender. **$800**

Lionel Trains, Inc. reproduction of American Flyer 4689 "Mayflower" locomotive. (Carail Museum Collection)

4694 1931-34; 4692 die-cast zinc alloy steamer and 4693 rounded Vanderbilt tender; 27"; 4-4-2; black with green stripe on loco frame; may have bell-ringing mechanism; remote control reverse; reproduced by Rich-Art. *$750*

4695 Catalog number for the locomotive only, included in the Nos. 4681 and 4696 locomotive and tender sets; reproduced by Rich-Art. *$850*

4696 1933-35; 4695 die-cast zinc alloy steamer and 4693 rounded Vanderbilt tender; 27"; 4-4-2; black with green stripe on loco frame, plus extra brass piping on sides; bell-ringing mechanism; remote control reverse; reproduced by Rich-Art. *$1,000*

4743 C. 1927, uncataloged; NH box cab; 12"; 0-4-0; red with yellow windows and black frame; very scarce. **$800**

4753 C. 1927, uncataloged; NH box cab; 12"; 0-4-0; red with yellow windows and black frame; very scarce. **$800**

Boucher Standard Gauge Locomotives

STEAM LOCOMOTIVES AND TENDERS

Boucher produced three steam locomotives, although the two largest differed only in number of wheels. Only the highest priced version, with its 4-6-2 wheel arrangement, was correctly described in the catalog as a "Pacific" locomotive. The mid-priced engine had the same boiler and cab but lacked the two trailing wheels, yet the company still called it a "Pacific." The smaller locomotive was a 4-4-0, but for its catalog description ("Atlantic") to be correct, it should have been a 4-4-2. Each of these engines was accompanied by the same coal-type tender.

Values for Boucher products are speculative; examples rarely change hands due to very limited production numbers. The prices given reflect their relative rarity and are comparable to products of other low-volume companies.

2100 1922-29; steam locomotive and rectangular tender; 14-3/4"; 4-4-0; black. **$3,250**

2222 1922-29; steam locomotive and rectangular tender; 20-1/2"; 4-6-0; black. **$3,500**

2500 1922-29; steam locomotive and rectangular tender; 20-1/2"; 4-6-2; black. **$3,750**

Dorfan Wide (Standard) Gauge Locomotives

STEAM LOCOMOTIVE AND TENDER

Dorfan sold a version of the Ives 1134 locomotive and tender, painted either black or green and carrying Dorfan decals on the tender in place of the Ives brass plates. This was the only Wide (Standard) Gauge steamer the company marketed.

ELECTRIC-TYPE LOCOMOTIVES

The company's first Standard Gauge electric locomotive (1926) was an impressive design patterned after a Pennsylvania prototype, with a squared-off body that had a raised center cab and lower hood extensions at each end, flanked by stamped-steel handrails. The die-cast body had no separate frame. Instead, the journal boxes and axle mounts were a part of the body. The 4-4-4 wheel arrangement featured two swiveling pilot trucks. Dorfan packaged these locomotives either ready to run or as take-apart kits ("Loco Builder" models) which could be assembled with a screwdriver. Trim included two small pantographs on the raised cab and a headlight on the end of each hood.

A second and smaller St. Paul type with an 0-4-0 mechanism appeared in 1927, also frameless and in built up or kit form. Trim was similar to the larger model, with two pantographs and two headlights, but the handrails were heavy wire instead of stamped-steel. Later models of both electric-type locomotives came with ball bearings on the axles, which improved operation and durability. Unfortunately, the bodies were cast from often impure zinc alloy, and were subject to deterioration. Dorfan improved its casting technique and material as the problem became evident, but many of their products are found today in very poor condition. All entries have a manual reverse except as indicated.

Dorfan No. 3920 St. Paul-style electric locomotive. (Carail Museum Collection)

1134 *Ca. 1929, uncataloged; Ives 1134 steamer and rectangular tender with Dorfan trucks, couplers and decals; 23-1/2"; 4-4-2; black or green with red trim; reproduced by Rich-Art.* **$2,400**

3920 1927-30; St. Paul electric; 13"; 0-4-0; orange, red, gray, green, maroon, or ivory with contrasting painted or brass windows; premium for latter colors. **$600**

3930 1926-30; Penn electric; 4-4-4; orange, gray, green, black, or blue; separate window frames beginning in 1928; some 1930 models with remote control reverse; premium for latter colors; extremely scarce. **$2,600**

3931 1930; Penn electric; 4-4-4; ivory with red windows and wheels; some with remote control reverse; extremely scarce. **$4,500**

3932 1927; Penn electric; 4-4-4; black with red windows and wheels; very rare. . . . . **(no value established)**

Ives Wide (Standard) Gauge Locomotives

STEAM LOCOMOTIVES AND TENDERS

Ives was the first of the three principal American toy train manufacturers to produce realistic steam locomotives in Wide (Standard) Gauge, beginning in 1921. Lionel's primitive and toy-like sheet metal locomotives appeared in 1906 and were phased out in 1926, and the first of their modern styles, the 390E, did not appear until 1929. By contrast, Ives had been producing large and well-proportioned cast-iron steamers, powered by spring-wound clockwork motors, since 1904, in the then-popular No. 1 Gauge. In

1915 the company produced a new and more modern design driven by an electric motor.

By 1920, however, it was apparent that Lionel's Standard Gauge dimensions were capturing an ever-increasing share of the market, and were in fact dominating the sales of large toy trains in America. In order to meet market demand, Ives converted its large No. 1 Gauge line to Wide Gauge, which measured 2-1/8" between the outer rails just like Lionel Standard Gauge. By increasing the width between the drive and pilot wheels and the tender trucks, they were able to convert the existing No. 1 Gauge locomotives to run on the new track. This model (1132) was produced through 1926 and was replaced the following year by another handsome cast-iron locomotive, numbered 1134 and patterned after the "President Washington" of the Baltimore & Ohio Railroad.

In 1928 Ives introduced a new and extremely realistic die-cast locomotive, featuring a smooth zinc alloy boiler and tender and a cab-mounted motor that allowed a prototypical open area between the boiler and drive wheels. This graceful and beautiful locomotive had a smooth and powerful ball bearing drive, and carried the same catalog number, 1134, as the 1927 cast-iron locomotive. The two designs were entirely different, however.

During the same year, the Ives Company was forced into bankruptcy and was reorganized under the joint management of both Lionel and American Flyer. The 1134 was produced under the Ives nameplate through 1930 and was also modified for the American Flyer line, as described earlier in this chapter. Another version was provided to and marketed by Dorfan. Unfortunately, the new casting technique had not yet been perfected, and many of these locomotives have deteriorated due to impurities in the zinc alloy used to produce them.

In 1930 the onset of the Great Depression sharply curtailed toy train sales, and Lionel cut back and finally eliminated production at the Ives factory in Bridgeport. Beginning in 1931, Ives trains were built in Lionel's Irvington, New Jersey plant, and most of the line consisted of regular Lionel items with Ives decals or brass nameplates and couplers. In 1932 the Lionel latch coupler was substituted, thus making it impossible for purchasers to couple the new products with their existing Ives trains. The Ives line now existed in name only, and the following year it was dropped entirely. During this transitional period, two Lionel locomotives were sold with Ives nameplates, the 1760 (Lionel 384) and 1770 (Lionel 390).

ELECTRIC-TYPE LOCOMOTIVES

Both Lionel and Ives introduced large models of New York Central S-Class electric locomotives in 1910, but they were constructed very differently. While Lionel's locos were made of sheet metal and rode on Standard Gauge track, the Ives design was cast-iron and built to the slightly smaller No. 1 Gauge standards.

S-Class locomotives are somewhat similar in profile to the St. Paul-style, with a raised center cab and an elongated hood on either end. Unlike the St. Paul, however, they are much more angular, with sharper edges on the body work

Ives 1134 locomotives (die-cast zinc models); the black version with a boiler-top headlight dates from 1929, while the red engine with headlight in the boiler front is 1930 production. (Carail Museum Collection)

and a more boxy design. The Ives version was much more realistic and faithful to the prototype than the Lionel, with such details as rivets cast into the body and frame and journal boxes over the drive wheels. Both firms powered these models electrically.

The popularity of Lionel's Standard Gauge forced Ives to adopt the new size in 1921, and their first Wide (Standard) Gauge electric types were No. 1 Gauge models with widened axles, sold under catalog number 3240. The company quickly developed a sheet metal version of the S-Class locomotive and sold it through 1928 in differing trim and price levels. The mid-priced 3242 had more trim than the economical 3241, while the elaborate 3243 rode on a larger frame and had a pair of four-wheel pilot trucks.

In 1924 a new and smaller body style appeared, much simpler in design and more economical to manufacture. This cab is usually referred to as a New Haven type, but is without the roof overhang characteristic of that railroad's design, so that it also resembles the New York Central T-Class design produced by American Flyer and Lionel. Two trim levels were offered, with the 3236 having more applied detail than the 3235. The latter was produced through 1927, while the former was catalogued from 1925 through 1930.

A very handsome St. Paul-style cab was introduced in 1927 and was used on two different models, the 0-4-0 3237 and the elaborate 4-4-4 "Olympian." Ives also built a version of this cab with extended ends and mounted it on an elongated 4-4-4 frame. These models are normally referred to as "short cab" and "long cab" "Olympian" versions. These impressive locomotives were catalogued with the long and graceful passenger coaches that Ives borrowed from American Flyer under the new management that followed their bankruptcy.

After Lionel assumed full control of the Bridgeport company, the Lionel 8 body was modified to fit the Ives

3236 frame. This modification consisted of adding a shaped metal strip around the bottom of the cab to raise it up enough to clear the taller Ives motor and applying Ives name and number plates. A Lionel 10 with Ives plates was also sold. Lionel made one final attempt to continue a separate Ives identity by creating a handsome 4-4-4 New Haven model in 1932, but this relatively high priced toy failed to sell well and is very hard to find today.

In the listings that follow, entries with "R" or "E" following the catalog number (e.g., 1132R, 1770E) have remote control reverse mechanisms.

10, 10E 1931-32; Lionel 10 St. Paul electric; 12"; blue with brass Ives nameplates. **$250**

40 Tender number only from various locomotive and tender sets; stamped-steel version reproduced by Rulon Taylor; die-cast version reproduced by Rich-Art. $200

1132, 1132R 1921-26; cast-iron steamer and 40 stamped-steel tender; 0-4-0; black; 75% premium for tan, 125% premium for white, and 200% premium for black with Wanamaker Department Store lettering; tender reproduced by Rulon Taylor. **$850**

1132 1928; cast-iron steamer and 40 die-cast tender (same as early 1134); 23-1/2"; 4-4-0; black. **$1,800**

1134, 1134R 1927; cast-iron steamer and stamped-steel or die-cast tender; 4-4-0; modeled after B & O President Washington locomotive; tender rubber-stamped "B.&O. R.R."; green, black; die-cast tender reproduced by Rich-Art; steel tender reproduced by Rulon Taylor. **$1,800**

1134, 1134R 1928-30; die-cast zinc alloy steamer and 40 die-cast tender; 23-1/2"; 4-4-2; black; 35% premium for green, 100% premium for red, 150% premium for copper plated or nickel plated; reproduced by Rich-Art; steel tender reproduced by Rulon Taylor. $1,800

1760, 1760E 1931; Lionel 384 steamer with Lionel 390T tender; 21"; 2-4-0; black with Ives brass plates. Caution: plates have been reproduced to disguise Lionel production as Ives models. **$800**

1764E 1932; NH box cab; 4-4-4 with swiveling pilot trucks; terra cotta with maroon roof and frame; very rare; reproduced by James Cohen (may be unmarked). $2,800

1770, 1770E 1932; Lionel 390 steamer with Lionel 390T tender; 22-1/4"; 2-4-2; black with Ives brass plates and Lionel latch couplers. Caution: plates have been reproduced to disguise Lionel production as Ives models. **$1,000**

3235, 3235R 1924-27; NH box cab on cast-iron (early) or stamped-steel frame; 12-1/4" (cast-iron frame) or 11-3/4" (steel frame); 0-4-0; brown, green, red, gray, or blue with contrasting window frames; 1000% premium for scarce maroon with Wanamaker Department Store lettering. **$175**

Clockwise from left: Ives 3236 locomotive with Lionel 8 body, steel frame and brass plates; 3241 locomotive with cast-iron frame and stamped lettering; 3235 locomotive with cast-iron frame and stamped lettering; 3236 locomotive with Ives body, cast-iron frame and brass plates. Locos with brass plates are later than those with stamped lettering, and they may have either cast-iron (earlier) or stamped-steel (later) frames.

3236, 3236R 1925-30; NH box cab on cast-iron (early) or stamped-steel frame; 12-1/4" (cast-iron frame) or 11-3/4" (steel frame); 0-4-0; brown, red, tan, or maroon with contrasting window frames; value undetermined for scarce maroon version. .**$185**

3236, 3236R 1925-30; NYC box cab (modified Lionel 8) on Ives stamped-steel frame; 11-3/4"; 0-4-0; blue, red, or green on black frame, or black on orange frame, with brass windows; value undetermined for scarce maroon version. **$275**

3237, 3237R 1926-30; St. Paul electric on stamped-steel frame with cast-iron or die-cast pilots; 13-1/4"; 0-4-0; green or blue on black frame, or black on orange frame, with brass windows; 50% premium for plates lettered "SOUTHERN PACIFIC"; reproduced by Rich-Art. $900

3240 1921; NYC-S cast-iron box cab on cast-iron frame, converted from earlier No. 1 Gauge production; 14-1/2"; 0-4-0; black. $900

Above: Ives 3237 St. Paul-style electric locomotive.

Ives 3245R St. Paul Olympian locomotive. (Carail Museum Collection)

3241, 3241R 1921-25; NYC-S box cab on cast-iron frame; 12-1/2" (early) or 13"; 0-4-0; green, red, or maroon with contrasting window frames; 500% premium for scarce maroon with Wanamaker Department Store lettering. **$175**

3242, 3242R 1921-30; NYC-S box cab on cast-iron (early) or stamped-steel frame; 12-1/2" (early cast-iron) or 13" (later cast-iron and steel); 0-4-0; brown, green, red, tan, orange, gray, blue, or dark blue on black frame, or black on orange or red frame, with contrasting window frames; 100% premium for gray, blue, and black with orange or red frame; 500% premium for scarce maroon with Wanamaker Department Store lettering; value not determined for rare dark blue version. **$250**

3243, 3243R 1921-28; NYC-S box cab on cast-iron (early) or stamped-steel frame; 4-4-4 with swiveling pilot trucks; green, orange, red, black, and blue on black frame, or black on red frame, with contrasting window frames; 150% premium for blue, black, and black with red frame; 500% premium for white; value undetermined for scarce maroon, with or without Wanamaker Department Store lettering. **$750**

3245, 3245R *1928-30; short or long St. Paul Olympian box cab on stamped-steel frame with cast-iron or stamped-steel pilots; 18"; 4-4-4 with swiveling pilot trucks; black, blue, or green on black frame, or black on orange frame, with brass windows; reproduced by Sirus & Varney and Rich-Art. $2,500*

Lionel Standard Gauge Locomotives

STEAM LOCOMOTIVES AND TENDERS

The first Standard Gauge trains were Lionel trains, sold beginning in 1906 and built of steel or brass with rubber-stamped lettering. Most were painted, but there were special versions of some models in polished brass and nickel. These early models were toy-like portrayals of small nineteenth century steam locomotives, lacking in realism but with a great deal of charm. Two sizes were manufactured with 0-4-0 and 4-4-0 wheel arrangements under several catalog numbers, the last being offered in 1926, when all steamers were dropped from the line.

Lionel reintroduced steam locomotives with the No. 390E in 1929, a much larger and more realistic interpretation than the early designs. It was soon joined by four other models in various sizes under five different catalog numbers. All were of mixed stamped-steel and die-cast construction, and while there were impurities in the zinc alloy material employed, Lionel steamers have survived intact in greater numbers than the Ives design. The most common failure is a broken frame, and reproduction frames are available for all models. It can be very difficult to identify a reproduction frame that has been properly painted and installed.

Four different tenders accompanied the engines. The smallest was a coal-carrying style sold with several models under catalog numbers 384T and 390T. A large twelve-wheel coal tender came with the large 392 loco, and the biggest 400 engine had its own Vanderbilt oil type tender. Lionel also borrowed the dies that Ives had used for its tenders and packaged them with two of their own models, the 385E and the 1835E.

ELECTRIC-TYPE LOCOMOTIVES

Following the success of the early steam designs, Lionel introduced interpretations in 1910 of electric-type locomotives that were familiar to residents of the eastern United States, the New York Central S-Class design. Early in the century, steam locomotives were banned from the tunnels that serviced the island of Manhattan, and electrified lines rapidly became common in that and other urban areas. Construction of the Lionel models was of steel or brass, and like the steamers, most were painted and had rubber-stamped lettering, although there were a few polished brass versions. They varied in size, number of wheels and number of motors (one or two), and were priced accordingly. The

The three major manufacturers all modeled St. Paul locomotives, but with very different results. Foreground: Ives 3237; background: Lionel 10 (left) and American Flyer 4683.

earliest had squared-off, rectangular body parts, but after the first few years of production, around 1913, the locomotives received more rounded bodies.

As Lionel refined and improved its manufacturing processes, the firm gradually replaced these early designs with a new series of locomotives and broadened the scope of prototypes represented. New versions of the New York Central S-Class (318, 402, and 408) were joined by NYC T-Class (8) and St. Paul models (10, 380, and 381). As with the earlier designs, most were driven by a single motor, with only the large 402 and 408 0-4-4-0 locos having two powered trucks. Two of the new designs (9U, 381U) came in screwdriver-assembly kits, identified by the letter "U" in the catalog number. All bodies were steel with brass inserts for windows and doors, and brass and die-cast trim pieces.

Lionel steam locomotives built between 1929 and 1939, and electric locomotives built between 1923 and 1936, are often referred to as coming from the "Classic Period."

5 *1906-26; sheet metal steamer without tender; 11-1/2"; 0-4-0; black with red trim on windows and pilot; 50% premium for drive wheels with thin rims (early); reproduced by James Cohen, Joseph Mania, and McCoy.* *$900*

5 SPECIAL 1906-11; sheet metal steamer with slope-backed, eight-wheel tender; 18"; 0-4-0; black with red trim on windows, tender and pilot; 75% premium for four-wheel tender. **$1,100**

6 *1906-23; sheet metal steamer with rectangular tender; 22"; 4-4-0; black with red trim on windows, tender and pilot; 100% premium for drive wheels with thin rims (early); reproduced by James Cohen, Joseph Mania, and McCoy.* *$1,100*

6 SPECIAL 1908-09; sheet metal steamer with rectangular tender; 22"; 4-4-0; brass and nickel finish with red trim on windows, tender and pilot. **$3,000**

7 *1910-23; sheet metal steamer with rectangular tender; 22"; 4-4-0; brass and nickel finish with red trim on windows, tender and pilot; same as 6 Special; 20% premium for drive wheels with thin rims; reproduced by James Cohen, Joseph Mania, McCoy, and Lionel Trains Inc.* *$2,500*

Lionel 5 Special locomotive, with 181 Combine and 180 Pullman; restored. Also visible are the top of a 78 Train Control Signal (behind locomotive), the base of a 92 Floodlight Tower (right) and a 200 Turntable (right foreground). Although the 181 Combine and a matching 182 Observation Car have been found in this yellow-orange shade of enamel, no matching 180 Pullman is known to exist. This restoration assumes that such a car probably was made to match the other two.

Lionel 6 locomotive; note the thin rims on the drive wheels, signifying early production (1906-1911). (Carail Museum Collection)

8, 8E 1925-32; NYC box cab electric; 11"; 0-4-0; maroon, green, red, Mojave; 200% premium for peacock blue; value undetermined for peacock blue with Macy's Department Store lettering or chrome plating. **$150**

9, 9E, 9U *1928-36; NYC box cab electric; 14-1/2"; 0-4-0 or 2-4-2; gunmetal, orange, two-tone green; 75% premium for dark green 9 (without remote control reverse); 20% premium for 9U kit assembled; 200% premium for 9U unassembled kit in original box; reproduced by Williams Reproductions and Mike's Train House.* **$1,000**

10, 10E 1925-30; St. Paul electric; 11-1/2"; 0-4-0; peacock blue, Mojave, gray; 125% premium for peacock blue with dark green frame; 150% premium for brown with dark green frame; 500% premium for red. **$160**

33 1913-24; NYC-S electric; 10-3/8"; 0-6-0 (1913) or 0-4-0 (1913-24); green, black, gray; 400% premium for factory repaints in red, maroon and peacock blue; 500% premium for 0-6-0 model; value undetermined for scarce dark blue version made for Montgomery Ward Department Store. **$90**

Lionel 9E locomotive in Stephen Girard colors. (Carail Museum Collection)

34 1912-13; NYC-S electric; 10-3/8"; 0-6-0 (1912) or 0-4-0 (1913); green; 125% premium for 0-6-0 model. **$300**

38 1913-24; NYC-S electric; 10-3/8"; 0-4-0; black, gray, green; 100-200% premium for maroon, brown, peacock blue, pea green, Mojave, and red (probable factory repaints). **$150**

42 1912-23; NYC-S electric; 15-1/2"; 0-4-4-0; one (early) or two motors; black, Mojave, gray; 100-200% premium for green, maroon, and peacock blue; reproduced by James Cohen, unmarked. $400

50 1924; NYC-S electric; 11-1/8"; 0-4-0; gray or green; 25% premium for Mojave; 100% premium for maroon. **$150**

51 1912-23; sheet metal steamer with slope-backed, eight-wheel tender; 18"; 0-4-0; black with red trim on windows, tender, and pilot; later version of 5 Special. **$1,100**

53 1911-14; NYC-S electric; 12"; 0-4-4-0; square, sharp-edged body; maroon; later version of 1911 Special. **$1,750**

53 1915-21; NYC-S electric; 12-1/4" (through 1919) or 11-1/8" (from 1920); 0-4-0; maroon or orange; 35% premium for green or Mojave; undetermined value for rare brown. **$700**

Lionel 42 locomotive; restored. (Carail Museum Collection)

Lionel 33 locomotive. (Carail Museum Collection)

54 1912; NYC-S electric; 15-1/2"; 0-4-4-0; square, sharp-edged body; brass; later version of 1912 Special; reproduced by James Cohen and McCoy, unmarked. $3,500

54 1913-23; NYC-S electric; 15-1/2"; 0-4-4-0; one (early) or two motors; rounded body edges; brass; 50% premium for two motors; reproduced by James Cohen and McCoy, unmarked. . $2,500

60 Ca. 1913-17; NYC-S electric; 10-3/8"; black; same as 33 but stamped "FAOS 60" for F. A. O. Schwarz Department Store; very scarce. ....**(no value established)**

61 Ca. 1913-17; NYC-S electric; 16"; black; same as 42 but stamped "FAOS 61" for F. A. O. Schwarz Department Store; very scarce. ....**(no value established)**

62 Ca. 1913-17; NYC-S electric; 11-1/8"; black; same as early 38 but stamped "FAOS 62" for F. A. O. Schwarz Department Store; very scarce.....................**(no value established)**

318, 318E 1924-35; NYC-S electric; 12-1/2"; 0-4-0; green, Mojave, gray; 75% premium for brown; 500% premium for black. **$200**

380, 380E 1923-29; St. Paul electric; 13-1/2"; 0-4-0; maroon, green; 75% premium for Mojave. **$300**

381, 381E, 381U 1928-29; St. Paul "Olympian" electric; 18"; 4-4-4; green; 20% premium for 381U kit assembled; 100% premium for 381U unassembled kit in original box; reproduced by Williams Reproductions, Mike's Train House, and Lionel Trains Inc. $3,000

384, 384E 1930-32; steel and die-cast steamer and 384T tender; 21"; 2-4-0; black with or without green stripe; 50% premium for crackle finish tender; reproduced by Lionel Trains Inc. . $450

385E 1933-39; steel and die-cast steamer and 384T or 385T (Ives casting) tender; 23-1/2"; 2-4-2; gunmetal; reproduced by Mike's Train House. $650

Lionel 318 locomotive. (Carail Museum Collection)

Lionel 381 St. Paul Olympian locomotive. (Carail Museum Collection)

Lionel 384 locomotive with two 309 Pullman Cars; bottom: American Flyer 4654 New Haven Locomotive with two 4151 Pullman Cars. (Carail Musuem Collection)

Lionel 385E (top) and 390E locomotives.
(Carail Museum Collection)

390, 390E 1929-31, 1933; steel and die-cast steamer and 390T tender; 22-1/4"; 2-4-2; black with or without orange stripe; 100% premium for two-tone blue; 200% premium for two-tone green; 15% premium for 390 (without remote control reverse). **$650**

392E *1932-39; steel and die-cast steamer and 384T (through 1934) or 392T twelve-wheel tender (from 1935); 25 or 27-1/4"; 4-4-2; black, with or without green stripe on tender; 50% premium for gunmetal with 392T tender; 75% premium for black with 392T tender; reproduced by Mike's Train House.* **$1000**

400E *1931-39; steel and die-cast steamer and 400T twelve-wheel Vanderbilt tender; 31-3/8"; 4-4-4; black or gunmetal; 25% premium for two-tone blue; 200% premium for crackle finish black, black with red stripe, all dark blue, or all nickel trim; reproduced by Mike's Train House and Lionel Trains Inc.* **$1,800**

402, 402E 1923-29; NYC-S electric; 17-1/2"; 0-4-4-0; Mojave. **$400**

408E *132 1927-36; NYC-S electric; 17-1/2"; 0-4-4-0; green, Mojave; 100% premium for two-tone brown; 120% premium for dark green; reproduced by Williams Reproductions, Mike's Train House and Lionel Trains Inc.* **$400**

1835E 1934-39; die-cast steamer and 384T or 1835T (Ives casting) tender; 23-1/2"; 2-4-2; black; 15% premium for 1835T tender. **$650**

1910 1910-12; NYC-S electric; 9-3/4"; 0-6-0; square, sharp-edged (early) or rounded body; green; 50% premium for square body. **$1,000**

1911 *1910-13; NYC-S electric; 11-1/4" (through 1912) or 11-1/8"; 0-4-0; square, sharp-edged (through 1912) or rounded body like 38; green or maroon; 100% premium for square body; reproduced by McCoy, unmarked.* **$1,000**

1911 SPECIAL 1911-12; NYC-S electric; 12"; 0-4-4-0; square, sharp-edged body; maroon. **$2,000**

1912 *1910-12; NYC-S electric; 15-1/2"; 0-4-4-0; square, sharp-edged body; green; reproduced by James Cohen and McCoy, unmarked.* **$3,500**

1912 SPECIAL *1910-12; NYC-S electric; 15-1/2"; 0-4-4-0; square, sharp-edged body; brass; reproduced, unmarked.* **$3,500**

Lionel 408E locomotive, in Mojave enamel. (Carail Museum Collection)

Lionel 392E locomotive in gunmetal gray enamel with twelve-wheel 392T tender; bottom: 392E locomotive in black enamel with eight-wheel 384T tender. (Carail Museum Collection)

Lionel Trains, Inc. reproduction of Lionel 400E steam locomotive; also visible are 424, 425 and 426 Stephen Girard passenger cars, three orange 60 Telegraph Posts beside track, and 137 Station at right, flanked by two 58 Lampposts. (Carail Museum Collection)

Alone among the major manufacturers of Standard Gauge trains, Lionel produced a line of trolleys and interurbans between 1906 and 1916. The term "trolley" is a misnomer when applied to these designs, since that term correctly refers to the electric pickup device (trolley pole) on the roof of a motorized coach that contacts an overhead wire. Since the Lionel models had no trolley poles, they represent the type of streetcar that derived its power from a ground-level third rail.

The Lionel interpretations are very attractive toys, and their proportions are quite faithful to prototype designs. Steel was used in the relatively complex construction, with such features as open end platforms, opening doors and neatly formed seats. They were powered by electric motors mounted between the wheels so that they did not intrude into the interior of the bodies. Some of the larger designs had two motors. The interurban models resemble the regular Lionel passenger coaches that were sold in sets with locomotives, but with differing window arrangements, distinctive identifying rubber-stamped lettering, and headlights on some models.

Judging by the numbers that survive, the trolleys and interurbans did not sell as well as the steam and electric-type locomotives, perhaps because they were seen by consumers to have less play value. While a locomotive could pull various combinations of freight or passenger cars, and young railroaders could add to their rolling stock one piece at a time, the trolleys were mostly stand-alone toys. Unpowered trailer versions were made, but a two-car trolley consist is inherently less interesting than a freight train with several different types of cars, or a long consist of lighted passenger cars. Lionel discontinued the trolley line during the First World War, and didn't make another until the plastic O Gauge No. 60 appeared in 1955.

Lionel 2 Trolley. (Carail Museum Collection)

1 1906-14; open platform trolley; 8-1/2", 9-9/16", 10-5/16" or 11-5/8"; 4 wheels; five (through 1907) or six (from 1908) windows; combinations of cream, orange, blue, green, and red. . .**$2,500**

1 1906-14; unpowered trailer version of 1 Trolley **$2,500**

2 1906-16; open (through 1909) or closed (from 1910) platform trolley; 10-5/16" or 11-5/8"; 4 wheels; six windows; combinations of cream, red, and blue. **$2,200**

2 1906-16; unpowered trailer version of 2 Trolley. . . .**$2,200**

3 1906-13; open (through 1909) or closed (from 1910) platform trolley; 13-7/8" (through 1909) or 15-1/4"; 8 wheels; nine windows; combinations of cream, orange, and green. . . .**$3,200**

3 1906-13; unpowered trailer version of 3 Trolley. . . .**$3,200**

4 1906-13; open (through 1909) or closed (from 1910) platform trolley; 13-7/8" or 15-1/4"; 8 wheels; nine windows; combinations of cream, orange, and green. **$5,200**

4 1906-13; unpowered trailer version of 4 Trolley. . .**$5,200**

*8 1908-16; closed platform trolley; 17-3/4" or 20-1/4"; 8 wheels; nine (through 1909) or eleven (from 1910) windows; combinations of cream, orange, and green; reproduced by Williams Reproductions. **$5,200**

9 1909-12; closed platform trolley; 17-3/4" or 20-1/4"; 8 wheels; nine (through 1909) or eleven (from 1910) windows; combinations of cream, orange, and green. **$5,200**

10 1910-16; interurban; 15-5/16"; 8 wheels; green; 50% premium for roof with large knobs; 100% premium for maroon. **$1,300**

*100 1910-16; closed platform trolley; 10-7/16" or 11-1/2"; 4 wheels; five (through 1914) or six (from 1914) windows; combinations of blue, red and cream; reproduced by Lionel Trains, Inc.
. . . .$2,500*

101 1910-14; open body summer trolley; 10-3/8"; 4 wheels; five benches; combinations of blue, red, and cream. **$2,500**

202 1910-14; open body summer trolley; 11-1/2"; 4 wheels; six benches; red and cream. **$2,500**

303 1910-14; open body summer trolley; 15"; 8 wheels; eight benches; green, cream, and maroon. **$3,000**

1000 1910-16; unpowered trailer version of 100 Trolley. . . . .
. . . .**$2,500**

1010 1910-16; unpowered trailer version of 10 Interurban. . . .
. . . .**$1,800**

1100 1910-14; unpowered trailer version of 101 Trolley. . . .
. . . .**$2,500**

2200 1910-14; unpowered trailer version of 202 Trolley. . . . .
. . . .**$2,000**

3300 1910-14; unpowered trailer version of 303 Trolley. . . . .
. . . .**$2,500**

The American Flyer 14" coach at right has fourteen individual windows cut out of the side, with a separate brass window frame fitted into each opening. The observation car has wider openings, a style of window that was also used on the dining cars.

12

PASSENGER CARS

Value Guide

The toy trains listed in this chapter are arranged according to manufacturer, in alphabetical order. The entries are listed in the numerical order of their catalog numbers. Each entry contains the following information: catalog number; dates of manufacture; length in inches (minus couplers); brief description for identification; color and/ or significant variations (if any); and value in *Very Good* (*VG*) condition. Colors are listed in order from most to least common.

For an explanation of grading criteria and how to evaluate condition, see Chapter 10. Buyers should expect to pay a premium for items in better than *Very Good* condition, with the upward price differential being greater for scarce or expensive items. The values for items in less than *Very Good* condition are generally lower than those shown, with the downward price differential being greater for common or inexpensive items.

The value of restored pieces depends upon the quality of the restoration work, the scarcity of the item, and the use to which the piece will be put (operation or display; see Chapter 10). In general, the average value of restored items is comparable to the most common version in *Very Good* condition.

Items which are known to have been reproduced are shown in italics. While most reproductions are so marked, there is always the possibility of unmarked or fraudulent items being presented as originals. Novices should obtain the advice of experienced collectors before purchasing high value toy trains. The catalog numbers for items which were advertised but not known to have been made are omitted from this chapter.

Items purchased in sets (locomotive plus cars, with or without track, transformer, and accessories) and those purchased with original boxes and/or original instruction books or other literature will command a premium, with the upward price differential depending upon scarcity. The premium for boxes depends upon condition (presence or absence of tears in the cardboard, end flaps, etc.) and scarcity of the set. Collectors place substantial value upon prewar boxes, especially set boxes, in *Very Good* or better condition.

Note that the term "Standard Gauge" was exclusive to Lionel and Boucher lines, and that the products of other manufacturers are referred to as "Wide gauge." The distance between the outer rails of the track, however, is the same (2-1/8") for all manufacturers. The term "Standard Gauge" is used in this book to describe all trains built to 2-1/8" gauge.

The earliest American Flyer Standard Gauge sets (1925) were passenger trains, as the company did not design its own freight cars until 1927. The first cars were 14" long and lithographed, and carried a variety of imaginative names according to which set or sets they came in. The catalogs gave graphic names to various sets: "The Eagle", "The Hamiltonian", and "The Lone Scout", for example. Individual cars were lettered "BUNKERHILL", "YORKTOWN", "AMERICA", "PLEASANT VIEW", etc.

The early cars were made in three body styles: baggage, coach, and observation. The baggage cars were lettered as RPO (Railway Post Office) cars, and had a pair of large sliding doors and five windows on each side. The passenger coaches (normally called "Pullman" after the most famous prototype manufacturer, the Pullman Car Company, and therefore capitalized) and the observation cars had fourteen windows per side, with the latter featuring an open rear deck. The windows on these cars were tall and narrow, and grouped in pairs, except for single lavatory windows at each end.

The lithography process gave these coaches much realistic detail, such as rivets, window frames, door panels, and paneled lavatory windows. Beginning in 1929, some of the 14" cars were enameled instead of lithographed, with brass trim around the windows. The detail of the earlier cars was no longer present, but with a glossier finish and a lot of bright work, they are handsome cars, although not as realistic. For two years, both litho and enameled cars were sold, with the latter being considered more desirable, and therefore higher priced.

American Flyer revised the construction of these cars when they introduced the enameled versions and built them in four body styles. Instead of a baggage/mail car, the new sets included a combination baggage and passenger coach ("combine") with one large sliding door and ten windows per side. (American Flyer called this style a "Club Car.") The fourteen-window coach was continued, with a separate brass window frame for each of the fourteen openings. However, some versions were built differently. Instead of punching out all fourteen window openings, just six wide and two narrow rectangles were cut in each side. The wide openings were fitted with brass frames with a vertical divider strip in the center, thus simulating the tall, narrow windows of the earlier lithographed cars.

By omitting the center strip in these window frames, American Flyer could change the appearance of a car substantially. This gave rise to a new style, a diner with just six

wide windows and two lavatory windows per side. This window style was also used for some observation cars.

A larger series of cars appeared in the 1926 catalog as part of the premium "President's Special" set. The bodies measured 19" long, and had highly detailed lithography. The earliest versions had four-wheel trucks, but six-wheel versions were soon added. As was done with the 14" cars, the company revised construction details and began enameling these expensive cars in 1928. The lithographed versions were made only in 1926 and 1927, and were not continued in the catalog along with the painted versions.

The large lithographed cars came in baggage (mail), coach and observation configurations, and were very similar in appearance to the 14" series, differing mainly in the number of windows. The baggage car had eight per side, and the coach and observation eighteen. When the enameled versions were introduced, four body styles comparable to the smaller enameled cars were made. The combine (club car) had a large door and fourteen windows per side, all with individual frames, and the coach had eighteen. A diner with eight wide and two narrow (lavatory) windows was introduced, again following the pattern used with the 14" cars. The observation car was unique, having nine of the tall and narrow windows toward the front of the car, and four wide ones at the open platform end.

These long cars are graceful and impressive, especially when pulled by the large, twelve-wheeled New York Central box cab electric locomotive. Sets were made in several different trim levels, with the most expensive being the chrome-plated "Mayflower" set. The large cars were also used for Ives passenger sets when Lionel and American Flyer took over that company in 1928.

All cars are identified below according to catalog numbers, which appear on their sides. They are all lighted and have four-wheel trucks, except as indicated.

American Flyer 4340 Club Car.

American Flyer "Eagle" passenger sets, each containing two 4151 Pullman Cars and one 4152 Observation Car; on the lower shelf, the roofs on the cars have been restored. (Carail Museum Collection)

4040 1925-27; **MAIL/BAGGAGE**; 14"; lithographed maroon, red, or green with contrasting trim and black trucks. **$95**

4041 1925-27; **PULLMAN**; 14"; lithographed maroon, red, or green with contrasting trim and black trucks. **$95**

4042 1925-27; **OBSERVATION**; 14"; lithographed maroon, red, or green with contrasting trim and black trucks. **$95**

4141 1927; **PULLMAN**; 14"; lithographed green, orange or red with contrasting trim and black trucks. **$95**

4142 1927; **OBSERVATION**; 14"; lithographed green, orange or red with contrasting trim and black trucks. **$95**

4080 1926-27; MAIL/BAGGAGE; 19"; lithographed tan with contrasting trim and black trucks; reproduced by Rich-Art. $220

4081 1926-27; PULLMAN; 19"; lithographed tan with contrasting trim and black trucks; reproduced by Rich-Art. $220

4082 1926-27; OBSERVATION; 19"; lithographed tan with contrasting trim and black trucks; reproduced by Rich-Art. .$220

4090 1927; MAIL/BAGGAGE; 19"; lithographed blue with contrasting trim and black six-wheel trucks; reproduced by Rich-Art. $325

4091 1927; PULLMAN; 19"; lithographed blue with contrasting trim and black six-wheel trucks; reproduced by Rich-Art. $325

4092 1927; OBSERVATION; 19"; lithographed blue with contrasting trim and black six-wheel trucks; reproduced by Rich-Art. $325

4151 1928-31; **PULLMAN**; 14"; lithographed green, orange, or red with contrasting trim and gray trucks. **$95**

4152 1928-31; **OBSERVATION**; 14"; lithographed green, orange, or red with contrasting trim and gray trucks. **$95**

4250 1929-31; **CLUB CAR**; 14"; lithographed green with contrasting trim and gray trucks. **$125**

4251 1929-31; **PULLMAN**; 14"; lithographed green with contrasting trim and gray trucks. **$125**

4252 1929-31; **OBSERVATION**; 14"; lithographed green with contrasting trim and gray trucks. **$125**

4331 1931-36; **PULLMAN**; 14"; enameled red with brass trim and gray trucks. **$135**

4332 1931-36; **OBSERVATION**; 14"; enameled red with brass trim and gray trucks. **$135**

4340 1928-32; **CLUB CAR**; 14"; enameled tan with gray trucks or red with green trucks; brass trim. **$165**

4341 1928-32; **PULLMAN**; 14"; enameled tan with gray trucks or red with green trucks. **$165**

4342 1928-32; **OBSERVATION**; 14"; enameled tan with gray trucks or red with green trucks; brass trim. **$165**

American Flyer 4342 Observation Car.

4343 1928-32; **DINER**; 14"; enameled tan or red with brass trim, and gray trucks. **$225**

4350 1931; **CLUB CAR**; 14"; enameled blue-green with red roof, brass trim, and gray trucks. **$125**

4351 1931; **PULLMAN**; 14"; enameled blue-green with red roof, brass trim, and gray trucks. **$125**

4352 1931; **OBSERVATION**; 14"; enameled blue-green with red roof, brass trim, and gray trucks. **$125**

4380 1928-29, 1931-32; CLUB CAR; 19"; enameled dark blue or tan with brass trim and gray or black trucks; reproduced by Rich-Art. $425

Above: American Flyer 4080 RPO (Railway Post Office) Mail and Baggage Car. (Carail Museum Collection)

Reproduction by Lionel Trains, Inc. of American Flyer "Mayflower" passenger cars; also visible are a Lionel 79 Highway Signal (left) and a Lionel 60 Telegraph Post (foreground). (Carail Museum Collection)

4381 *1928-29, 1931-32;* **PULLMAN**; *19"; enameled dark blue or tan with brass trim and gray or black trucks; reproduced by Rich-Art.* $425

4382 *1928-29, 1931-32;* **OBSERVATION**; *19"; enameled dark blue or tan with brass trim and gray or black trucks; reproduced by Rich-Art.* $425

4390 *1928-34;* **CLUB CAR**; *19"; enameled blue with brass trim and six-wheel trucks; 100% premium for chrome-plated "MAYFLOWER" version; reproduced by Rich-Art.* $575

4391 *1928-34;* **PULLMAN**; *19"; enameled blue with brass trim and six-wheel trucks; 100% premium for chrome-plated "MAYFLOWER" version; reproduced by Rich-Art and Lionel Trains, Inc.* $575

4392 *1928-34;* **OBSERVATION**; *19"; enameled blue with brass trim and six-wheel trucks; 100% premium for chrome-plated "MAYFLOWER" version; reproduced by Rich-Art and Lionel Trains, Inc.* $575

4393 *1928-34;* **DINER**; *19"; enameled blue with brass trim and six-wheel trucks; 100% premium for chrome-plated "MAYFLOWER" version; reproduced by Rich-Art and Lionel Trains, Inc.* $575

Boucher Standard Gauge Passenger Cars

Boucher adapted four passenger car designs from the former Voltamp line: a combination car, a Pullman, a coach, and an observation car. The Pullman had two doors and two oval windows flanking four double windows per side. The double windows were topped by a rounded transom. The observation car was identical, except that the sides were shortened at the rear by eliminating the door, and fitted with an open platform. The combine was similar to the Pullman, but lacked one oval and one double window per side, leaving the forward end blank except for the passenger door. There was no baggage door.

The final design (the coach) differed from the first three by having nine separate window openings per side in place of the four double windows. The doors and oval windows at each end were the same as on the Pullman. All cars were 18" long and could be lighted inside by a wiring accessory, consisting of a socket and a 28"-long cord that connected to a power terminal on the tender or to the next adjacent car. This system was also used by Lionel, prior to the introduction of pickup rollers on individual cars.

Values for Boucher products are speculative; examples rarely change hands, due to very limited production numbers. The prices given reflect their relative rarity, and are comparable to products of other low-volume companies.

2105 1922-29; **PASSENGER COACH**. $495

2107 1922-29; **PULLMAN CAR**. $550

2140 1922-29; **OBSERVATION CAR**. $550

2141 1922-29; **COMBINATION CAR**. $550

Dorfan entered the Standard Gauge field with a series of 13-1/4"-long cars, finished either with lithography or enamel, and some versions had tiny passengers in the windows, a feature none of the other manufacturers offered. They were very sturdily built, with major panels held together by rivets. Separate window frames painted in contrasting colors were fitted into the window openings on each side of the coach (six openings) and observation car (five openings). These frames had a central vertical strip, thus giving the impression of twice as many windows. The baggage car had two large doors and no windows on each side.

Some of the cars were lighted, with current supplied by a third-rail pickup roller. They came with either stamped-steel or die-cast wheels and truck frames, and most of the latter have suffered deterioration over the years due to impurities in the alloy used to make them. It is common to find Dorfan cars with replacement trucks from other manufacturers. A wide variety of catalog numbers identified cars in different colors or trim options, as used in various sets, but all Dorfan passenger cars are essentially the same in construction.

__770__ 1928-30; **BAGGAGE**; enameled green with contrasting trim; cataloged as 995 or 998. . . . . **$295**

__771__ 1928-30; **PULLMAN**; enameled green or red with contrasting trim and passengers; lettered "SAN FRANCISCO"; cataloged as 994 or 997. . . . . **$235**

__772__ 1928-30; **PULLMAN**; enameled green or red with contrasting trim and passengers; lettered "WASHINGTON"; cataloged as 994 or 997. . . . .**$235**

__773__ 1928-30; **OBSERVATION**; enameled green, red, or maroon with contrasting trim and passengers; cataloged as 996. .**$225**

__780__ 1928-30; **PULLMAN**; lithographed red, tan, or orange with contrasting trim. **$175**

__781__ 1928; **PULLMAN**; lithographed red with contrasting trim. **$175**

__785__ 1928-29; **PULLMAN**; enameled green with contrasting trim and passengers. **$175**

__786__ 1928-29; **OBSERVATION**; enameled green with contrasting trim and passengers. **$195**

__787__ 1928-30; **PULLMAN**; enameled red with contrasting trim and passengers. **$195**

__788__ 1928-30; **BAGGAGE**; enameled red with contrasting trim. **$195**

__789__ 1928-30; **OBSERVATION**; enameled red with contrasting trim and passengers. **$225**

__789__ C. 1927-28; **PULLMAN**; lithographed maroon, tan, or orange with contrasting trim; lettered "MOUNTAIN BROOK" . **$195**

__790__ 1927-28; **PULLMAN**; lithographed maroon, red, or orange with contrasting trim; lettered "PLEASANT VIEW". . . **$195**

__790__ 1927-28; **OBSERVATION**; lithographed maroon with contrasting trim; lettered "PLEASANT VIEW". **$265**

__791__ 1928; **PULLMAN**; lithographed red with contrasting trim; lettered "PLEASANT VIEW". **$195**

__890__ 1926-28; **PULLMAN**; enameled orange with brass trim and passengers. **$195**

__891__ 1926; **PULLMAN**; enameled orange with brass trim and passengers; lettered "SAN FRANCISCO". **$195**

__990__ 1927-28; **PULLMAN**; enameled gray, green, brown, or maroon with brass or contrasting painted trim; lettered "WASHINGTON" or "CHICAGO". **$195**

Lithographed Dorfan 790 "Pleasant View" Pullman. (Carail Museum Collection)

Enameled Dorfan 994 "Washington" Pullman, showing hand-painted, die-cast passenger figures in the windows. (Carail Museum Collection)

991 1927; **PULLMAN**; enameled gray with brass or orange trim; lettered "SAN FRANCISCO". **$225**

992 1927-28; **OBSERVATION**; enameled gray, green, brown, or maroon with brass or contrasting painted trim. **$225**

992 1928-29; **PULLMAN**; enameled blue with tan trim and passengers; scarce. **$700**

993 1928-29; **OBSERVATION**; enameled blue with tan trim and passengers; scarce. **$700**

994 1928-30; **PULLMAN**; enameled green or red with contrasting trim and passengers; lettered "771 SAN FRANCISCO" or "772 WASHINGTON". **$235**

995 1928-30; **BAGGAGE**; enameled green or red with contrasting trim and passengers; numbered "770". **$295**

996 1928-30; **OBSERVATION**; enameled green, red, or maroon with contrasting trim and passengers; numbered "773". .**$225**

997 1928-30; **PULLMAN**; enameled green with contrasting trim and passengers; lettered "771 SAN FRANCISCO" or "772 WASHINGTON". **$235**

997-1 1930; **PULLMAN**; enameled ivory with red roof and passengers; lettered "FLORIDA LIMITED"; very scarce. . . **$825**

998 1928-30; **BAGGAGE**; enameled green with contrasting trim; numbered "770". **$225**

998-1 1928-30; **BAGGAGE**; enameled ivory with red roof; lettered "FLORIDA LIMITED"; very scarce. **$825**

999 1928-30; **OBSERVATION**; enameled green with contrasting trim and passengers. **$225**

999-1 1928-30; **OBSERVATION**; enameled ivory with red roof; lettered "FLORIDA LIMITED"; very scarce. **$825**

Ives Wide (Standard) Gauge Passenger Cars

Like American Flyer, Ives built its Standard Gauge passenger cars in only two sizes, until bankruptcy in 1928 forced the sale of the company to Lionel and American Flyer. Thereafter Ives cars appear with a variety of bodies borrowed from the other two companies. The original Ives designs were based upon the firm's experience with No. 1 gauge trains, first introduced in 1904 and thus predating Lionel's similarly-sized Standard Gauge line by two years. Ives converted the No. 1 gauge line to Standard Gauge in 1921, under pressure of sales competition from Lionel, but since the sizes were much alike, the change only required using wider trucks and wheel sets.

Of all the major manufacturers, Ives' construction techniques were the most labor intensive, with many pieces and a great number of solder joints required. Each car was enameled, with added details such as contrasting window frames and transoms. Some of the early cars had especially attractive "rainbow" transoms, painted in three overlapping colors. This and other expensive methods of production eventually led to some of the company's economic difficulties in the latter 1920s, as the products could not be sold at competitive prices and still realize a profit.

Both the large and small series came in three-car sets: a combination baggage and passenger car ("combine") called a "Buffet" or "Club" car in the catalog; a coach or Pullman (Ives called it a "Parlor" car); and an observation car. On the 13-3/4" cars, the Club Car featured a sliding baggage door on each side and four main windows, plus a smaller lavatory window at one end. The coach and observation each had five large windows and two lavatory windows, although they differed slightly from each other in design. The 17" cars had more windows, but otherwise were similar in appearance to the smaller series.

In the mid-1920s, Lionel switched from painted trim and rubber-stamped lettering to brass trim and identification plates, and since these details proved very successful in attracting customers, Ives and American Flyer soon followed suit. By 1928, Ives had announced plans for an entirely new series of cars that, at 21-1/2" long, would rival the largest Lionel offerings. However, the failure of the company intervened, and when Lionel and American Flyer took over, the complicated method of assembling Ives passenger cars proved too expensive to be continued.

From that time onward, first American Flyer and then Lionel car bodies were mounted on Ives trucks and provided with Ives plates or decals. As the Great Depression began, Lionel found it increasingly difficult to maintain dif-

Ives 186 Observation Car with brass plates; restored.

Ives 247 Club Car with Lionel body. (Carail Museum Collection)

Comparison of Ives 244 Club Car with American Flyer body (top) and 246 Dining Car with Lionel body. The Dining Car is very hard to find and came in a 1930 set called "The National Limited," pulled by a red 1134 steam locomotive and tender. (Carail Museum Collection)

ferences for the adopted line, and beginning in 1931, Ives cars were identified only by decals or paper strips applied to 100% Lionel products. However, Lionel did make one final effort to keep the Ives name alive, with a distinctive new locomotive (No. 1764) and a set of relatively small passenger cars, the 1766-67-68 series. When in 1933 the Ives brand name was finally abandoned, Lionel continued to market these cars with Lionel name plates, but the attractive 1764 locomotive was dropped.

In the list below, all cars are enameled and have black four-wheel trucks except as indicated. Those with interior lights are so noted. Early cars (through 1925) are rubber-stamped, while later cars have brass plates. Combination cars (passenger section plus baggage door at one end) were called Buffet cars through 1925, and Club cars thereafter, but are structurally similar.

170 1925-26; **BUFFET CAR**; 13-3/4"; green or tan with contrasting trim. **$135**

171 1924; **BUFFET CAR**; 13-3/4"; green with maroon trim; rainbow transoms. **$135**

171-3 1924; **BUFFET CAR**; 13-3/4"; green with maroon trim; rainbow transoms; lighted. **$135**

171 1925-28; **PARLOR CAR (PULLMAN)**; 13-3/4"; green or tan with contrasting trim. **$135**

172 1924; **PARLOR CAR (PULLMAN)**; 13-3/4"; green with maroon trim. **$135**

172-3 1924; **PARLOR CAR (PULLMAN)**; 13-3/4"; green with maroon trim; lighted. **$135**

172 1925-26; **OBSERVATION**; 13-3/4"; green or tan with contrasting trim. **$135**

173 1924; **OBSERVATION**; 13-3/4"; green with maroon trim. **$135**

173-3 1924; **OBSERVATION**; 13-3/4"; green with maroon trim; lighted. **$135**

180 1925-28; **BUFFET CAR**; 17"; six-wheel trucks; various colors; lighted. **$225**

181 1925-28; **PARLOR CAR (PULLMAN)**; 17"; six-wheel trucks; various colors; lighted. **$225**

182 1925-28; **OBSERVATION**; 17"; six-wheel trucks; various colors; lighted. **$225**

184 1921-25; **BUFFET CAR**; 13-3/4"; various colors with contrasting trim. **$75**

184 1926-30; CLUB CAR; 13-3/4"; various colors with contrasting trim; 25% premium for orange with black roof; 50% premium for blue or light green; 50% premium for black diaphragms; reproduced for the Ives Circus Train by Harry A. Osisek. $75

185 1921-30; PARLOR CAR (PULLMAN); 13-3/4"; various colors with contrasting trim; 25% premium for orange with black roof; 50% premium for blue or light green; 50% premium for black diaphragms; reproduced for the Ives Circus Train by Harry A. Osisek. $75

186 1922-30; OBSERVATION; 13-3/4"; various colors with contrasting trim; 25% premium for orange with black roof; 50% premium for blue or light green; 50% premium for black diaphragms. Reproduced for the Ives Circus Train by Harry A. Osisek. $75

187 1921-25; **BUFFET CAR**; 17"; four-wheel trucks; various colors; some lighted; 500% premium for white with gold trim. **$225**

187-1 1922-24; **BUFFET CAR**; 17"; four-wheel trucks; various colors; lighted. **$225**

187-3 1925; **BUFFET CAR**; 17"; four-wheel trucks; orange with green trim or white with red trim; lighted. **$325**

187 1926-28; **CLUB CAR**; 17"; four-wheel trucks; various colors; lighted; 100% premium for blue, green, or gray with brass plates. **$225**

188 1921-28; **PARLOR CAR (PULLMAN)**; 17"; four-wheel trucks; various colors; some lighted; 100% premium for blue, green, or gray with brass plates; 500% premium for white with gold trim. **$225**

188-1 1922-24; **PARLOR CAR (PULLMAN)**; 17"; four-wheel trucks; various colors; lighted; 500% premium for white with gold trim. **$225**

188-3 1925; **PARLOR CAR (PULLMAN)**; 17"; four-wheel trucks; orange with green trim or white with red trim; lighted. **$325**

189 1921-28; **OBSERVATION**; 17"; four-wheel trucks; various colors; some lighted; 100% premium for blue, green, or gray with brass plates; 500% premium for white with gold trim. .. **$225**

189-1 1922-24; **OBSERVATION**; 17"; four-wheel trucks; various colors; lighted; 500% premium for white with gold trim. **$225**

189-3 1921-28; **OBSERVATION**; 17"; four-wheel trucks; orange with green trim or white with red trim; lighted. **$325**

241 1928-29; CLUB CAR (American Flyer 4390); 19"; black with red roof and red Ives six-wheel trucks; Ives couplers; lighted; 75% premium for green or orange; 100% premium for copper plated; reproduced by Sirus & Varney and Rich-Art. $1,500

242 1928-29; PARLOR CAR (American Flyer 4393 diner); 19"; black with red roof and red Ives six-wheel trucks; Ives couplers; lighted; 75% premium for green or orange; 100% premium for copper plated; reproduced by Sirus & Varney and Rich-Art. $1,500

243 1928-29; OBSERVATION (American Flyer 4392); 19"; black with red roof and red Ives six-wheel trucks; Ives couplers; lighted; 75% premium for green or orange; 100% premium for copper plated; reproduced by Sirus & Varney and Rich-Art. $1,500

244 1929; **CLUB CAR** (American Flyer 4390); 19"; light green with Ives four-wheel trucks; Ives couplers; lighted. . . **$3,500**

245 1929; **PARLOR CAR** (American Flyer 4393 diner); 19"; light green with Ives four-wheel trucks; Ives couplers; lighted. **$3,500**

246 1929; **OBSERVATION** (American Flyer 4392); 19"; light green with Ives four-wheel trucks; Ives couplers; lighted. **$3,500**

246 1930; **DINING CAR** (Lionel 431); 18-1/4"; blue with red roof; six-wheel Ives trucks and couplers; lighted; 100% premium for orange with black roof, or black with red roof. . . **$2,100**

247 1930; **CLUB CAR** (Lionel 419); 18-1/4"; blue with red roof; six-wheel Ives trucks and couplers; lighted; 100% premium for orange with black roof, or black with red roof. **$2,100**

248 1930; **PULLMAN** (Lionel 418); 18-1/4"; blue with red roof; six-wheel Ives trucks and couplers; lighted; 100% premium for orange with black roof, or black with red roof. **$2,100**

249 1930; **OBSERVATION** (Lionel 490); 17-5/8"; blue with red roof; six-wheel Ives trucks and couplers; lighted; 100% premium for orange with black roof, or black with red roof. . . . **$2,100**

332 1931-32; **BAGGAGE CAR** (Lionel 332); 12"; peacock blue with green roof and orange trim; Lionel trucks and couplers; lighted. **$175**

*Ives 249 Observation Car with Lionel body.
(Carail Museum Collection)*

Ives 248 Pullman with Lionel body. (Carail Museum Collection)

339 1931-32; **PULLMAN** (Lionel 339); 12"; peacock blue with green roof and orange trim; Lionel trucks and couplers; lighted.
. . . .**$175**
341 1931-32; **OBSERVATION** (Lionel 341); 12"; peacock blue with green roof and orange trim; Lionel trucks and couplers; lighted. **$175**

418 *1931; PARLOR CAR (Lionel 418); 18-1/4"; green; six-wheel Lionel trucks and couplers; lighted; reproduced by Williams Reproductions.* **$850**

419 *1931; BAGGAGE/PARLOR CAR (Lionel 419); 18-1/4"; green; six-wheel Lionel trucks and couplers; lighted; reproduced by Williams Reproductions.* **$850**

431 *1931; DINING CAR (Lionel 431); 18-1/4"; green; six-wheel Lionel trucks and couplers; lighted; reproduced by Williams Reproductions.* **$1,600**

490 *1931; OBSERVATION (Lionel 490); 18-1/4"; green; six-wheel Lionel trucks and couplers; lighted; reproduced by Williams Reproductions.* **$850**

1766 *1932; PULLMAN; 15"; terra cotta with maroon roof and cream trim; six-wheel trucks and Lionel couplers; lighted; reproduced by Mike's Train House.* **$950**

1767 *1932; BAGGAGE CAR; 15"; terra cotta with maroon roof and cream trim; six-wheel trucks and Lionel couplers; lighted; reproduced by Mike's Train House.* **$950**

1768 *1932; OBSERVATION; 15"; terra cotta with maroon roof and cream trim; six-wheel trucks and Lionel couplers; lighted; reproduced by Mike's Train House.* **$950**

Lionel Standard Gauge Passenger Cars

Lionel's first passenger car—the 29 day coach—appeared in 1908 and used a body borrowed from the No. 3 Trolley. The first Pullman car, numbered 1910, was very similar in design to the interurban car (Chapter 11) and was added to the line about a year later. These were soon followed by a series of cars slightly over 16" in length and made in three styles: a combine (combination baggage and passenger car), Pullman, and observation car. Although these models appeared in the 1906 catalog, it is believed that they were not made until 1910, a year or two after the early 29 and 1910 designs. However, at that time the Lionel factory was already at work developing a more comprehensive line of cars to go with their expanding series of locomotives.

From as early as 1912, Lionel offered Standard Gauge passenger cars in three distinct sizes and price ranges. The early cars were soldered, enameled, and detailed with contrasting trim, in much the same way as those made by Ives. With their large arched windows, ornate roofs, and fancy observation platforms, they present a charming toy-like appearance, less realistic than the Ives cars but very attractive to buyers.

Lionel catalogs and advertisements were aggressive and exaggerated in extolling the virtues of their products, especially when promoting what they considered to be their superior construction and durability. The early Lionel cars did seem to be somewhat more rugged than Ives, but the difference was not great. However, Joshua Cowen's engineers soon developed a patented construction variation that gave Lionel a distinct advantage over its principal competitor. Whereas the early cars from both manufacturers had single-thickness walls, with window openings cut out and trimmed with paint, Lionel added a new twist. In order to provide the early cars with contrasting window frames, it had been necessary to paint them individually—a time-consuming technique. Lionel's new process eliminated this step, and simultaneously increased the strength and rigidity of the car sides.

The revised passenger cars, first introduced in 1923, had conventional stamped-steel sides with the window and door openings cut out as before. These new cars were fitted with a steel insert, effectively doubling the side walls. Windows were cut out of these inserts, but the openings were smaller than those in the car sides. When placed inside the car, these inserts formed recessed frames around the windows. Instead of painting each window frame separately, Lionel could paint the entire insert, and in one step instead of many, contrasting trim was provided for all the windows.

The double-wall concept improved the appearance, imparted added realism, and gave the cars added weight and stiffness. As the company refined the concept, additional cutouts were made in the car sides where the contrasting color of the insert would show through. These cutouts were placed to simulate name and number plates. On smaller cars, the inserts were folded to form longitudinal bench seats on each side of the car, giving the structure even greater strength.

Lionel's competitive edge in the marketplace strengthened with the introduction of this improvement in a series of large (18") cars in 1923, and the concept was applied to the small and medium cars as well, in 1925 and 1926 respectively. Sales figures increased throughout the 1920s, and despite American Flyer's entry into the Standard Gauge market in 1925, Lionel continued to dominate the field, eventually forcing Ives into bankruptcy.

American Flyer challenged the Lionel patent with their first Standard Gauge locomotive, the 4019 New York Central model of 1925. This loco was built with Lionel-style inserts that formed separate window frames and doors, but it was found to infringe upon the Lionel patent. American Flyer was forced to revert to single wall construction for all subsequent locomotives and rolling stock.

Lionel's passenger car numbering system was somewhat more irregular than that used by the competition, or even for its own freights. The cars usually came in three- or four-car sets, consisting of a combine, Pullman, and observation car, and sometimes a baggage car or a diner. But the numbers were not always consecutive. While Ives numbered the three types of their large cars consecutively (187, 188, and 189 for combine, coach, and observation), Lionel used 18, 19, and 190. When these cars were revised, the numbers became 418, 419, and 490. Later large cars were more closely numbered (412, 413, 414, and 416), although 415 was skipped.

The early medium-sized cars were logically numbered 180, 181, and 182, but the revised versions (1926) skipped a number. One sequence used 309 for the Pullman, 310 for the baggage car, and 312 for the observation. Another series of the same-size cars was 319, 320, and 322. It may be speculated that 311 and 321 were reserved for a car that was planned, but never made, such as a combine.

Numbering on the smaller cars seems more haphazard, but there is consistency in the system. The early four-car sequence, 31, 32, 35, and 36 for combine, baggage, Pullman, and observation respectively, was replaced by two sequences: 337 Pullman, and 338 observation, and 339 Pullman and 341 observation. A 332 baggage car sometimes came with either of these pairs.

Lionel expanded its size range even more, beginning in 1929, with a set of redesigned large cars measuring a full 21-1/2" in length. These magnificent toys were fitted with immense detail inside: individual seats, interior doors, and even miniature plumbing fixtures in the washrooms. These cars were named after, and lettered for, California,

Colorado, Illinois, and New York, and have come to be known to collectors as "State Cars." Accompanying this new series in 1930 was a slightly smaller version of the same design. Measuring 18-3/4" in length, they were painted two-tone blue for the new "Blue Comet" set.

By this time, Lionel was producing passenger cars in four different sizes, with a fifth about to be added. Lionel's purchase of the Ives line was proving to be a considerable burden as the economic problems of the early 1930s deepened, and the company could no longer afford to produce two independent brand names. Most Ives products were that in name only, being Lionel products with Ives name plates. However, Lionel designed a new locomotive and passenger car set especially for the Ives brand name in 1932, and when that marque was abandoned the following year, the cars (but not the loco) were retained in the line and identified as Lionel products. At 15" in length, these sleek, low-silhouette designs bridged the gap between the boxy 309-type cars and the very expensive "State" and "Blue Comet" cars. Because of the Depression, however, these cars were not big sellers and they are hard to find today.

In the summary that follows, all cars have four-wheel trucks, except as indicated. Some early cars were unlighted, but Lionel sold lighting kits which could be connected to a wiring post on the locomotive body. All later cars were fitted with interior lights and roller-type power pickups on the trucks.

Lionel 19 Combination Car (baggage and coach). (Carail Museum Collection)

18 1906-27; **PULLMAN**; 16-1/4"; green or Mojave with contrasting trim; 250% premium for orange; 750% premium for roof with high wooden knobs. **$275**

19 1906-25; **COMBINE**; 16-1/4"; green or Mojave with contrasting trim; 250% premium for orange; 750% premium for roof with high wooden knobs. **$275**

Lionel 29 Day Coach. (Carail Museum Collection)

29 1908-27; **DAY COACH** (3 Trolley body); 13-7/8" (through 1909) or 15-1/4"; dark green or maroon; open end platforms with railings; lettered "NEW YORK CENTRAL LINES" or "PENN-SYLVANIA R.R."; 250% premium for short body lettered "N.Y.C. & H.R.R.R."; 125% premium for long body lettered "N.Y.C. & H.R.R.R.". $750

31 1921-25; **COMBINE**; 10-3/4"; green, maroon, or brown; 100% premium for orange. $75

32 1921-25; **MAIL/BAGGAGE**; 10-3/4"; green, maroon, or brown; 100% premium for orange. $75

35 1912-26; **PULLMAN**; 10-1/2"; green, maroon, or brown; 100% premium for orange; 500% premium if lettered "PENN-SYLVANIA"; 1000% premium for dark blue. **$50**

36 1912-26; **OBSERVATION**; 10-1/2"; green, maroon, or brown; 100% premium for orange; 500% premium if lettered "PENN-SYLVANIA"; 1000% premium for dark blue. **$50**

180 1911-21; **PULLMAN**; 12-1/2"; maroon or brown with contrasting trim. **$150**

181 1911-21; **COMBINE**; 12-1/2"; maroon or brown with contrasting trim; 75% premium for orange. **$150**

182 1911-21; **OBSERVATION**; 12-1/2"; maroon or brown with contrasting trim; 75% premium for orange. $150

190 1910-27; **OBSERVATION**; 16-1/4"; green or Mojave with contrasting trim; 250% premium for orange; 750% premium for roof with high wooden knobs. **$275**

309 1926-40; **PULLMAN**; 13-1/4"; various colors; 50% premium for two-tone blue; 75% premium for two-tone green **$165**

310 1926-40; **BAGGAGE**; 13-1/4"; various colors; 50% premium for two-tone blue; 75% premium for two-tone green. $165

312 1926-40; **OBSERVATION**; 13-1/4"; various colors; 50% premium for two-tone blue; 75% premium for two-tone green. $165

Lionel 181 Combination Car (baggage and coach).

319 1924-30; **PULLMAN**; 13-1/4"; maroon with Mojave trim; 75% premium if lettered "LIONEL LINES". **$165**

320 1924-30; **BAGGAGE**; 13-1/4"; maroon with Mojave trim; 75% premium if lettered "ILLINOIS CENTRAL" or "LIONEL ELECTRIC RAILROAD". **$165**

322 1924-30; **OBSERVATION**; 13-1/4"; maroon with Mojave trim; 75% premium if lettered "LIONEL LINES". **$165**

332 1926-33; **BAGGAGE**; 12"; various colors; 75% premium for Mojave or green; 200% premium for two-tone brown; 225% premium for peacock blue with orange trim and lettered "MACY SPECIAL". $75

337 1925-32; **PULLMAN**; 12"; various colors; 225% premium for pea green with cream trim (made for R. H. Macy Department Store, but not marked as such). **$125**

338 1925-32; **OBSERVATION**; 12"; various colors; 225% premium for pea green with cream trim and lettered "MACY SPE-CIAL". **$125**

339 1925-33; **PULLMAN**; 12"; peacock blue or gray with contrasting trim; 75% premium for Mojave; 150% premium for two-tone brown; 225% premium for peacock blue with orange trim and lettered "MACY SPECIAL". **$75**

Lionel 182 Observation Car.

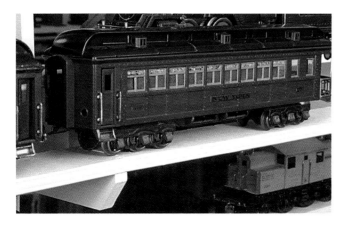

Lionel 416 "New York" Observation Car, part of the State set. (Carail Museum Collection)

<u>341</u> 1925-33; **OBSERVATION**; 12"; peacock blue or gray with contrasting trim; 75% premium for Mojave; 150% premium for two-tone brown; 225% premium for peacock blue with orange trim and lettered "MACY SPECIAL". **$75**

<u>412</u> 1929-35; **PULLMAN**; 21-1/2"; two-tone green or two-tone brown; six-wheel trucks; lettered "CALIFORNIA"; reproduced by Williams Reproductions and Lionel Trains, Inc. **$2,000**

<u>413</u> 1929-35; **PULLMAN**; 21-1/2"; two-tone green or two-tone brown; six-wheel trucks; lettered "COLORADO"; reproduced by Williams Reproductions and Lionel Trains, Inc. **$2,000**

<u>414</u> 1929-35; **PULLMAN**; 21-1/2"; two-tone green or two-tone brown; six-wheel trucks; lettered "ILLINOIS"; reproduced by Williams Reproductions and Lionel Trains, Inc. **$2,000**

<u>416</u> 1929-35; **OBSERVATION**; 21-1/2"; two-tone green or two-tone brown; six-wheel trucks; lettered "NEW YORK"; reproduced by Williams Reproductions and Lionel Trains, Inc. . . . **$2,000**

42 Locomotive and 19 Combination Car (baggage and coach); foreground: Lionel 9U Bild-A-Loco and 429 Combination Car. The 429 combine is incorrectly positioned; the baggage doors should be at the head end, next to the locomotive. (Carail Museum Collection)

Lionel 422 "Tempel" Observation Car; part of Blue Comet set. (Carail Museum Collection)

Lionel 424 "Liberty Bell" Pullman; part of Stephen Girard set. (Carail Museum Collection)

<u>418</u> 1923-32; **PULLMAN**; 18-1/8"; four- or six-wheel trucks; Mojave or green with contrasting trim; 100% premium if lettered "ILLINOIS CENTRAL"; reproduced by Williams Reproductions. **$250**

<u>419</u> 1923-32; **COMBINE**; 18-1/8"; four- or six-wheel trucks; Mojave or green with contrasting trim; 100% premium if lettered "ILLINOIS CENTRAL"; reproduced by Williams Reproductions. **$250**

<u>420</u> 1930-40; **PULLMAN**; 18-3/4"; two-tone blue; six-wheel trucks; lettered "FAYE"; reproduced by Mike's Train House and Lionel Trains, Inc. **$950**

<u>421</u> 1930-40; **PULLMAN**; 18-3/4"; two-tone blue; six-wheel trucks; lettered "WESTPHAL"; reproduced by Mike's Train House and Lionel Trains, Inc. **$950**

<u>422</u> 1930-40; **OBSERVATION**; 18-3/4"; two-tone blue; six-wheel trucks; lettered "TEMPEL"; reproduced by Mike's Train House and Lionel Trains, Inc. **$950**

<u>424</u> 1931-40; **PULLMAN**; 16"; two-tone green with brass trim; six-wheel trucks; lettered "LIBERTY BELL"; 15% premium for nickel trim; reproduced by Mike's Train House and Lionel Trains, Inc. **$500**

<u>425</u> 1931-40; **PULLMAN**; 16"; two-tone green with brass trim; six-wheel trucks; lettered "STEPHEN GIRARD"; 15% premium for nickel trim; reproduced by Mike's Train House and Lionel Trains, Inc. **$500**

Lionel 490 Observation Car; also visible is a 440 Signal Bridge (left background).

Lionel 425 "Stephen Girard" Pullman; part of Stephen Girard set. (Carail Museum Collection)

426 *1931-40;* **OBSERVATION**; *15-3/4"; two-tone green with brass trim; six-wheel trucks; lettered "CORAL ISLE"; 15% premium for nickel trim; reproduced by Mike's Train House and Lionel Trains, Inc.* *$500*

428 *1926-30;* **PULLMAN**; *18-1/8"; four-wheel trucks; green with contrasting trim; 150% premium for orange; reproduced by Williams Reproductions.* *$300*

429 *1926-30;* **COMBINE**; *18-1/8"; four-wheel trucks; green with contrasting trim; 150% premium for orange; reproduced by Williams Reproductions.* *$300*

430 *1926-30;* **OBSERVATION**; *17-5/8"; four-wheel trucks; green with contrasting trim; 150% premium for orange; reproduced by Williams Reproductions.* *$300*

431 *1927-32;* **DINER**; 18-1/8"; four- or six-wheel trucks; Mojave, green, or orange with contrasting trim. **$550**

490 *1923-32; OBSERVATION; 17-5/8"; four- or six-wheel trucks; Mojave or green with contrasting trim; 100% premium if lettered "ILLINOIS CENTRAL"; reproduced by Williams Reproductions.* *$250*

Lionel 426 "Coral Isle" Observation Car; part of Stephen Girard set.

1766 *1934-40;* **PULLMAN**; *15"; terra cotta or red with maroon roof; six-wheel trucks; similar to Ives 1766; reproduced by Mike's Train House.* *$750*

1767 *1934-40;* **BAGGAGE**; *15"; terra cotta or red with maroon roof; six-wheel trucks; similar to Ives 1766; reproduced by Mike's Train House.* *$750*

1768 *1934-40;* **OBSERVATION**; *15"; terra cotta or red with maroon roof; six-wheel trucks; similar to Ives 1766; reproduced by Mike's Train House.* *$750*

1910 1909-10; **PULLMAN**; 16-1/4"; green with maroon trim.
. . . .**$1,750**

Ives 195 Caboose; restored.

13

FREIGHT CARS

Value Guide

The freight cars listed in this chapter are arranged according to manufacturer, in alphabetical order. Entries are listed in the numerical order of their catalog numbers. Each entry contains the following information: catalog number; dates of manufacture; length in inches (minus couplers); brief description for identification; color and/or significant variations (if any); and value in *Very Good* (*VG*) condition. Colors are listed in order from most to least common.

For an explanation of grading criteria and how to evaluate condition, see Chapter 10. Buyers should expect to pay a premium for items in better than *Very Good* condition, with the upward price differential being greater for scarce or expensive items. The values for items in less than *Very Good* condition are generally lower than those shown, with the downward price differential being greater for common or inexpensive items.

The value of restored pieces depends upon the quality of the restoration work, the scarcity of the item, and the use to which the piece will be put (operation or display; see Chapter 10). In general, the average value of restored items is comparable to the most common version in *Very Good* condition.

Items which are known to have been reproduced are shown in italics. While most reproductions are so marked, there is always the possibility of unmarked or fraudulent items being presented as originals. Novices should obtain the advice of experienced collectors before purchasing high value toy trains. The catalog numbers for items which were advertised, but not known to have been made, are omitted from this chapter.

Items purchased in sets (locomotive plus cars, with or without track, transformer, and accessories), and those purchased with original boxes and/or original instruction books or other literature, will command a premium, with the upward price differential depending upon scarcity. The premium for boxes depends upon condition (presence or absence of end flaps, tears in the cardboard, etc.) and scarcity of the set. Collectors place substantial value upon prewar boxes, especially set boxes, in *Very Good* or better condition.

Note that the term "Standard Gauge" was exclusive to Lionel and Boucher, and that the products of other manufacturers are referred to as "Wide Gauge." The distance between the outer rails of the track, however, is the same (2-1/8") for all manufacturers. The term "Standard Gauge" is used in this book to describe all trains built to 2-1/8" gauge.

The first American Flyer Standard Gauge train sets were restricted to passenger cars, as the firm didn't produce its own style of freight cars for two more years. In the interim year of 1926, Lionel provided Flyer with four of its early large freights (stock car, boxcar, gondola, and caboose), each of which was stamped on the underside with the appropriate Flyer number. It is presumed that since the Lionel Corporation was already well advanced with the production of its new line of freight cars and was discontinuing the old designs, allowing American Flyer to sell their old stock would not be considered a competitive threat.

When the American Flyer-designed line of freight cars finally appeared in 1927, it was distinctively different from both the old and the new versions made by Lionel. Not only were they an inch-and-a-half longer than Lionel's biggest, their overall proportions seemed much more like the real thing than the handsome but chunky Lionel cars. However, the variety was more limited, with nothing comparable to Lionel's dump car, searchlight car, or crane in play value. In addition, Lionel offered freights in two sizes and price ranges, thus accommodating the economy market. American Flyer produced only the large 14" cars.

Conventional steel construction was used for all of the cars, and they were trimmed with brass plates and brake wheels. The tank car was especially handsome, with brass ladders and tie-down straps. On most cars, the truck side frames were flexibly mounted to swivel when traveling over rough track, and the coupler design provided very strong connections between the cars and excellent tracking ability. However, the couplers were mounted in male and female pairs, so that the cars could be run in only one direction. The caboose had only female couplers, and locomotives were fitted with the male type on both ends.

There were just seven car styles, although one of them was marketed under two different descriptions. The 4022 Machinery Car (1928 to 1933) and the later 4023 Log Car cannot be distinguished from one another except by number plates and the presence of a load of wood on the latter. The number plates are not a reliable guide, however, since the American Flyer factory was notoriously inconsistent in mounting these plates, and cars are often found with two different numbers on opposite sides. And, the wood load was removable, turning a log car into a machinery car, for all practical purposes.

All of the cars are reasonably easy to find except for the hopper, which was included in fewer sets than the others. The sand car (gondola) and the caboose are the most common pieces.

4000 1927; 4012 **FLATCAR** with ten stakes (same style as 4023 log car but without wood load); 14"; dark blue with black trucks. $225

4000 1927; **CABOOSE**; 14"; yellow with tan roof on black frame with black trucks, no window frames or smokestack; no interior light; very rare. . . . .(value not established)

4005 1926; **STOCK (CATTLE) CAR**; 11-1/4"; Lionel 13 with hook couplers and black American Flyer trucks; green. . $150

4006 1931-36; HOPPER CAR; 14"; red with gray trucks; reproduced by Rich-Art. $400

4007 1926; **SAND CAR**; 11-14"; Lionel 12 gondola with hook couplers and black American Flyer trucks; gray. $150

American Flyer 4006 Hopper Car. (Carail Museum)

4007 1927; **SAND CAR** (gondola); 14"; maroon with black frame and trucks. $85

4008 1926; **BOXCAR**; 11-1/4"; Lionel 14 with hook couplers and black American Flyer trucks; orange. $150

4008 1927; **BOXCAR**; 14"; orange with orange or red roof and black frame and trucks. $225

4010 1928-36; **TANK CAR**; 14"; cream tank with dark blue frame and gray trucks; 100% premium for blue tank; 100% premium for "A.F. AIR SERVICE" decal. $250

4011 1926; **CABOOSE**; 11-1/4"; Lionel 17 with hook couplers and black American Flyer trucks; red with black roof. . . $150

4011 1927-32; **CABOOSE**; 14"; red with red roof on black frame with black or gray trucks; brass window frames and smokestack; no interior light; 25% premium for yellow with tan roof (early) on black frame with black trucks, no window frames or smokestack. $120

4012 1927; **FLATCAR** with ten stakes (same style as 4023 log car but without wood load); 14"; dark blue with black trucks. $225

American Flyer 4010 Tank Cars in blue and yellow enamel. (Carail Museum Collection)

4017 1928-36; **SAND CAR** (gondola); 14"; green with green or black frame and black or gray trucks; 20% premium for orange body and frame with gray trucks; 200% premium for scarce maroon with black frame and trucks. **$50**

4018 1928-36; **AUTOMOBILE (BOX) CAR**; 14"; tan with blue roof and door and gray trucks. **$190**

4020 1928-36; **STOCK (CATTLE) CAR**; 14"; blue with dark blue roof and gray trucks. **$210**

4021 1928-36; **CABOOSE**; 14"; red with red or dark red roof and frame and gray trucks; brass window frames and smokestack; interior light. **$90**

4022 1928-33; **MACHINERY (FLAT) CAR** with ten stakes (same as 4023 log car but without wood load); 14"; orange with orange or blue side bars and gray trucks. **$65**

4023 1934-36; **LOG CAR** with ten stakes (same as 4022 machinery car but includes wood load); 14"; orange with gray trucks. **$65**

4677 Ca. 1928-36; 4017 **SAND CAR** (gondola); 14"; green with green frame and gray trucks; brass plates lettered "NATIONWIDE LINES". **$600**

4677 Ca. 1928-36; 4018 **AUTOMOBILE (BOX) CAR**; 14"; tan with blue roof and door; brass plates lettered "NATIONWIDE LINES". **$600**

4677 Ca. 1928-36; 4021 **CABOOSE**; 14"; red with red or dark red roof and frame and gray trucks; brass window frames and smokestack; interior light; brass plates lettered "NATIONWIDE LINES". **$600**

Boucher Standard Gauge Freight Cars

Boucher manufactured eight freight car designs, all adapted from the Voltamp line and constructed of stamped steel. They differed from Voltamp production in the style of lettering and the trucks, which were a new design to fit Standard Gauge track. All measured 13-1/2" long, and except for the caboose, all had brake wheels at both ends. All are hard to find, with the dump car, gondola, and hopper being the least common. Around 1978, John E. Harmon reproduced all but the caboose; he reports that another hobbyist produced copies of that car at about the same time.

Values for Boucher products are speculative; examples rarely change hands, due to very limited production numbers. The prices given reflect their relative rarity, and are comparable to products of other low-volume companies.

2108 1922-29; *BOXCAR*; *reproduced by John E. Harmon.* *$300*

2109 1922-29; *FLATCAR*; *reproduced by John E. Harmon.* *$275*

2110 1922-29; *CABOOSE*; *reproduced (maker unknown).* *$300*

2111 1922-29; *GONDOLA*; *reproduced by John E. Harmon.* *$325*

2112 1922-29; *COAL HOPPER*; *reproduced by John E. Harmon.* *$350*

2113 1922-29; *OIL TANK CAR*; *reproduced by John E. Harmon.* *$300*

2114 1922-29; *CATTLE CAR*; *reproduced by John E. Harmon.* *$300*

2115 1922-29; *DUMP CAR*; *reproduced by John E. Harmon.* *$350*

Dorfan Wide (Standard) Gauge Freight Cars

Dorfan built only six different types of freight cars, but they were very handsome models. Each measured 14" without the couplers, comparable to American Flyer's products, and the first five were lithographed rather than enameled. The litho process allowed inclusion of many fine details on the cars, including rivets, plentiful dimensional and capacity lettering and road heralds. This resulted in a high degree of realism. They were nicely trimmed with journals, handrails, ladders and other details. The tank car also sported shiny domes and tie-down straps. Only the lumber car, which appeared a year after the other five, was enameled instead of lithographed.

As on the American Flyer cars, matched pairs of male and female couplers permitted operation in only one direction. The truck frames and wheels were die cast and provided good performance, but impurities in the material resulted in early deterioration, and these cars are almost always found with steel replacements.

800 1928-30; **GONDOLA**; 14"; orange with black frame and trucks. **$250**

801 1928-30; **BOXCAR**; 14"; green with red or green roof and black frame and trucks. **$250**

804 1928-30; **TANK CAR**; 14"; blue with black frame and trucks. **$250**

805 1928-30; **HOPPER CAR**; 14"; dark red with black frame and trucks. **$275**

806 1928-30; **CABOOSE**; 14"; brown with blue-green or red roof, brown or red cupola, red cupola roof and black frame and trucks. **$250**

809 1929-30; **LUMBER CAR**; 14"; black frame with eight red enameled stakes, plus six pieces of wood 3/4" x 3/4" x 11-5/8" each. **$600**

Ives Wide (Standard) Gauge Freight Cars

When Ives converted its No. 1 Gauge trains to conform to the popular Lionel Standard Gauge track requirements in 1921, the company already had tooling for six freight cars, dating from 1915. These steel cars were hand soldered from many different pieces, and were very well detailed and realistic for such early models. Measuring 11-1/2" long, the No. 1 Gauge cars were almost identical in length to the largest of Lionel's contemporary production. Adapting them to the new size track consisted primarily of replacing the No. 1 Gauge trucks with wider versions.

Over the next decade some changes were made in these designs, such as the addition of sides to the flatcar and the provision of a full size frame for the tank car. (Early tank cars are distinguished by a very narrow, thin strip frame and a narrow walkway surrounding the lower portion of the tank.) Other changes were of a minor nature: the addition of journals, an interior light in the caboose, coupler modifications, and new colors, for example. It was not until American Flyer and Lionel took over the bankrupt company in 1928, however, that any major changes took place.

Producing an Ives freight car demanded a great many worker hours, a factor which led in part to the firm's economic difficulties during the 1920s. The bodies of the cars were made from many separate pieces and required a lot of individual soldered joints. Painting was also laborious, requiring several more steps than comparable competing cars. In 1928, Lionel and Flyer quickly dropped some of these complex cars from the Ives line and substituted their own designs, fitted with Ives trucks, couplers, and identity plates. The Flyer caboose, boxcar, stock car, tanker, and gondola designs were used in 1928 and early 1929, after which Lionel substituted their 200-series cars. In the case of the 190 tank car, parts from all three manufacturers were used on one car: a Lionel 215 tank, a Flyer frame, and Ives trucks and couplers. The Ives-designed 191 Coke Car, 194 Coal Car and 196 Flatcar were continued through 1930 and then dropped.

Although considerable savings were realized by dropping the original Ives designs, the onset of the Depression meant that further savings were necessary. In 1931 Lionel closed the Bridgeport factory where Ives trains had been built, and all production moved to the Lionel plant in Irvington, New Jersey. Instead of continuing to use the large and more expensive 200-series cars, the firm applied Ives name plates to the smaller 500-series designs. As a final economy step, the last vestiges of Ives design (the trucks and couplers) were replaced with Lionel components, and except for the brass plates, the cars became identical to their Lionel counterparts. There no longer seemed any advantage to maintaining a separate Ives identity, and the brand name disappeared after 1932.

The economic decline of Ives during the 1920s was due in part to increased competition and in part from a failure to institute changes that would lead to more economical production. The company's engineers were talented and imaginative. They had produced the first successful remote control reverse unit early in the decade, as well as a superior cab-mounted motor for the 1928 release of the 1134 steam locomotive. Both locomotives and rolling stock were well designed and built, but the need to remain competitive with Lionel and Flyer forced Ives to sell its products at prices that failed to cover costs, much less realize a profit.

Nevertheless, in the dying days of independent operation Ives created some of the most memorable toy trains ever produced: the 1134 steamer, the St. Paul Olympian locomotives, and especially the Standard Gauge circus train. This beautiful and imaginative set was packaged with an assortment of cardboard accessories acquired from the Coca-Cola company, and overprinted with Ives lettering. The cutouts depicted a circus tent, entrance gate, horse-drawn wagons, elephants, and even a circus band.

The train was pulled by an 1134 steam locomotive, and consisted of regular Ives freight cars in 1928. Three flatcars carried two animal cages each, and a stock car, box, and passenger coach (called a "Performers' Pullman" that year) were relettered for the Ives Railway Circus. Twelve animal figures were included, and there were even canvas covers for the cages to simulate protection for the livestock while in transit. The circus train was an impressive toy with a considerable amount of play value, but it arrived just as the company was failing, and few were made. Even if it had been created earlier, it is doubtful that the circus train would have done much to improve the company's fortunes. The problem of complex construction meant that the price for the set would have been substantial, and despite the relative prosperity of the late 1920s, most families could not afford such a high ticket item. Ives' lower priced Standard Gauge trains were selling reasonably well, but the firm was losing money on many of them.

In an effort the keep the circus concept alive, the Lionel-Flyer management substituted American Flyer bodies for the stock and boxcars in 1929. The remaining components were the same as in the previous year. While marginally more sets were sold than in 1928, it was not a great success, and the circus train was discontinued in 1930.

The circus cars and the Lionel and Flyer versions are scarce, with a few approaching rarity, but examples of most other Ives freight cars are fairly plentiful. They are hard to find in *Excellent* condition, however, due to the problem of flaking paint that plagues most of the company's products. They are also somewhat more fragile than either Lionel or American Flyer cars, and examples with good paint, bold lettering and all small trim parts present command a substantial premium.

Ives 195 Caboose; restored.

190 1921-28; **TANK CAR**; 11-1/4"; orange tank (many variations in shade from yellow to almost red) with black trucks; narrow, thin strip frame and surrounding strip walkway, with small auxiliary tank centered below main tank (through 1922), or full sized orange frame (from 1923); 20% premium for narrow frame version; 300% premium for maroon lettered for Wanamaker Department Store. $185

190 1929-30; **TANK CAR** (Lionel 215 tank); 14"; orange with black American Flyer frame and Ives trucks; Ives couplers and identity plates. $525

191 1921-30; **COKE CAR**; 11-1/4"; open body with four transverse bulkheads joined by four thin longitudinal strips on each side; brown, green, red, or blue with black trucks; 300% premium for maroon lettered for Wanamaker Department Store. . $185

192 1921-28; **MERCHANDISE (BOX) CAR**; 11-1/4"; brown, tan, orange, green or white with black trucks and trim and Santa Fe herald; some with contrasting roof color; 300% premium for maroon lettered for Wanamaker Department Store. . . . $225

192-C 1928; CIRCUS EQUIPMENT (MERCHANDISE) CAR; 11-1/4"; yellow with red roof, green trim and black trucks; rubber-stamped "THE IVES R.R. CIRCUS" or "THE IVES RAILWAY SHOW". Reproduced by Harry A. Osisek. $1,250

192 1930; **MERCHANDISE (BOX) CAR** (Lionel 214); 12-1/2"; orange with peacock-blue roof, black Ives trucks; Ives couplers and identity plates. $725

193 1921-28; **STOCK (CATTLE) CAR**; 11-1/4"; brown, maroon, or green with black trucks; some with contrasting roof color; 300% premium for maroon lettered for Wanamaker Department Store. $200

193 1930; **STOCK (CATTLE) CAR** (Lionel 213); 12-1/2"; orange with red roof and black Ives trucks; Ives couplers and identity plates. $900

193-C *1928; CIRCUS ANIMAL (STOCK) CAR; 11-1/4"; yellow with red roof with green trim and black trucks; rubber-stamped "THE IVES R.R. CIRCUS" or "THE IVES RAILWAY SHOW"; 10% premium if stamped "THE IVES R.R. SHOW". Reproduced by Harry A. Osisek.* ***$1,250***

194 1921-30; **COAL (HOPPER) CAR**; 11-1/4"; green, very dark green or gray with black trim and trucks, or black with red trim and black trucks; Pennsylvania Railroad keystone and lettering; 100% premium for black with red trim and red Ives decal instead of keystone; 300% premium for maroon lettered for Wanamaker Department Store. **$225**

195 1921-28; **CABOOSE**; 11-1/2"; five windows each side, red wit red, dark orange, brown or maroon roof and cupola; interior light from 1927; 500% premium for very scarce version with two windows each side, red with maroon roof and cupola (1928 only). **$235**

195 1930; **CABOOSE** (Lionel 217); 12-1/2"; red with maroon roof, blue or peacock-blue cupola, and black Ives trucks; Ives couplers and identity plates. **$200**

196 1922-1930; **FLATCAR**; 11-1/4"; no sides until 1924; green or orange with black trucks; 300% premium for maroon lettered for Wanamaker Department Store. **$100**

196-C *1928-29; CIRCUS FLATCAR; 11-1/4"; yellow with green trim and black trucks; rubber-stamped "THE IVES RAILWAY CIRCUS" or "THE IVES RAILWAY SHOW"; includes two 72 cage wagons or two 73 tent pole wagons; valued at approximately 50% if wagons are missing. Reproduced by Harry A. Osisek.* ***$1,200***

197 1928-29; **LUMBER CAR**; 11-1/2"; green or orange with black trucks; four upright stakes per side, with load of six long rectangular wood pieces. **$275**

197 1930; **LUMBER CAR** (Lionel 211); 12-1/2"; green with black Ives trucks and one-piece wood load; Ives couplers, with or without rubber-stamped Ives identification plates. **$300**

198 1930; **GRAVEL CAR** (Lionel 212 Gondola); 12-1/2"; black, green, or maroon with black Ives trucks; Ives couplers and identity plates. **$175**

199 1929-30; **DERRICK** (Lionel 219); 12-1/2"; peacock-blue with red boom and windows, and red or dark green roof; black Ives or Lionel trucks; Ives couplers and identity plates. **$1,050**

1771 1931-32; **LUMBER CAR** (Lionel 511); 11-1/2"; green with black Lionel trucks and Lionel couplers and one-piece wood load; rubber-stamped Ives identification on bottom. **$125**

1772 1931-32; **GONDOLA** (Lionel 512); 11-1/2"; peacock-blue with black Lionel trucks and Lionel couplers; Ives identity plates. **$125**

1773 1931-32; **STOCK (CATTLE) CAR** (Lionel 513); 11-1/2"; green with orange roof and black Lionel trucks and Lionel couplers; Ives identity plates. **$325**

1774 1931-32; **BOXCAR** (Lionel 514); 11-1/2"; yellow with orange roof and black Lionel trucks and Lionel couplers; Ives identity plates. **$325**

1775 1931-32; **TANK CAR** (Lionel 515); 11-1/2"; white with black Lionel trucks and Lionel couplers; Ives identity plates. **$425**

1776 1931-32; **COAL (HOPPER) CAR** (Lionel 516); 11-1/2"; red with black Lionel trucks and Lionel couplers; Ives identity plates. **$725**

1777 1931-32; **CABOOSE** (Lionel 517); 11-1/2"; green with red roof and cupola ends, and green cupola sides; black Lionel trucks and Lionel couplers; Ives identity plates. **$125**

1778 1931-32; **REFRIGERATOR CAR** (Lionel 514R); 11-1/2"; white with peacock-blue roof and black Lionel trucks and Lionel couplers; Ives identity plates. **$400**

1779 1931; **DERRICK** (Lionel 219); 12-1/2"; peacock-blue with red boom and windows and black roof; black Lionel trucks and Lionel couplers; Ives identity plates. **$1,050**

20-190 1928; **TANK CAR** (American Flyer 4010); 14"; orange tank and frame with black Ives trucks, Ives couplers and identity plates. **$650**

20-192 1928-29; **MERCHANDISE (BOX) CAR** (American Flyer 4018); 14"; yellow with blue or red roof and black Ives trucks, Ives couplers and identity plates; 50% premium for green with red roof. **$325**

20-192-C 1929; **CIRCUS EQUIPMENT CAR**(American Flyer 4018); 14"; orange with red roof; black Ives trucks and Ives couplers; rubber-stamped "THE IVES R.R. CIRCUS". . . **$1,200**

20-193 1928-29; **STOCK (CATTLE) CAR** (American Flyer 4020); 14"; orange with red roof and black Ives trucks, Ives couplers and identity plates; 20% premium for green with red roof. **$275**

20-193-C 1929; **CIRCUS ANIMAL (STOCK) CAR** (American Flyer 4020); 14"; orange with red roof; black Ives trucks and Ives couplers; rubber-stamped "THE IVES R.R. CIRCUS". **$1,200**

20-194 1929; **GRAVEL CAR** (gondola; American Flyer 4017 Sand Car); 14"; black with black Ives trucks, Ives couplers and identity plates; same as 20-198. . . . . **$175**

20-195 1928-29; **CABOOSE** (American Flyer 4021); 14"; red with maroon roof and maroon or peacock-blue cupola; black Ives trucks, Ives couplers and identity plates; brass window frames and smokestack; interior light; 150% premium for light green. **$90**

20-198 1929; **GRAVEL CAR** (gondola; American Flyer 4017 Sand Car); 14"; black with black Ives trucks, Ives couplers and identity plates; same as 20-194. . . . . **$175**

Lionel Standard Gauge Freight Cars

Almost from the beginning of Standard Gauge production, Joshua Cowen understood the marketing advantage of building his trains in two different price ranges. The large series of cars (normally referred to by collectors as the 10 series) first appeared in 1906 and was joined just four years later by the smaller and more economical 100 series. From then until the end of Standard Gauge production, just prior to World War II, two sizes of freight cars were offered at all times. A similar lineup of large and small freights was cataloged in O Gauge as well.

The initial 10 series of large cars was built to accompany the Nos. 5 and 6 steam locomotives that inaugurated Standard Gauge in 1906. They were simply constructed of soldered sheet steel and rode on pairs of large, unpainted eight-wheel trucks. Decorative details included brake wheels and rubber-stamped road name lettering on some of the cars. Most of them were embossed with "LIONEL MFG. CO." until 1918, when the company changed its legal identity to The Lionel Corporation. Later cars were rubber-stamped on the bottom to identify this change. Over the years, the design of the trucks was changed several times, and there were minor alterations in construction of the bodies themselves, but overall appearance of the cars remained essentially constant.

Along with the new line of electric locomotives which appeared in 1910, Lionel introduced the smaller and less expensive 100 series of freight cars. Only five designs were made: gondola, boxcar, stock car, ballast car, and caboose. (The more extensive 10 series also included a flatcar and a tank car.) The company maintained a consistency in its catalog numbers that was continued throughout Standard Gauge production. The final digit identifies the type of car. For example, boxcars are numbered 1*4*, 11*4*, 21*4*, and 51*4*; stock cars are numbered 1*3*, 11*3*, 21*3*, and 51*3*, etc. Construction was similar to the larger cars.

As Lionel improved its manufacturing techniques, more refined locomotives with highly detailed bodies and more powerful motors were introduced, beginning with the 380 St. Paul model in 1923. Recognizing the need for cars of comparable quality, the company dropped the 10 series in 1926, and replaced them with the new 200 series. Construction was much heavier, and the earlier rubber-stamped decoration was replaced with brass plates. Colors were brightened considerably. While each of the earlier cars was mostly painted in one relatively somber color, the new series had contrasting roofs and door guides, and a much wider variety of hues. These colors were not really representative of prototype railroad practice, but the success of these cars suggests that buyers were attracted more by color than by authenticity.

The new cars also had considerable play value. While only the early ballast cars of the 10 and 100 series had any operating features (levers that dumped the load), there were three 200 series cars that allowed young engineers to handle the freight. The dump car had a gear mechanism that tilted the body and allowed the side to swing open, and the hopper car had doors on the underside that opened. Most attractive of all was the derrick (crane) car, with its three big knobs that swiveled the cab, and raised and lowered the boom and hook. In addition, two cars were lighted: the caboose and the floodlight car.

Just as these new cars were introduced, the early steam locomotives disappeared from the catalog, and the only motive power available came in the form of electric-outline models of various sizes. The 200 series cars looked fine with big engines like the 380, but were out of proportion to the smaller 8 and 10 locos. In 1927, Lionel scrapped the 100 series and replaced it with a new line of small, but still substantial, freight cars. This new 500 series was almost as varied as the large line, lacking only the dump car and derrick. Like the large cars, they were substantially constructed, had brass plates instead of rubber stamping, and were decorated in a variety of bright colors.

Lionel's two-tier line and price structure gave it a very definite advantage in the marketplace, and throughout the 1920s the firm continued to capture an increasingly greater share of the market. The company benefited from superior engineering that made assembly easy and kept production costs low, and the heavy-gauge steel used in construction made the trains very durable. Ives cars, for example, were more realistic and prototypical, but in their darker colors they appeared drab by comparison with the Lionel products. Burdened by the need for a high degree of hand fabrication, Ives trains cost too much to produce, and the company folded in 1928, to be taken over jointly by Lionel and American Flyer, and finally by Lionel alone.

As the Great Depression loomed, Lionel was well placed to dominate the market. The firm offered two sizes of trains (Standard and O Gauges) and two price levels within each gauge. The least expensive O Gauge models were accessible to most families, while the largest and fanciest entries in the Standard Gauge line represented the most magnificent and desirable toys ever offered to the American public.

Lionel 13 Stock Car (left) and 17 Caboose. (Carail Museum Collection)

11 *1906-26;* **FLATCAR**; *11-1/4"; maroon, brown, red and gray, with shiny steel trucks, each assembled with one rivet per side; 20% premium if embossed "LIONEL MFG. CO."; 100% premium for orange; 300% premium for early three-rivet trucks; reproduced by James Cohen and Joseph L. Mania.* **$75**

12 *1906-26;* **GONDOLA**; *11-1/4"; red, brown, or gray, with or without contrasting trim; shiny steel trucks assembled with one rivet per side; 20% premium if embossed "LIONEL MFG. CO."; 800% premium for early three-rivet trucks; reproduced by James Cohen and Joseph L. Mania.* **$75**

13 *1906-26;* **STOCK (CATTLE) CAR**; *11-1/4"; green with shiny steel trucks assembled with one rivet per side; 20% premium if embossed "LIONEL MFG. CO."; 300% premium for early three-rivet trucks; reproduced by James Cohen and Joseph L. Mania.* **$90**

14 *1906-26;* **BOXCAR**; *11-1/4"; orange or red with shiny steel trucks assembled with one rivet per side; 20% premium if embossed "LIONEL MFG. CO."; 200% premium for early three-rivet trucks; 500% premium for "HARMONY CREAMERY" lettering; reproduced by James Cohen and Joseph L. Mania.* . . **$90**

15 *1906-26;* **TANK CAR**; *10-3/4"; maroon, red or brown, with shiny steel trucks assembled with one rivet per side; 200% premium for early three-rivet trucks; reproduced by James Cohen and Joseph L. Mania.* **$75**

Lionel 214 Boxcar (left) and 213 Stock Car (right). Also visible among the many accessories are 155 Station Platforms (background), 438 Switch Tower (center), 25 Bumper (left foreground), 83 Traffic Signal (right foreground) and 440 Signal Bridge (left). (Carail Museum Collection)

Lionel No. 14 Boxcar. (Reproduction by Joseph L. Mania, photograph by Sean Smyth)

Lionel 15 Tank Car (left) and 16 Ballast Car. (Carail Museum Collection)

16 *1906-26;* **BALLAST CAR**; *10-3/4"; maroon, red, brown, or green, some with contrasting trim; shiny steel trucks assembled with one rivet per side; 200% premium for early three-rivet trucks; reproduced by James Cohen and Joseph L. Mania.* **$150**

17 *1906-26;* **CABOOSE**; *11-1/4"; maroon, red, or brown with black roof; shiny steel trucks assembled with one rivet per side; 50% premium for early version with awnings over windows; 20% premium if embossed "LIONEL MFG. CO."; 200% premium for early three-rivet trucks; reproduced by James Cohen and Joseph L. Mania.* **$100**

112 *1910-26;* **GONDOLA**; *7" (early) or 9-1/2"; gray, green, brown, maroon, or red, some with contrasting trim and/or interior; 300% premium for early short version.* **$60**

113 *1912-26;* **STOCK (CATTLE) CAR**; *9-1/2"; green.* **$75**

114 *1912-26;* **BOXCAR**; *9-1/2"; orange or red.* **$75**

116 *1910-26;* **BALLAST CAR**; *9-1/2"; maroon, brown, green, or gray.* **$65**

117 *1912-26;* **CABOOSE**; *9-1/2"; maroon, red, or brown with black roof.* **$60**

211 *1926-40;* **FLATCAR**; *12-1/2"; black with lumber load; reproduced by Mike's Train House.* **$100**

Lionel 214R Refrigerator Car. (Carail Museum Collection)

Lionel 216 Hopper Car; restored.

Lionel 214 Boxcar. (Carail Museum Collection)

212 *1926-40;* **GONDOLA***; 12-1/2"; maroon with black frame; 50% premium for gray or green; 100% premium for dark green; reproduced by Mike's Train House.* ***$125***

213 *1926-40;* **STOCK (CATTLE) CAR***; 12-1/2"; terra cotta with green roof and black frame; 25% premium for Mojave or terra cotta with maroon roof; 150% premium for cream with maroon roof; reproduced by Mike's Train House.* ***$220***

214 *1926-40;* **BOXCAR***; 12-1/2"; cream with orange roof and black frame; 75% premium for terra cotta with green roof; 150% premium for yellow with brown roof; reproduced by Mike's Train House.* ***$220***

214R *1929-40;* **REFRIGERATOR CAR***; 12-1/2"; ivory with peacock-blue roof and black frame; 50% premium for white with light blue roof; reproduced by Mike's Train House.* ***$525***

215 *1926-40;* **TANK CAR***; 12-1/2"; green tank with black frame; 75% premium for ivory tank, with or without Sunoco decal; 125% premium for aluminum tank, with or without Sunoco decal; reproduced by Mike's Train House.* ***$165***

216 *1926-38;* **HOPPER CAR***; 12-1/2"; dark green with black frame; reproduced by Mike's Train House.* ***$275***

217 *1926-40;* **CABOOSE***; 12-1/2"; red with peacock-blue roof, red or peacock-blue cupola, and black frame; lighted rear deck; 10% premium for red with red roof and cupola; 100% premium for orange with maroon roof (early); reproduced by Mike's Train House.* ***$200***

218 *1926-38;* **DUMP CAR***; 12-1/2"; Mojave with brass or Mojave ends and black frame; value undetermined for gray or green; reproduced by Mike's Train House.* ***$260***

219 *1926-40;* **DERRICK***; 12-1/2"; peacock-blue cab with dark green roof, red boom and black frame; 100% premium for yellow cab with red roof and red or green boom; 125% for white or ivory cab with green boom; reproduced by Mike's Train House.* ***$200***

220 *1931-40;* **FLOODLIGHT CAR***; 12-1/2"; terra cotta with brass lights and black frame; 50% premium for green with nickel lights; reproduced by Mike's Train House.* ***$300***

511 *1927-40;* **FLATCAR***; 11-1/2"; green with black frame.* ***$50***

512 *1927-39;* **GONDOLA***; 11-1/2"; peacock-blue with black frame; 25% premium for green.* ***$50***

Lionel 217 Caboose. (Carail Museum Collection)

Lionel 218 Dump Car, in tilted position; restored.

Lionel 514R Refrigerator Car. (Carail Museum Collection)

513 1927-38; **STOCK (CATTLE) CAR**; 11-1/2"; orange with pea green roof and black frame; 50% premium for green with orange roof; 250% premium for cream with maroon roof. . . .
. . . .**$100**

514 1929-40; **BOXCAR**; 11-1/2"; sliding doors; cream with orange roof and black frame; 35% premium for yellow with brown roof; same number as the 1928-29 version of the refrigerator car.
. . . .**$120**

514, 514R 1927-40; **REFRIGERATOR CAR**; 11-1/2"; hinged doors with latch; ivory or white with peacock-blue roof; 100% premium for 514 plates (no "R", 1927-28 version); 150% premium for white with light blue roof or ivory with Stephen Girard green roof. **$200**

515 1927-40; **TANK CAR**; 11-1/2"; terra cotta, ivory or aluminum tank with black frame; with or without Sunoco decal; 200% premium for scarce orange tank with Shell decal. .**$165**

516 1928-40; **HOPPER CAR**; 11-1/2"; red; 10% premium for coal load. **$200**

517 1927-40; **CABOOSE**; 11-1/2"; green with red roof and black frame; lighted rear deck; 50% premium for red with red roof; 600% premium for red with black roof (part of coal train set with 318 locomotive and three hopper cars). **$75**

520 1931-40; **FLOODLIGHT CAR**; 11-1/2"; terra cotta with brass lights and black frame; 25% premium for green with nickel lights. **$160**

Accessories made the difference between a train "set" and a model railroad, as promoted by Lionel's catalogs in the 1920s and 1930s. Lionel's stations, platforms, power stations, signals, and dwellings dominate this scene on the Carail Museum layout.

14

ACCESSORIES

Value Guide

Accessories were a vital component of the marketing strategy of early toy train manufacturers. A toy train set was often viewed as a Christmas toy, brought out yearly during the holiday season and stored away for the rest of the year. In order to promote the concept of year-round rail-roading, the manufacturers (and especially Lionel) empha-sized building permanent layouts, complete with signals, buildings, and scenery.

The toy train accessories listed in this chapter are arranged according to manufacturer, in alphabetical order. The entries are listed in the numerical order of their catalog numbers. Each entry contains the following information: catalog number; dates of manufacture; dimensions in inch-es; brief description for identification; color and/or signifi-cant variations (if any); and value in *Very Good (VG)* condition. Colors are listed in order from most to least common.

Each of the four manufacturers included in this chapter sold trains in two sizes, Standard Gauge and the smaller O Gauge. (Boucher accessories, except for track products, were made by Lionel.) However, they carried only one line of accessories and promoted them as usable with either gauge. Most of these items are quite large and look best with Standard Gauge trains. Some are grossly oversized for

O Gauge, but the problem of scale was not of great impor-tance to toy train purchasers in the first four decades of the twentieth century. It was not until the rise of scale model railroading, especially in the 1930s, that buyers became more sensitive to the huge discrepancies between the size of O Gauge trains and the accessories sold to go with them.

Lionel also built beautiful but far too tiny houses for the residents of Lionelville. Their bungalows, villas, and mansions were about half size for O Gauge, more appropri-ate for use with HO scale trains. Next to a Standard Gauge locomotive, they look almost ridiculous, yet many thou-sands were sold to owners of these large trains. If used in the background of a layout, their size adds to a feeling of perspective, making the layout seem larger. As foreground models, or when placed too close to stations or tracks, they tend to detract from any feeling of reality.

While most accessories were considered appropriate for either gauge, a few were specific to the smaller trains, such as the tunnels shaped to fit O Gauge track or the operating log loader or bascule bridge. These items could not be used with Standard Gauge trains and are not included in this chapter. Some operating accessories required a special sec-tion of track to make them work and were packaged in either Standard or O Gauge versions with the appropriate size of track. Otherwise they are identical, although the catalog numbers reflected the track size. For example, a Lionel 77 Crossing Gate came with Standard Gauge track, while the 077 Gate—exactly the same except for its number plate—was sold with an O Gauge track section.

For an explanation of grading criteria and how to evaluate condition, see Chapter 10. Buyers should expect to pay a premium for items in better than *Very Good* condition, with the upward price differential being greater for scarce or expensive items. The values for items in less than *Very Good* condition are generally lower than those shown, with the downward price differential being greater for common or inexpensive items.

The value of restored pieces depends upon the quality of the restoration work, the scarcity of the item, and the use to which the piece will be put (operation or display; see Chapter 10). In general, the average value of restored items is comparable to the most common version in *Very Good* condition.

Items which are known to have been reproduced are shown in italics. While most reproductions are so marked, there is always the possibility of unmarked or fraudulent items being presented as originals. Novices should obtain the advice of experienced collectors before purchasing high-value toy trains. The catalog numbers for items which were advertised, but not known to have been made, are omitted from this chapter.

Items accompanied by original boxes and/or original instruction books or other literature will command a premium, with the upward price differential depending upon scarcity. The premium for boxes depends upon condition (presence or absence of end flaps, tears in the cardboard, etc.) and scarcity. Collectors place substantial value upon prewar accessory boxes in *Very Good* or better condition, especially those which held multiple items (such as a set of five bungalows).

Note that the term "Standard Gauge" was exclusive to Lionel and Boucher, and that the products of other manufacturers are referred to as "Wide Gauge." The distance between the outer rails of the track, however, is the same (2-1/8") for all manufacturers. The term "Standard Gauge" is used in this book to describe all trains built to 2-1/8" Gauge.

American Flyer Wide (Standard) Gauge Accessories

Prior to the introduction of their Wide (Standard) Gauge trains in 1925, all American Flyer accessories were intended for use with their O Gauge trains. Some were large enough to look good with Standard Gauge trains, and they are listed below, but the smaller items are not included. Some of the earliest items, such as semaphores mounted on open girder poles, were manufactured in Germany.

During the years under consideration here, American Flyer built relatively few action accessories, just crossing gates, warning signals and lighted items such as lampposts and block signals. While some of these items are quite handsome and appealing, many are rather plain. However, a lot of their strictly decorative items were exceptionally well detailed. Using the lithograph process, for example, the company produced a succession of colorful and attractive freight and passenger stations. Exterior designs included brick, stucco, and wood siding patterns, and some windows had passenger and ticket agent figures in them. (Ives also built beautiful lithographed stations, but almost all of Lionel's equivalents were enameled in solid colors, and lacked complex decorations.)

Some of the stations were offered in lighted versions, with exterior lamp fixtures mounted under the roof eaves, interior lights, or both. When inside lamps were included, windows were cut out rather than lithographed, and some were glazed with a celluloid material. Flyer's largest—the Union Station—was constructed of wood instead of metal. Using this material, the company made the huge structure at a very competitive price. It was a beautiful toy, and was lighted with five bulbs, one of which lighted a four-sided clock in the central tower. Unfortunately, the Union Station was less durable than the metal stations, and fewer have survived.

American Flyer dropped Standard Gauge production after 1936, and when the company was sold to A. C. Gilbert two years later, a dramatic change in emphasis occurred. Gilbert redesigned the O Gauge train line to a scale of approximately 3/16" to one foot, one-fourth smaller than their previous offerings and Lionel's O Gauge trains. (These 3/16" trains were to be the foundation of American Flyer's S Gauge trains after World War II.) There was a corresponding switch to smaller accessories to accompany the new line, including new stations, a tool shed, an operating crane, a switch tower, figures (including an animated track gang accessory) and an operating water tower. These items are too small to look good with Standard Gauge trains, but the operating billboard, which contained a motorized whistle and first appeared in 1937, is one late accessory that Standard Gauge operators can use.

Collectors may find some accessories bearing four-digit numbers that begin with "2"; these are not listed below. If sold for Standard Gauge use, the numbers for these accessories began with the digit "4", while a "2" denoted O Gauge. Otherwise, the items were the same, and are listed under the appropriate Standard Gauge catalog number. To find a description of a *2116* Crossing Signal, for example, consult the listing for item *4116*.

When American Flyer first introduced Wide (Standard) Gauge trains, the firm had few accessories that were appropriate for such large trains. From 1926 through 1929 they purchased some items from Lionel, and resold them with American Flyer identification.

All accessories operate manually, unless automatic action is specified.

91 1931-32; **FAST FREIGHT STATION**; 6" x 4"; lithographed with red roof; lettered "FLYER TOWN FREIGHT 91" on ends. $20

91 1922-25; **OPEN PASSENGER STATION PLATFORM**; 15-1/8" x 4"; lithographed with green and white roof. $65

92 1929-33; **WATCHMAN'S TOWER**; 10" high; lithographed building on pole with ladder; bell below base of building. $35

93 1928-31; **PASSENGER STATION**; 6" x 4"; lithographed with green roof; lettered "SUBURBAN WEST BOUND TRAINS"; lighted. $50

95 1926-27; **FREIGHT STATION**; 12" x 7-1/2"; lithographed. $95

96 1923-35; **PASSENGER STATION**; 9-1/2" x 5-1/2"; imitation brick lithography with green or red roof; lettered "WAITING ROOM", "BAGGAGE ROOM", "TICKET OFFICE", etc. $75

97 1928-34; **FREIGHT STATION**; 12" x 7-1/2"; lithographed; similar to 95, with front dormer and lighted; also found mounted on 19" x 8-1/8" base with O Gauge crane. $95

97 1923-26; **PASSENGER STATION**; 12" x 7-1/2"; lithographed with green roof; lettered "FLYER TOWN STATION NO. 97". $95

98 1923-26; **PASSENGER STATION**; 12" x 7-1/2"; lithographed with green roof; similar to 97; lettered "FLYER TOWN STATION NO. 97"; lighted inside with glazed windows. $95

99 1923-26; **PASSENGER STATION**; 12" x 7-1/2"; lithographed with green roof; similar to 97; lettered "FLYER TOWN STATION NO. 97"; lighted inside with glazed windows; two exterior lights. $125

100 1922-23; **PASSENGER STATION**; 12-3/4" long; imitation brick lithography with maroon roof; lithographed ticket agent in window. $225

101 1925-27; **PASSENGER STATION**; 13-1/2" x 8"; imitation brick lithography with red roof; lithographed ticket agent and passengers in windows. $200

102 1928-38; **PASSENGER STATION**; 12-1/4" x 8-1/2"; imitation brick lithography with green roof; brass dormer; lettered "CENTRAL STATION"; lighted inside; two exterior lights. $225

104 1925-37; **PASSENGER STATION**; 9-1/2" x 5-1/2"; imitation brick lithography with green or red roof, or imitation stucco and wood siding with green, red or orange roof; lettered "WAITING ROOM", "BAGGAGE ROOM", "TICKET OFFICE", etc.; similar to 96, but lighted. $95

105 1927; **PASSENGER STATION**; 12" x 7-1/2"; imitation brick and stucco lithography with maroon roof; similar to 97; lettered "FLYER TOWN STATION NO. 97"; two exterior lights. $125

107 1916-17; **SEMAPHORE**; stamped-steel with one signal arm. $25

107 1928-32; **PASSENGER STATION**; 12" x 7-1/2"; imitation brick and stucco lithography with orange or multicolored roof; dormer lithographed or with brass plate; similar to 97; lettered "FLYER TOWN STATION NO. 97"; two exterior lights. $175

108 1929-34; **SWITCH TOWER**; 11-5/16" x 9"; orange or maroon base; tan or green first story; cream second story; green or red roof with two contrasting chimneys; six operating knife switches on back. $1,000

110 1928; **PASSENGER STATION**; 29" x 17-3/4"; wood construction; red with white trim and green roof; landscaped base; brass plate lettered "UNION STATION AMERICAN FLYER LINES"; five lights inside. $2,000

201 1936; **BOXED SIGNAL SET**; contains 202, 206, 218, and 221. . . . .$95

202 1930-38; **BANJO SIGNAL**; red or green; lettered "R.R. DANGER". $10

203 1930-32; **FLASHING SIGNAL**; lettered "DANGER RAILROAD CROSSING". $10

205 Ca. 1910; **SEMAPHORE**; open girder pole; platform with railing and three smaller poles supporting three signal arms; three oil lamps. $135

205 1936; **BOXED EQUIPMENT SET**; contains 202, 206, 218, 221, 234, 242, 253, and 2005. . . . .$110

206 1920-32; **WARNING SIGN**; red; lettered "RAILROAD CROSSING DANGER AMERICAN FLYER R.R.". $10

206 Ca. 1949; **LAMPPOST**; open girder pole; mechanism to raise and lower large glass globe. **$100**

207 1910-32; **SEMAPHORE**; stamped-steel with one signal arm. **$25**

208 1916-31; **SEMAPHORE**; stamped-steel with two signal arms. **$15**

209 Ca. 1914; **SEMAPHORE**; open girder pole; platform with railing and two smaller poles supporting two signal arms; two oil lamps. **$100**

209 1920-39; **TELEGRAPH POLE**; 8-3/4" high; single or double crossarm. **$10**

210 1937-38; **BOXED EQUIPMENT SET**; contains 202, 206, 218, 221, and 234. . . . . **$95**

211 1931-32; **TRESTLE BRIDGE**; 28" long; wood, painted red. **$50**

213 1931-32; **TRESTLE BRIDGE**; 27-1/2" long; wood, painted red; lighted lithographed watchman's shed on top. **$55**

214 1934-38; **WATCHMAN'S TOWER**; 10" high; lithographed building on pole with ladder; bell below base of building; similar to 92; lighted. **$35**

215 1934-40; **WATER TOWER**; 9-1/2" high; red tank with four black legs and green or yellow ladder; similar to 2020. . **$15**

218 1931-32; **SEMAPHORE**; stamped-steel with two signal arms. **$15**

219 1931-32; **TELEGRAPH POLE**; 8-3/4" high. **$10**

220 1930-32; **STATION CLOCK**; 6-3/4" high; green; movable clock hands. **$15**

221 1930-38; **CROSSING GATE**. **$10**

222 1930-32; **BANJO SIGNAL**; red or green; lettered "R.R. DANGER". **$10**

223 1930-32; **FLASHING SIGNAL**; lettered "DANGER RAIL-ROAD CROSSING". **$10**

233 1933-39; **LAMPPOST**; 7-3/8" or 8-1/8" high; green or blue stamped-steel with crossarm and two lamps. **$25**

234 1933-38; **PASSENGER STATION**; 6" x 4"; lithographed with red roof; lettered "SUBURBAN WEST BOUND TRAINS"; similar to 93; lighted. **$50**

235 1933-35; **WATER TOWER SET**; 15-1/4" x 4"; rectangular base with 215 Water Tower, lighted lithographed shed and semaphore. **$75**

236 1933-35; **CROSSING SET**; 15-1/4" x 4"; red base with 206 Warning Sign, 214 Watchman's Tower and 2021 Crossing Gate; lighted. **$55**

237 1933-38; **PASSENGER AND FREIGHT STATIONS** on single base; 17-1/8" x 6-1/2"; 104 Passenger Station and 91 Freight Station buildings; lighted; semaphore and lamppost on base. **$200**

240 1933-34; **BOXED EQUIPMENT SET**; contains 218, 220, 221, 222, and six 240A. **$150**

240A 1933-34; **TELEGRAPH POLE**; 8-3/4" high; green. **$10**

246 1935; 15-1/2" long; **TUNNEL**; lighted. **$65**

250 1910-14; **PASSENGER STATION**; 14" x 10"; stamped-steel with embossed details; railing and telegraph pole on the roof; central building flanked by open platforms with curved roofs; German manufacture. **$350**

577 1939-42; **BILLBOARD** with circus poster; 8-3/8" x 2-3/4"; contains motorized whistle; sold for use with O Gauge, but usable with Standard Gauge. **$55**

579 1939-42; **LAMPPOST**; die-cast green pole; upright bulb with cap. **$20**

580 1939-42; **LAMPPOST**; die-cast silver pole; crossarm with two upright bulbs with caps. **$20**

2005 1935-39; **TRIANGLE LIGHT SIGNAL**; blue or green with manual switch. **$20**

2009 1920-26; **LAMPPOST**; 10-7/8" high; brass pole; cast-iron base and gooseneck; green; single bulb. **$65**

2010 1920-26; **LAMPPOST**; 13" high; brass pole; cast-iron base and double gooseneck; green; two bulbs. **$85**

2011 1922-34; **SEMAPHORE**; orange base and open girder construction pole; single arm. **$20**

2012 1922-34; **SEMAPHORE**; peacock-blue base and open girder construction pole with ladder; single arm; lighted. . . . **$25**

2013 1927-28; **LAMPPOST** (Lionel 57); 7-1/2" high; yellow die-cast base and brass pole; rectangular steel lamp housing with celluloid sides and street signs. **$90**

2014 1922-23; **SEMAPHORE**; open girder construction pole with ladder; single arm; automatic operation. **$25**

2017 1925-27; **WARNING SIGN** with ladder; lighted. . **$20**

2018 1925-26; **BLOCK SIGNAL** with ladder and two lights. **$25**

2020 1922-33; **WATER TOWER**; 9-1/2" high; red or orange tank; similar to 215 and Ives 89, and probably built by Flyer for Ives. $15

2021 1925-33; **CROSSING GATE**. $10

2022 1925-33; **CROSSING GATE**; lighted. $20

2029 1937-38; **BILLBOARD** with steam locomotive poster; 8-3/8" x 2-3/4"; contains motorized whistle; sold for use with O Gauge, but usable with Standard Gauge. **$55**

2040 1931-34; **SEMAPHORE**; die-cast base with one signal arm; lighted; may be wired for manual train stop operation. . . **$35**

2043 1930-39; **SEMAPHORE**; die-cast base; one signal arm; lighted; remote control train stop circuit. **$45**

2050 1928-34; **FLAGPOLE**; 23-1/2" high; white pole with gold-painted eagle on top, on large blue base with brass plates; American flag (can be moved up and down pole). **$60**

2109 1926-27; **LAMPPOST**; 9-5/8" high; maroon stamped-steel, one bulb. $20

2110 1926-27; **LAMPPOST**; 9-5/8" high; maroon or brown stamped-steel, two bulbs. $35

2209 1928-35; **LAMPPOST**; 10-1/8" high; blue, maroon or red stamped-steel, one bulb. $20

2210 1928-35; **LAMPPOST**; 11-1/2" high; green stamped-steel base, with green, gray and/or orange upper parts, two bulbs. $35

2216 1928-34; **WARNING SIGN**; die-cast base, diamond-shaped warning sign. $15

2222 1928-34, 1936-39; **CROSSING GATE**; red circular (1928-34) or green rectangular (1936-39) base; lighted. **$25**

2290 1928-33; **TELEGRAPH POLE**; cast base, cast crossarm and decorative cap; green. $20

2294 1928; **BOXED SET OF FOUR 2290 TELEGRAPH POLES** with cord to simulate wires. $110

4004 (2004) 1936; **CROSSING SET**; 9-1/2" x 5-1/2"; base with 214 Watchman's Tower and 2222 Crossing Gate; automatic operating bell. $45

4015 (2015) 1927-29; **SEMAPHORE**; stamped-steel with ladder and one lighted signal arm. **$25**

4016 (2016) 1927; **WARNING SIGN** with operating bell; green. $25

4032 (2032) 1926-29; **CROSSING GATE** (Lionel 77); green and maroon or black; automatic. **$35**

4033 (2033) 1926-29; **BLOCK SIGNAL** (Lionel 78); die-cast base and signal head; automatic train stop circuit. **$85**

4042 (2042) 1930-36; **CROSSING GATE**; die cast; lighted; automatic operation. $35

4116 (2116) 1928-36; **WARNING BELL**; stamped-steel; round (through 1935) or rectangular (1936) base; diamond-shaped warning sign; automatic operation. $35

4122 1928-32; **MAIL BAG PICKUP**; pole, hook, and three mail bags, for use with Standard Gauge baggage cars. $35

4206 (2206) 1928-34, 1936-39; **HIGHWAY WARNING FLASHER**; die-cast (through 1934) or stamped-steel (1936-39) base; crossarm with automatic alternate flashing red bulbs; 50% premium for early version. $25

4218 1925-27; **TRESTLE BRIDGE**; 56" long; wood, painted red. $85

4218 (2218) 1928-31, 1936; **BLOCK SIGNAL**; die-cast (through 1931) or steel (1936) base; steel target with red and green lights offset from pole; automatic operation with two special contact rail track sections. $45

4219 1925-33; **TRESTLE BRIDGE**; 56" long; wood, painted red; brass plates at ends. **$85**

4220 1928-33; **TRESTLE BRIDGE** with approach ramps; 70-1/2" long (bridge span 42"); red with brass plates; telegraph pole at each end, two warning lights on top at ends. $160

4230 1928-35; **WARNING SIGNAL**; rectangular base with circular sign enclosing flashing light. $45

4254 1928; **TUNNEL**; 19-1/2" long; composition, or papier-mâché. $35

4255 1925-27; **TUNNEL**; 18" long; composition or papier-mâché. $55

4256 1925-27; **TUNNEL**; 22" long; composition or papier-mâché. $65

4257 1928; **TUNNEL**; 23" long; composition or papier-mâché. $65

4266 1929-33; **TUNNEL**; 16" or 19" long; composition or papier-mâché; 50% premium for 19" version. $55

4267 1929-34; **TUNNEL**; 23" long; composition or papier-mâché; two telegraph poles. $175

4268 1934; **TUNNEL**; 18" long; composition or papier-mâché; lighted with two bulbs. $85

The Dorfan Company's train production enjoyed a relatively brief life span—just a decade from when the factory was established in 1924. Wide (Standard) Gauge production was even more fleeting, from 1926 through 1930. Nevertheless, the small enterprise produced a fair variety of accessories. While not as plentiful as those offered by the three larger American competitors, Dorfan's accessory lineup included all the essentials: stations, signals, bridges, crossing gates, lampposts, tunnels, and one magnificent item not offered by the others until years later: a huge operating stationary crane.

As is the case with American Flyer, some Dorfan accessories were supplied by the Lionel factory, which was located nearby. Others, such as the big signal light bridge (418 and 419), were clearly imitative of Lionel products, although they exhibit a distinctive Dorfan character. Dorfan accessories were produced and sold in fewer numbers than those of Lionel, Ives, and Flyer, and are therefore less plentiful to collectors. Some have suffered from the company's inadequate die casting technique in the early years. The signal bridge, for example, is usually found broken or badly warped.

Using Dorfan accessories on a layout imparts a nice variety, especially when they appear in conjunction with the other companies' products. The stations are distinctive, with some showing the German design heritage of the parent Fandor company. The mechanical components, such as die-cast control boxes, have a pleasing, bulky appearance.

Some items that required special track sections to operate were sold for use with both O Gauge and Standard Gauge trains, with similar but not identical catalog numbers. The accessories themselves were the same for either gauge, but were accompanied by the correct section of track (either O or Standard) according to the catalog number. The O Gauge numbers had three digits, while the Standard Gauge equivalent had the prefix "1" added. Thus the 402 semaphore sold for O Gauge use was labeled *1402* when intended to accompany Standard Gauge trains. Collectors who find an item with a three-digit number that is not listed below should consult the four-digit equivalent. Accessories limited to O Gauge applications, such as bridges and small tunnels, are omitted from the list below. Those made originally only for O Gauge, but adaptable to Standard Gauge, are included. Accessories operate manually, unless automatic action is specified.

70 1929-30; **MOTORIZED CRANE**; 10-1/4" x 10-1/4", 20" high; four green girders mounted on red die-cast base support tan rotating cab with red roof and green boom; motor and gear box on base rotates cab and raises and lowers hook; usually subject to casting deterioration. **$2,800**

319 1930; **TUNNEL**; 8-1/4" long, 8" high; composition. .**$45**

321 1927-30; **TUNNEL**; 11-1/4" long, 8-1/4" high; composition. **$45**

322 1927-30; **TUNNEL**; 12-1/4" long, 11-3/4" high; composition. **$55**

323 1927-30; **TUNNEL**; 14-1/4" long, 12" high; composition. **$65**

400 1925-30; **BLOCK SIGNAL**; red or blue; die cast, similar to 1401, but without train stop mechanism; lights change as train passes; sold only with O Gauge track sections, but can be adapted to Standard Gauge use. **$60**

405 1925-26; **SWITCH BOARD**; 6-1/2" high; control panel with six knife switches. **$50**

406 1926-27; **SWITCH TOWER**; 9-1/2" high; with 405 switch board; very scarce. **$300**

407 1926-30; **SWITCH BOARD**; 6-1/2" high; control panel with six knife switches; similar to 405. . . . .**$50**

413 1927-30; **BRIDGE**; 42" long; single span. **$85**

414 1929-30; **BRIDGE**; 56" long; two spans. **$145**

414-L 1929-30; **BRIDGE**; 56" long; two spans; four lighted corner posts; very scarce. **$300**

417 1930; **POSITION LIGHT SIGNAL**; pole with round target; five lights arranged like a plus sign; includes manual control box. **$100**

417 1927-29; **PASSENGER STATION**; 12-1/2" long; lithographed and lettered "NEWARK CENTRAL"; lighted. .**$250**

418 1930; **SIGNAL BRIDGE**; spans two tracks, with one 417 position light target and manual control box; scarce, and usually subject to casting deterioration. **$300**

418 1927-29; **PASSENGER STATION**; 7-1/2" long; lithographed and lettered "MONTCLAIR". **$85**

419 1930; **SIGNAL BRIDGE**; spans two tracks, with two 417 Position Light Targets and manual control box; scarce, and usually subject to casting deterioration. **$375**

Dorfan 414-L Bridge. (Carail Museum Collection)

419 1929; **PASSENGER STATION**; 7-1/2" long; lithographed and lighted. $85

420 1925-30; **LAMPPOST**; 7" high; yellow base with red or blue pole and gooseneck lamp. $25

425 1930; **PASSENGER STATION**; 8-3/4" long; cream or blue with red roof and clock face; flag on roof; lighted. **$165**

426 1930; **PASSENGER STATION**; 12-1/2" long; lithographed and lettered "NEWARK CENTRAL"; lighted; similar to 417.
. . . .$250

427 1930; **PASSENGER STATION**; 18-1/2" long; cream with red windows and two clock faces; flag on roof; lighted; very scarce.
. . . .$495

430 1925-30; **LAMPPOST**; 8-1/2" high; upright bulb. . . .$25

431 1930; **LAMPPOST**; 13-1/2" high; gooseneck; 110 volt with circuit breaker. $25

432 1930; **FLAGPOLE**; 20-1/2" high; American flag (can be moved up and down pole). $45

433 1930; **LAMPPOST**; 13-1/2" high; gooseneck; similar to 431; low voltage. $25

1401 (401) 1929-30; **BLOCK SIGNAL**; red or blue; die cast with manual train stop circuit; lighted. $65

1402 (402) 1929-30; **SEMAPHORE**; 12" high; green with one signal arm; die cast, with manual train stop circuit. $65

1406 (406) 1928-30; **BELL SIGNAL**; 8-1/2" high; automatic.
. . . .$45

1416 (416) 1927-30; **WARNING SIGNAL**; 8-1/2" high; lighted (two flashing red bulbs). $45

1421 (421) 1929-30; **CROSSING GATE**; rectangular base with warning sign and Lionel crossing gate; automatic. **$60**

Ives Wide (Standard) Gauge Accessories

Like the other three manufacturers, Ives produced the same accessories for Standard and O Gauge trains with little regard for scale. All items carried a single catalog number, except in the case of operating signals, where special track sections in either size were required to make them function. Operating accessories had three-digit numbers for Standard (Wide) Gauge and the suffix "-0" for O Gauge. For example, a Standard Gauge 331 Target Signal was labeled 331-0 for O Gauge.

Some Lionel accessories were cataloged after the 1928 bankruptcy, although in many cases the Ives catalog numbers were retained. Some items were assembled from both Ives and Lionel parts, but many Ives pieces were discontinued. The Ives factory in Bridgeport, Connecticut was closed in 1931, and Lionel moved the operation to their own Irvington plant, and used Lionel-designed accessories with three- and four-digit catalog numbers for the Ives line. Some of these items were continued as Lionel items after

the company abandoned the Ives brand name in 1933. (Some late production accessories had different numbers for Standard and O Gauge use, such as the No. 1883 [Standard Gauge] and 1884 [O Gauge] Warning Bells. In these listings, the O Gauge number is in parentheses.)

Some of the earliest Ives accessories were manufactured in Germany, and since they could accompany the large No. 1 Gauge trains as well as the O Gauge line, they are suitable for use with the Standard Gauge trains made in 1921 and later (excepting those with No. 1 Gauge track installed, such as bridges). The imported items had a distinctly European flavor. From about 1906, the company designed its own line of stations and signals, which more closely approximated the appearance of American railroads.

Ives produced some beautiful and impressive lithographed stations, rich in detail and brightly colored. The styles were changed periodically, and the same catalog numbers were often retained through a number of design changes. Lighted stations had open window areas, while some of the unlighted versions displayed extremely complex and realistic windows and doors. The most elaborate had simulated stained glass, figures of ticket agents and dispatchers, and small details like simulated clocks on interior walls. An impressive glass dome station platform was made to be placed next to the largest stations.

Ives made some items strictly for O Gauge, such as the smaller tunnels, and these are not included in the following list. All accessories operate manually, unless automatic action is specified.

72 *1928-30; **POLE WAGON**; steel; maroon, lettered "THE IVES R.R. CIRCUS"; came with circus set flatcars; reproduced by Harry A. Osisek.* *$200*

73 *1928-30; **ANIMAL CAGE WAGON**; steel; white; came with circus set flatcars; reproduced by Harry A. Osisek.* *$200*

74 *1928-30; **ANIMAL FIGURE SET**; came with circus set flatcars; reproduced by Harry A. Osisek.* *$200*

75 *1928-30; **RAMP**; steel; part of circus set, for loading wagons on flatcars; reproduced by Harry A. Osisek.* *$50*

80 1906 07; **SIX SCENIC PANELS**; 20" long, 15" high each; lithographed; value undetermined. . . .**(value not established)**

86 1906-30; **TELEGRAPH POLE.** $10

86 1906-08; **BOXED SET OF TWELVE TELEGRAPH POLES**, with string to simulate wire. $150

87 1923-30; **FLAGPOLE**; American flag (can be moved up and down pole); some 1930 versions with Lionel flagpole. . . .$65

89 1923-29; **WATER TOWER**; 9-1/2" high; orange tank with four black legs; similar to American Flyer 2020, and probably built by Flyer for Ives. $15

89 *1930; **WATER TOWER**; yellow tank with blue roof on Lionel 438 Signal Tower base; scarce; reproduced.* *$300*

95 1929-30; **TRUSS BRIDGE**; center span with two ramps. $85

96 1929-30; **TRUSS BRIDGE**; two center spans with two ramps. $125

97 1929-30; **TRUSS BRIDGE**; three center spans with two ramps. $125

99-2-3 1922-26; **TRUSS BRIDGE**; 58" long; two center spans with two ramps. $85

100 1930; **BOXED ACCESSORY SET**; contains crossing gate, warning sign, two signals, clock, and five telegraph poles. $85

100 1931-32; **TWO BRIDGE RAMPS** (Lionel 100); 28-1/4" long. $25

101 1931-32; **BRIDGE** (Lionel 101); 42-1/4" long; 104 span with two 100 ramps. $90

104 1931-32; **BRIDGE** (Lionel 104); 14" long. $40

106 1929-30; **TUNNEL**; 19" long; composition. $40

107 1929-30; **TUNNEL**; 23" long; composition. $45

111 1912-30; **WARNING SIGN**; (Lionel 068 in 1930). .$12

113 1906-28; **PASSENGER STATION**; 13-1/2" x 9-3/4" or 12-3/4" x 8"; various lithographed designs and colors. $200

113-3 1924-28; **PASSENGER STATION**; 12-3/4" x 8"; various lithographed designs and colors; lighted; similar to 113. .$200

114 1903-1911; **PASSENGER STATION**; cast-iron door and window frames; various sizes, lithographed designs and colors; earliest versions German. $550

114 1912-22; **PASSENGER STATION**; lithographed door and window frames; various sizes, lithographed designs and colors. $160

114 1923-1928; **PASSENGER STATION**; lithographed (early) and enameled. $75

115 1903-22; **FREIGHT STATION** with high base, most with ramp; various sizes, lithographed designs and colors; earliest versions German. $200

115 1923-28; **FREIGHT STATION** with low base, no ramp; various sizes, lithographed designs and colors. $90

116 1903-11; **PASSENGER STATION**; 18-1/2" x 8"; V-shaped bay window area; various lithographed designs and colors $725

116 1912-28; **PASSENGER STATION**; 18-1/2" x 8"; rectangular bay window area; various lithographed designs and colors $225

116-3 1926-28; **PASSENGER STATION**; 18-1/2" x 8"; rectangular bay window area; lithographed; four exterior lights. .$275

117 1903-23; **OPEN STATION PLATFORM**, designed to fit on both sides of track; eight poles; two benches on base; 100% premium for simulated iron decorations on roof. $195

117 1924-28; **OPEN STATION PLATFORM**, designed to fit on both sides of track; six poles; four benches on base. $195

118 1905-12; **OPEN STATION PLATFORM**; small base, single pole and roof. $175

119 1905-14; **OPEN STATION PLATFORM**; 11-1/2" x 3-1/2"; two poles. $175

120 1905-16; **OPEN STATION PLATFORM**; 18-1/2" x 4"; four poles; railings on base. **$195**

121 1905-09; **OPEN STATION PLATFORM** with elaborate multi-panel glass roof, designed to fit over track; eight poles; two benches on lithographed base. **$1,600**

121 1910-23; **OPEN STATION PLATFORM** with eight-panel glass roof, designed to fit over track; six poles; two benches on lithographed base. **$1,100**

121 1924-27; **OPEN STATION PLATFORM** with eight-panel glass roof, designed to fit over track; six poles; four benches on enameled base. **$700**

122 1905-23; 116 **STATION** with 121 glass dome and platform attached; 100% premium for early multi-panel glass roof. **$1,350**

123 1905-23; two 116 **STATIONS** with 121 glass dome (without poles) supported between them; 100% premium for early multi-panel glass roof. **$1,600**

200 1923-28; **FREIGHT STATION**; 9" long; lithographed. **$115**

200 1910-14; **POWER STATION**; simulated brick lithography, with external chimney; designed to cover batteries. **$750**

Ives 331 Target Signal (left) and 113 Station. (Carail Museum Collection)

201 1923-28; **PASSENGER STATION**; 9" x 6"; lithographed. **$115**

201-3 1923-28; **PASSENGER STATION**; 9" x 6"; lithographed, with two exterior lights. **$115**

201 1910-14; **POWER STATION**; simulated brick lithography, with external chimney; contains AC transformer; similar to 200. . . . .**$750**

202 1910-14; **POWER STATION**; simulated brick lithography, with external chimney; contains DC transformer; similar to 200. . . . .**$750**

203 1912-14; **POWER STATION**; simulated brick lithography, with external chimney; contains two AC transformers; similar to 200. . . . .**$750**

216 1923-27; **CROSSING GATE**; 14" long; with road and fences; hand operated. **$75**

220 1929-30; **FREIGHT STATION**; 9" long; lithographed; similar to 200. . . . .**$115**

221 1929-30; **PASSENGER STATION**; 9" x 6"; lithographed; similar to 201. . . . .**$115**

225 1929-30; **PASSENGER STATION** (Lionel 127); enameled white, with green base and red or orange roof and chimney; lighted. **$165**

226 1929-30; **PASSENGER STATION** (Lionel 126); enameled pale orange, with green base and red or green roof; lighted; 75% premium for maroon 1930 version. $195

228 1924-28; **OPEN STATION PLATFORM**; six poles; four benches on base; similar to 117, but without opening for track. $145

230 1929-30; **PASSENGER STATION** (Lionel 122); 14" long; embossed brick walls, white or yellow with red roof; lighted; some with external Ives 88 lamp over door. $295

230-3 1929-30; **PASSENGER STATION** (Lionel 122); 14" long; embossed brick walls, white or yellow with red roof; lighted; similar to 230 with two external Ives 88 lamps. $325

230-3X 1929; 230 **PASSENGER STATION** (Lionel 122) with 228 station platform. $475

230-3XX 1929; 230 **PASSENGER STATION** (Lionel 122) with two 228 station platforms. $595

250 1929-30; **HOUSE** (Lionel 184 Bungalow); 4-3/4" long; lighted. $100

251 1929-30; **HOUSE** (Lionel 189 Villa); 5-1/2" long; lighted. $200

252 1929-30; **HOUSE** (Lionel 191 Mansion); 7-1/8" long; lighted. $300

253 1929-30; **POWER STATION** (Lionel 435); 7-1/2" x 6"; cream with green base and orange trim, or ivory with brown base and red trim. $295

254 1929; **POWERHOUSE** (Lionel 436); 9-1/8" x 7-5/8". $350

255 1929-30; **SIGNAL TOWER** (Lionel 438); 10-1/2" high; two knife switches on back. $425

300 1922-30; **SEMAPHORE**; 14" high; cast-iron base with steel pole; one signal arm; lighted. $65

301 1922-30; **SEMAPHORE**; 15" high; cast-iron base with steel pole; two signal arms; lighted. $95

302 1922-28; **SEMAPHORE**; 13" high; cast-iron base with steel pole; two short poles on elevated platform; two signal arms; lighted. $125

306 1922-32; **LAMPPOST**; 12" high; cast-iron (through 1923) or die-cast base; one bulb. $65

307 1922-31; **LAMPPOST**; 12" high; cast-iron (to 1923) or die-cast base; two bulbs. $95

308 1928-30; **LAMPPOST**; 8-1/2" high; became Lionel 53 in 1931; one upright bulb. $65

310 1923-25; **SEMAPHORE**; 14" high; cast-iron base with steel pole; one signal arm; similar to 300; unlighted. $45

311 1923-25; **SEMAPHORE**; 15" high; cast-iron base with steel pole; two signal arms; similar to 301; unlighted. $65

312 1923-25; **SEMAPHORE**; 13" high; cast-iron base with steel pole; two short poles on elevated platform; two signal arms; similar to 302; unlighted. $125

330 1924-31; **SEMAPHORE**; 14" high; Lionel mechanism in 1930-31; lighted with automatic operation. $95

331 1924-30; **TARGET SIGNAL**; 3-1/2" diameter target; cast-iron base with steel pole; lighted with automatic operation. $95

332 1924-30; **WARNING BELL**; 8-1/2" high; cast-iron base with steel pole; automatic operation; Lionel bell in 1930. . . . . $95

333 1924-30; **BANJO SIGNAL**; cast-iron base with steel pole; banjo shaped target with flashing red light; 25% premium for 1930 version with Lionel bell mechanism. $95

334 1928-30; **CROSSING GATE**; 20-1/4" long base, with fence, shed, roadway and Lionel gate arm; automatic operation. $175

338 1924-30; **TELLTALE SIGNAL**; cast-iron base with steel pole; 24 cords (through 1928) or six or seven chains hanging from crossarm. $60

339 1928-30; **BUMPER** (Lionel 25); lighted. $25

340 1929-30; **BUMPER** (Lionel 23); lighted. $15

349 1929-30; **FLASHING SIGNAL** (Lionel 79); 11-1/2" high; two red bulbs with heat-activated circuit. $100

350 1929-30; **TRAFFIC SIGNAL** (Lionel 83); blinking bulb with heat-activated circuit. $100

600 1913-27; **LAMPPOST**; various styles with hanging bulb. $50

601 1913-27; **LAMPPOST**; various styles with two hanging bulbs. $75

630 1923-27; **ACCESSORY SET**; boxed set of 89 Water Tank, 107-S Semaphore, 107-D Semaphore and 111 Warning Sign. $275

631 1923-27; **ACCESSORY SET**; boxed set of 300 semaphore, 306 Lamppost and 87 Flagpole. $250

632 1923-27; **ACCESSORY SET**; boxed set of 87 Flagpole and 301 Lamppost. $165

1563 1931; **TELEGRAPH POLE**; similar to 86. . . . . . . $10

1856 1932; **BUMPER** (Lionel 23); lighted. $15

1858 1932; **BUMPER** (Lionel 25); lighted. $25

1861 1931-32; **TUNNEL**; 19" long; composition; similar to 106. . . . .**$40**

1862 1931-32; **TUNNEL**; 23" long; composition; similar to 107. . . . .**$45**

1863 1931-32; **TELLTALE SIGNAL**; similar to 338. . . **$60**

1864 1931-32; **SEMAPHORE**; 12" high; one signal arm; lighted; similar to 300. . . . .**$65**

1865 1922-30; **SEMAPHORE**; 14" high; two signal arms; lighted; similar to 301. . . . .**$95**

1866 1931-32; **FLAGPOLE**; 17" high; American flag (can be moved up and down pole); either Ives 87 or Lionel 89. . .**$65**

1867 1931-32; **SIGNAL TOWER** (Lionel 438); 12" high; two knife switches on back. **$425**

1868 1931-32; **HOUSE** (Lionel 191 Mansion); 7-1/8" long; lighted; similar to 252. . . . .**$300**

1869 1931-32; **HOUSE** (Lionel 189 Villa); 5-1/2" long; lighted; similar to 251. . . . . **$200**

1870 1931-32; **HOUSE** (Lionel 184 Bungalow); 4-3/4" long; lighted; similar to 250. . . . .**$100**

1871 1931-32; **PASSENGER STATION** (Lionel 126); enameled red, with green roof; lighted; similar to 226. . . . . **$195**

1872 1931-32**; PASSENGER STATION** (Lionel 127); enameled white, with red roof; lighted; similar to 225 . . . .**$165**

1873 1931-32; **PASSENGER STATION** (Lionel 122); 14" long; embossed brick walls, white or yellow with red roof; lighted; similar to 230. . . . .**$325**

1874 1931-32; **PASSENGER STATION** (Lionel 122); 14" long; embossed brick walls, white or yellow with red roof; lighted; similar to 230-3. . . . . **$325**

1875 1931-32; **OPEN FREIGHT PLATFORM** (Lionel 155); 18" long. **$350**

1876 1931-32; **POWER STATION** (Lionel 435); 7-1/2" x 6"; cream with green base and orange trim, or ivory with brown base and red trim; similar to 253. **$295**

1879 (1878) 1931-32; **CROSSING GATE** (Lionel 77); lighted and automatic. **$50**

1880 1931-32; **FLASHING HIGHWAY SIGNAL** (Lionel 79); 12" high; two red bulbs with heat-activated circuit; similar to 349. . . . .**$100**

1881 1931-32; **TRAFFIC SIGNAL** (Lionel 83); 6" high; blinking bulb with heat-activated circuit; similar to 350. . . . . **$100**

1882 1928-30; **LAMPPOST**; 8-1/2" high; became Lionel 53 in 1931; one upright bulb; similar to 308. . . . .**$65**

1883 (1884) 1931-32; **WARNING BELL**; 8-1/2" high; cast-iron base with steel pole; automatic operation; similar to 332 or Lionel 69. . . . .**$95**

1885 (1886) 1931; **TARGET SIGNAL**; 3-1/2" diameter target; cast-iron base with steel pole; lighted with automatic operation; similar to 331. . . . .**$95**

1901 1932; **CONTROL PANEL** (Lionel 439); red; six knife switches; lighted. **$125**

1902 1932; **FLOODLIGHT TOWER** (Lionel 92); green; lighted with two bulbs. **$195**

1903 (1904) 1932; **SEMAPHORE** (Lionel 80); 15" high; automatic. **$115**

1905 1932; **LAMPPOST** (Lionel 54); 9-1/2" high; gooseneck; lighted with two bulbs. **$75**

1906 1932; **BOXED STATION ACCESSORIES** (Lionel 163); contains dump, baggage, and two hand trucks. **$250**

1908 (1907) 1932; **TRAIN CONTROL SIGNAL** (Lionel 78); lighted; automatic. **$90**

Lionel Standard Gauge Accessories

The Lionel Corporation owes a fair share of its reputation to the clever and imaginative accessories that graced the line for most of the twentieth century. While the majority of the best known animated pieces date from the post-World War II period, the company introduced automatic operation as early as 1921 with a ringing bell signal. This was quickly followed by automatic block signals, semaphores, and crossing gates. Most fascinating of all was the 78 Train Control Signal, with a clever heat-activated circuit that automatically stopped a train, held it for fifteen or twenty seconds, and then restarted it, as if for a station stop.

The firm sold Ives stations in the early years, but soon introduced a line of distinctive painted depots that were plainer than competitive lithographed models from Ives and

American Flyer, but were handsome and substantially built. In the mid-1930s, these stations received a train stop mechanism. A variety of other buildings (houses, power stations, signal towers, and a roundhouse, for example) made it possible to build a convincing scenic setting on a layout.

The company's most important achievement in this area, one which gave birth to the most popular toy train accessory of all time, was the use of a solenoid to animate a human figure. The 45 Gateman first appeared in 1935, and although it was oversized even for Standard Gauge trains, it was an instant hit. Like many other Lionel items, it was made for use with O Gauge trains as well. Catalog numbers for O Gauge versions of any accessories that required special track sections contained the prefix "0" (e.g., 40 and 045 Gateman) until 1936. Thereafter the track sections were replaced by a pressure operated switch (called a "contactor") that could be used with either gauge, and a single catalog number with the suffix "N" (e.g., 45N) was used.

Lionel used the die casting process for some accessories, and suffered the same problems that plagued the other manufacturers: deterioration of the castings due to impurities in the alloy. However, since many Lionel accessories enjoyed a long production life, the company had improved this material by the late 1930s, and many sound examples can be found. In addition, most of the cast parts have been reproduced for use by restorers.

Lionel provided well for the imaginary people who inhabited toy train layouts in the 1920s and 1930s, with three different sizes of houses, a diner, and tunnels with tiny houses mounted on the sides and served by embossed and painted roads. The individual houses were beautiful but diminutive, about half size for O Gauge and only about a quarter of the size that would have been appropriate for Standard Gauge trains. However, toy train buyers in those years were little concerned with matters of scale, and huge numbers were sold. They were also mounted on landscaped boards called "scenic plots," complete with lawns, trees and hedges.

Rounding out the line were lampposts, towers, and station accessories. In the latter 1930s, motorized items were introduced, including coal and log loaders, a magnetic crane and an operating lift bridge. These items were scaled for O Gauge use, however, and are not listed in this chapter. Also omitted are other items sized and catalogued specifically for the smaller line of trains. However, there are some late 1930s items that, although intended for O Gauge, are so oversized as to be ideal for Standard Gauge. These include, for example the 153 Block Signal and 154 Highway Warning Flasher, and are included below. All accessories operate manually, unless automatic action is specified.

24 1906-07; **PASSENGER STATION**; 11" x 7-1/2"; simulated ivory brick sides, red and black base, and maroon bay window; probably German. . . . . **(value not established)**

25 1906-07; **OPEN STATION PLATFORM**; 11" x 11"; designed to fit on both sides of track; includes one human figure; probably German. . . . . **(value not established)**

26 1906-07; **FOOT BRIDGE**; 24" long, 17" high; steel steps and elevated walkway to span track; probably German. . . . .**(value not established)**

27 1908-14; **PASSENGER STATION** (Ives 116); 21" x 9"; lithographed. . . . .**(value not established)**

28 1908-14; **DOUBLE PASSENGER STATION**; two 27 Stations supporting glass dome; similar to Ives 123; probably made by Ives. . . . .**(value not established)**

32 1909-18; **TWELVE HUMAN FIGURES**; seated to fit over pins in trolley seats. **$150**

35 1940-42, postwar; **LAMPPOST**; 6-1/8" high; die-cast gray or aluminum. **$40**

45 (045, 45N) 1935-42; **GATEMAN**; 7" x 5-3/4"; ivory or white building with red roof and door on green base; warning sign; animated figure with lantern; automatic. **$75**

49 1937-39; **AIRPORT**; 58" diameter; round two-piece lithographed cardboard mat. **$85**

50 1936; **REMOTE CONTROL AIRPLANE**; 12" wingspan; red steel aircraft suspended on wire from 30" high pylon; motorized. **$350**

51 1936, 1938; **AIRPORT**; square, two-piece lithographed heavy paper mat. **$75**

52 1933-41; **LAMPPOST**; 10-1/2" high; die-cast painted aluminum. **$55**

53 1931-42; **LAMPPOST**; 8-1/2" high; various colors; Ives casting. **$40**

54 1929-35; **LAMPPOST**; 9-1/2" high; cast-iron and steel gooseneck with two bulbs; maroon, green or brown. **$65**

55 1937-39; **REMOTE CONTROL AIRPLANE**; similar to 50, with aluminum painted wing and stabilizer. **$450**

56 1924-42, postwar; LAMPPOST; 7-3/4" high; die-cast base with steel pole and steel-capped bulb enclosure; various colors; 25% premium for copper finish; reproduced by Mike's Train House. $60

57 1922-42; LAMPPOST; 7-1/2" high; orange or yellow; die-cast base with steel pole and large steel-capped bulb enclosure lettered "BROADWAY" and "MAIN STREET"; 50% premium for other street names; reproduced by Mike's Train House. $60

An Ives 1134 locomotive and tender pass Lionel's most famous accessory: the 45 Gateman. To its left is a 77 Crossing Gate.

58 1922-42, postwar; **LAMPPOST**; 7-3/8" high; die cast and steel; gooseneck; various colors **$40**

59 *1920-36; LAMPPOST; 8-11/16" or 8-15/16" high; cast iron and steel; gooseneck; various colors; reproduced by Mike's Train House.* *$60*

60 (060) 1920-28; **TELEGRAPH POLE**; 8-3/4" high; steel; various colors. **$25**

61 1914-32, 1934-36; **LAMPPOST**; 12-3/4" high; cast iron and steel; gooseneck; various colors. **$70**

62 1920-32; **SEMAPHORE**; 8-3/4" high; green girder post; one signal arm; unlighted. **$30**

63 1915-21; **SEMAPHORE**; 14" high; black base, orange pole; one signal arm; unlighted. **$35**

63 1933-42; **LAMPPOST**; 12-3/4" high; die cast with crossarm and two upright bulbs; painted aluminum. **$150**

64 1915-21; **SEMAPHORE**; 14" high; two signal arms; similar to 63. . . . . **$45**

64 *1940-42, postwar; LAMPPOST; 6-3/4" high; green die cast and steel with offset arm and hanging bulb; reproduced by Mike's Train House.* *$55*

65 1915-26; **SEMAPHORE**; 14" high; one signal arm; lighted; similar to 63. . . . . **$55**

No. 53 Lamppost, in front of a 437 Signal Tower. A 280 Bridge is visible at right.

66 1915-26; **SEMAPHORE**; 14" high; two signal arms; lighted; similar to 64. . . . . **$55**

67 1915-32; **LAMPPOST**; 13" high; green cast-iron and steel; gooseneck. **$90**

68 (068) 1920-39; **WARNING SIGN**; 8-7/8" high; brass diamond-shaped sign on open girder post; various colors. **$12**

Lionel 060 Telegraph Posts (foreground), 84 Semaphore (left background, restored), 129 Terrace with 124 Station.

Left to right: Lionel 78 Train Control Block Signal, 76 Block Signal, 83 Traffic Signal, 69 Bell Signal, 87 Crossing Signal. (Carail Museum Collection)

69 (069, 69N) 1921-42; **BELL SIGNAL**; 8-1/2" high; open girder post, diamond-shaped warning sign and bell mechanism; automatic. **$30**

70 1921-32; **BOXED ACCESSORY SET**; contains 59, two 62, and 68. . . . . **$95**

71 (071) 1921-31; **BOXED TELEGRAPH POLE SET**; contains six 60 or 060. . . . .**$125**

76 (076) 1923-28; **BLOCK SIGNAL**; 8-3/4" high; white, mojave or green open girder post with narrow crossarm and two signal lights; automatic. **$35**

76 1939-42; **WARNING BELL SHACK**; 7" x 5-3/4"; white building on red base with orange roof; warning sign on post; automatic bell mechanism. **$160**

77 (077, 77N) 1923-39; **CROSSING GATE**; 11" long arm; steel base; with or without light in arm; automatic. **$35**

78 (078) 1924-32; **TRAIN CONTROL BLOCK SIGNAL**; 10-1/4" high; die-cast base and light housing on steel pole; two bulbs; automatic heat-activated train stop circuit. **$75**

79 1928-40; **FLASHING HIGHWAY SIGNAL**; 11-1/2" high; white, cream, ivory, or aluminum die-cast base and light sockets on steel pole; heat-activated flasher circuit; red light under base. **$75**

80 (080, 80N) 1926-42; **SEMAPHORE**; 15" high; terra cotta, green, orange, red or black die-cast base with steel pole; one signal arm. **$75**

82 (082, 82N) 1927-42; **SEMAPHORE**; 14-3/4" high; peacock-blue or green die-cast base with steel pole; one signal arm; automatic heat-activated train stop circuit. **$80**

83 1927-42; **TRAFFIC SIGNAL**; 6-1/4" high; die cast; cream housing on mojave or red base and white or tan diver's helmet-shaped lamp housing with blinking light inside. **$75**

Lionel 79 Flashing Highway Signal (right) and 126 Station (left, restored).

84 (084) 1927-32; **SEMAPHORE**; 15" high; green or maroon die-cast base with steel pole; one signal arm. **$75**

85 1929-42; **TELEGRAPH POLE**; 9" high; steel; orange or aluminum. **$30**

86 1929-42; **BOXED TELEGRAPH POLE SET**; contains six 85 pole. **$195**

87 1927-42; **CROSSING SIGNAL**; 6-3/4" high; die cast; orange, green, or cream housing on orange, mojave or dark green base, with ivory or white drum-shaped lamp housing with blinking light inside. **$75**

89 1923-34; **FLAGPOLE**; 14" high; ivory or white pole on steel base; American flag (can be moved up and down pole). . .**$45**

90 1927-42; **FLAGPOLE**; 14-3/4" high; ivory pole on steel base with landscaped plot; American flag (can be moved up and down pole). **$65**

92 *1931-42;* **FLOODLIGHT TOWER**; *20-1/4" high; terra cotta and green or red and aluminum-painted open girder tower; two lamp housings; reproduced by Williams Reproductions and Mike's Train House.* *$200*

94 *1932-42;* **HIGH-TENSION TOWER**; *24" high; open girder tower with three crossarms; terra cotta base with gray or mojave tower, or red base with gray or aluminum tower; reproduced by Williams Reproductions and Mike's Train House.* *$245*

Lionel 92 Floodlight Tower (center), 200 Turntable (lower left), 436 Power Station (right background), 91 Circuit Breaker (right foreground), 58 Lamppost (extreme right), 1835E Locomotive and 1835W Tender (background).

Lionel 83 Traffic Signal (left) and 56 Lamppost. (MTH reproduction)

99 (099, 99N) 1932-42; **TRAIN CONTROL BLOCK SIGNAL**; 12" high; die-cast base and light housing on steel pole; red, amber, and green lights in black target; automatic heat-activated train stop circuit. **$95**

100 1920-31; **TWO BRIDGE RAMPS**; 14" x 5-1/2" each; steel; cream with gray, black, or speckled roadbed. **$25**

101 1920-31; **BRIDGE**; 42" long; 104 Bridge with pair of 100 Ramps. **$65**

102 1920-31; **BRIDGE**; 56" long; two 104 Bridges with pair of 100 Ramps. **$105**

103 1920-31; **BRIDGE**; 70" long; three 104 Bridges with pair of 100 Ramps. **$145**

104 1920-31; **BRIDGE**; 14" x 6-1/2"; center span; steel; green and cream with gray, black, or speckled roadbed. **$40**

104 1909-14; **TUNNEL**; 13" x 9"; papier-mâché. **$85**

109 1913; **TUNNEL**; 25" x 14"; papier-mâché. **$95**

112 1931-34; **PASSENGER STATION**; 13-1/2" x 9-1/4"; ivory or beige embossed block walls on mojave, terra cotta, or red base, with skylight and two clock faces; lighted. **$225**

113 1931-34; **PASSENGER STATION**; 13-1/2" x 9-1/4"; 112 with two exterior light fixtures flanking doors. **$275**

114 1931-34; **PASSENGER STATION**; 19-1/2" x 9-1/4"; long version of 113; two skylights. **$1,050**

115 *1935-42, postwar;* **PASSENGER STATION**; *13-1/2" x 9-1/4"; 113 with ivory or beige walls and red base; automatic train stop device; reproduced by Lionel Trains, Inc.* *$275*

Four 94 High Tension Towers surrounding five Lionel 444 Roundhouse sections (reproductions); various other accessories. (Carail Museum Collection)

Lionel 104 Bridge Center Span (foreground) and 280 Bridge.

116 *1935-42; PASSENGER STATION; 19-1/2" x 9-1/4"; 114 with cream or beige walls and mojave or red base; automatic train stop device; reproduced by T-Reproductions and Lionel Trains, Inc.* *$1,100*

117 1935-42; **PASSENGER STATION**; 115 without exterior light fixtures. **$275**

119 1915-42; **TUNNEL**; 16" long (papier-mâché) or 12" x 9" (steel). **$75**

119L 1927-33; **TUNNEL**; 12" x 9"; steel; lighted. **$75**

120 1915-27; **TUNNEL**; 20" long (papier-mâché) or 17" x 12" (steel). **$85**

120L 1927-42; **TUNNEL**; 17" x 12"; steel; lighted by two bulbs. **$95**

121 1908-17; **PASSENGER STATION** (Ives 113); lithographed. . . . .**(value not established)**

121 1917-20; **PASSENGER STATION**; 13-1/2" x 9"; embossed wood and composition board; made by Schoenhut; lighted version catalogued 121X; rare. **$650**

121 1920-26; **PASSENGER STATION**; 13-1/2" x 9"; steel; brown walls with gray or speckled base and green roof; lettered "LIONEL CITY"; unlighted. **$180**

Lionel 116 (left) and 113 Stations. (Carail Museum Collection)

122 1920-31; **PASSENGER STATION**; similar to 121; lighted. **$180**

123 1920-23; **PASSENGER STATION**; 121 with 110 volt interior light. **$180**

124 1920-30, 1933-36; **PASSENGER STATION**; similar to 121; lighted plus two exterior light fixtures. **$200**

125 1923-25; **PASSENGER STATION**; 10" x 7"; simulated red brick lithographed walls on mojave base with green roof; lettered "LIONELVILLE"; unlighted. **$185**

126 *1923-36; PASSENGER STATION; lithographed or enameled 125; various colors; lighted; reproduced by Lionel Trains, Inc.* *$225*

Lionel's 117 Station contained the automatic train control circuit, but lacked outside lamp brackets and was therefore slightly less expensive than the similar 115.

127 1923-36; **PASSENGER STATION**; 8-1/2" x 4-3/8"; various colors; lettered "LIONELTOWN"; lighted. **$145**

128 1928-42; **PASSENGER STATION** and Terrace; 129 Terrace with 121, 122, 124, 112, 113, or 115 station. **$1,200**

129 *1928-42; TERRACE; 31-1/2" x 18"; elliptical mojave or cream steel structure with landscaped plots; recessed to fit 121, 122, 124, 112, 113, or 115 Station; reproduced by T-Reproductions in two sizes, to fit 115 or 116 Stations.* *$1,000*

134 1937-42; **PASSENGER STATION**; 124 with automatic train stop circuit; tan walls on green base with red roof. . . . **$275**

136 1937-42; **PASSENGER STATION**; 126 with automatic train stop circuit; cream or tan walls on green base with red roof. **$250**

137 1937-42, postwar; **PASSENGER STATION**; 127 with automatic train stop circuit; white or ivory walls on tan or cream base with red roof. **$175**

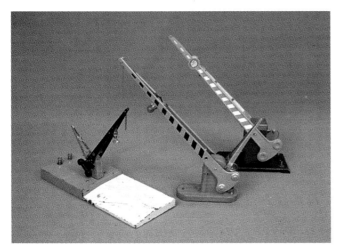

Lionel Crossing Gates, left to right: 46, 152, 77. The two larger models were sold for use with both O and Standard Gauge trains, but are actually much too large to look realistic with the former. Only the smaller 46 is closely scaled for O Gauge.

140L 1927-32; **TUNNEL**; 37" x 24-1/2"; steel; 90-degree curve; lighted by two bulbs. **$395**

152 1940-42; **CROSSING GATE**; 10-1/2" long arm; red die-cast base; light below arm; automatic. **$35**

153 1940-42, postwar; **BLOCK SIGNAL**; 9" high; green die-cast base with red and green bulbs in black target; automatic. .**$30**

154 1940-42, postwar; **FLASHING HIGHWAY SIGNAL**; 8-3/8" high; black die-cast base, and crossarm with two flashing red bulbs; automatic; 100% premium for orange base. **$30**

155 *1930-42; OPEN FREIGHT PLATFORM; 18" x 8-1/4"; yellow, terra cotta, green, and maroon, or white, red, and gray; two light fixtures under roof; reproduced by Mike's Train House.* *$325*

157 *1930-42; HAND TRUCK; 3-3/4" long; red die-cast freight station accessory; reproduced by Mike's Train House.* . . .*$30*

161 *1930-42; BAGGAGE TRUCK; 4-1/2" long; green die-cast freight station accessory; reproduced by Mike's Train House.* *$50*

162 *1930-42; DUMP TRUCK; 4-1/2" long; blue and orange die-cast freight station accessory; reproduced by Mike's Train House.* *$50*

163 *1930-42; BOXED FREIGHT STATION ACCESSORY SET; contains two 157, 161, 162; reproduced by Mike's Train House.* *$30*

184 *1923-42; BUNGALOW; 4-3/4" x 2-3/4"; lithographed or enameled steel; various colors; lighted; reproduced by Frank Bowers.* *$95*

185 *1923-24; BUNGALOW; 4-3/4" x 2-3/4"; unlighted 184.* *$95*

186 *1923-32; BOXED BUNGALOW SET; five 184.* *$495*

187 *1923-24; BOXED BUNGALOW SET; five 185.* *$495*

189 *1923-42; VILLA; 5-3/8" x 4-7/8"; enameled steel; various colors; lighted; reproduced by Frank Bowers.* *$200*

191 *1923-42; VILLA (MANSION); 7-1/8" x 5"; enameled steel with "sun porch" extension; various colors; lighted; reproduced by Frank Bowers.* *$275*

192 1923-32; **BOXED VILLA SET**; two 184, one 189, one 191. . . . .*$1,200*

194 1927-29; **BOXED ACCESSORY SET**; contains 69, 76, 77, 78, 80 and five track sections. **$400**

195 *1927-30; SCENIC PLOT; 22" x 19"; plywood landscaped platform; contains two 56, 90, 184, 189, 191; platform reproduced by Ron Morris.* *$750*

Lionel 128 Passenger Station and Terrace (124 model station).

Left to right: Lionel 161 Baggage Truck (green), two 157 Hand Trucks (red), 208 Tool Set, 209 Barrels. (Carail Museum Collection)

Lionel 162 Dump Trucks (foreground) and 205 LCL Freight Containers. (Carail Museum Collection)

196 1927; **BOXED ACCESSORY SET**; contains two 58, six 60, 62, 68, 127. . . . .**$345**

200 1928-33; **TURNTABLE**; 17" in diameter; track section on rotating disk; eight tracks to attach to sidings; green or black base with red, black, or mojave disk; reproduced by T-Reproductions and Mike's Train House. **$160**

205 1930-38; **BOXED SET OF THREE LCL FREIGHT CONTAINERS**; 3-1/2" x 3" x 4"; dark green steel box with hinged door; reproduced by Lyle Cain. **$295**

208 1928-42; **TOOL SET**; six miniature tools in hinged box; reproduced by Mike's Train House. **$85**

209 (0209) 1930-42; **BOXED SET OF FOUR OR SIX HOLLOW WOODEN BARRELS**; barrels may be opened; reproduced. **$15**

280 1931-42; **BRIDGE**; 14" long; green, gray, or red steel open girders with pedestrian walkway. **$40**

281 1931-40; **BOXED BRIDGE SET**; 28" long; two 280. . . . .**$95**

282 1931-40; **BOXED BRIDGE SET**; 42" long; three 280. . . . .**$155**

300 1928-42; **HELLGATE BRIDGE**; 28-3/4" x 11"; steel; open girder span between two towers with arches and windows; green, orange, and cream or green, orange, and terra cotta; 15% premium for red, ivory, and aluminum; reproduced by T-Reproductions and Mike's Train House. **$850**

308 1940-42, postwar; **BOXED SIGNS**; five assorted warning signs. **$45**

435 1926-38; **POWER STATION**; 7-1/2" x 6"; gray or green base, with orange, terra cotta, or cream walls; contrasting trim; built to enclose small transformer; reproduced by Mike's Train House. **$200**

436 1926-37; **POWER STATION**; 9-1/8" x 7-5/8"; gray or green base, terra cotta or cream walls, with contrasting trim; built to enclose large transformer; reproduced by Mike's Train House. **$200**

437 1926-37; **SIGNAL TOWER**; 10-1/4" x 8-3/8"; various color combinations; bay window on second story; six knife switches on back; reproduced by T-Reproductions, Mike's Train House, and Lionel Trains, Inc. **$350**

Lionel 184 and 185 Bungalows were made in many different color combinations, some enameled and others with highly detailed lithography, simulating bricks and foliage.

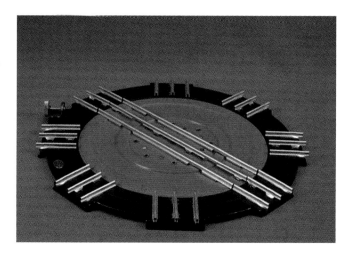

Lionel 200 Turntable, restored.

438 1927-39; **SIGNAL TOWER**; 6" x 4-3/4", 12" high; various color combinations; building elevated on tower; with or without two knife switches on back; reproduced by T-Reproductions and Mike's Train House. **$350**

439 1932-42; **PANEL BOARD**; 8-3/16" high, 7-1/8" high; six knife switches and area for mounting two switch control levers. **$100**

Lionel 440 Signal Bridge and 126 Station (restored);
Ives and American Flyer locomotives and rolling stock.

438 Signal Towers, late colors (left) and early colors (back view
showing knife switches). (Carail Museum Collection)

440 (0440, 440N) *1932-42;* **SIGNAL BRIDGE***; die-cast terra
cotta bases with mojave girder bridge and maroon walkway, or red
bases and walkway with aluminum-painted or gray girder bridge;
spans two tracks; two black die-cast position lights with five bulbs
each; includes 440C Control Panel; reproduced by Lionel Trains,
Inc.* *$300*

440C *1932-42;* **PANEL BOARD***, for operating 440 Signal
Bridge; 8-3/16" high; four knife switches, two signal control levers
and area for mounting two switch control levers; reprduced by
Lionel Trains, Inc.* *$100*

Lionel 300 Hellgate Bridge (early colors).
(Carail Museum Collection)

441 *1932-36;* **WEIGH STATION***; 29-1/2" x 9-1/2"; green base
with track section on moving platform; cream building enclosing
operating scale with miniature weights; rarely found operable due
to casting deterioration.* *$750*

442 *1938-42;* **DINER***; 10-5/8" x 5-1/2"; 610 O Gauge coach on
landscaped platform; cream or ivory with red roof; platform reproduced by Ron Morris.* *$200*

444 *1932-35;* **ROUNDHOUSE***; 24" x 8-3/4", widening to rear;
terra cotta with green roof and contrasting trim; multiple sections
could be linked; reproduced by T-Reproductions and Mike's Train
House; scarce.* *$2,000*

550 *1932-36;* **BOXED SET OF HUMAN FIGURES***; contains
551, 552, 553, 554, 555, 556; reproduced by Mike's Train House
and others.* *$195*

551 *1932-36;* **ENGINEER FIGURE***; 3" high; reproduced by
Mike's Train House, others.* *$25*

552 *1932-36;* **CONDUCTOR FIGURE***; 3" high; reproduced by
Mike's Train House, others.* *$25*

553 *1932-36;* **PORTER FIGURE***; 3" high; reproduced by Mike's
Train House, others.* *$25*

554 *1932-36;* **MALE FIGURE***; 3" high; reproduced by Mike's
Train House, others.* *$25*

555 *1932-36;* **FEMALE FIGURE***; 3" high; reproduced by Mike's
Train House, and others.* *$25*

556 *1932-36;* **RED CAP FIGURE***; 3" high; reproduced by Mike's
Train House, others.* *$25*

812T 1930-41; **BOXED SET OF THREE MINIATURE
TOOLS.** *$30*

840 *1928-40;* **POWER STATION***; 26" x 21-1/2"; cream or white
walls with contrasting trim; elevated base and three tall smoke-
stacks; built to enclose two large transformers; reproduced by T-
Reproductions and Mike's Train House.* *$200*

910 *1932-42;* **GROVE OF TREES***; 16" x 8"; landscaped platform; reproduced by Ron Morris.* *$750*

Lionel 436 Power Station, restored. This accessory was sold for use with either O or Standard Gauge trains, and is shown here amid O Gauge items. The same building in a Standard Gauge setting appears in a photo of a 92 Floodlight Tower earlier in this chapter (pg. 191).

Lionel 444 Roundhouse, flanked by 191 Villa (left) and 189 Villa. (Carail Museum Collection)

Lionel 912 Scenic Plot with 189 Villa; scenic plots came with a variety of hand-applied landscaping materials, and therefore differ significantly in appearance. (Carail Museum Collection)

Lionel 440C Control Panel (left) and 439 Panel Board, each with two switch controls mounted below knife switches. (Carail Museum Collection)

Lionel 441 Weigh Station; 23 bumper (left); 300 Hellgate Bridge (late colors, background). (Carail Museum Collection)

Lionel 442 Diner (left foreground), 83 Traffic Signal (right), 79 Flashing Highway Signal (behind 83 signal), plus various Scenic Park sections containing 184 bungalows and 189 and 191 villas. (Carail Museum Collection)

Lionel 550 Figure Set. (Carail Museum Collection)

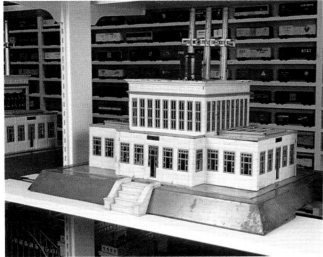

Lionel 840 Power Station. (Carail Museum Collection)

Lionel 917 Scenic Hillside, two 155 Freight Platforms, and 440 Signal Bridge (temporarily out of place, awaiting permanent installation). (Carail Museum Collection)

Lionel's 1045 Flagman is shown connected to a section of track with a short piece of insulated rail (left). When a train's wheels ground this rail, they complete a momentary circuit to a solenoid connected to the flagman's arm, making it wave. Most 1045 figures were molded in blue Bakelite, as shown at right. The figure on the accessory base has a dark brown uniform, but his swinging arm is blue.

911 *1932-42;* **SCENIC PLOT***; 16" x 8"; landscaped platform; contains 191; platform reproduced by Ron Morris. $375*

912 *1932-42;* **SCENIC PLOT***; 16" x 8"; landscaped platform; contains 189; platform reproduced by Ron Morris. $350*

913 *1932-42;* **SCENIC PLOT***; 16" x 8"; landscaped platform; contains 184; platform reproduced by Ron Morris. $325*

914 *1932-36;* **SCENIC PLOT***; 16" x 8-1/2"; landscaped platform; simulates a park, with cream urn; reproduced by Ron Morris. $225*

915 *1932-35;* **TUNNEL***; 60" or 65" x 28-1/2"; wood and composition; 90-degree curve; reproduced by Ron Morris. $275*

917 *1932-36;* **SCENIC HILLSIDE***; 34" x 15"; landscaped platform with two very small houses; reproduced by Ron Morris. $350*

918 *1932-36;* **SCENIC HILLSIDE***; 30" x 10"; landscaped platform with one very small house; reproduced by Ron Morris. $325*

920 *1932-33;* **SCENIC PLOT***; 57" x 31-1/2"; two plywood landscaped platforms; contains two 184, 189, 191, either 910 or 914, and 922; platform reproduced by Ron Morris. $2,000*

921 *1932-33;* **SCENIC PLOT***; 85" x 31-1/2"; three plywood landscaped platforms (920 plus 921C); platform reproduced by Ron Morris. $3,000*

921C *1932-33;* **SCENIC PLOT***; 28" x 31-1/2"; plywood landscaped platform; contains 184, 189, 191, either 910 or 914, and 922; platform reproduced by Ron Morris. $1,000*

922 *1932-36;* **SCENIC PLOT***; 13" x 3-3/4"; landscaped platform with 56 lamppost; reproduced by Ron Morris. $195*

923 *1933-42;* **TUNNEL***; 40" by 23"; wood and composition; 90-degree curve; reproduced by Ron Morris. $225*

927 *1937-42;* **SCENIC PLOT***; 16" x 8-1/2"; landscaped platform with flagpole; reproduced by Ron Morris. $175*

1045 *1938-42, postwar;* **FLAGMAN***; 4" x 4"; blue 4-1/4" figure with movable arm that waves flag; red steel base; automatic; 100% premium for brown figure. $40*

GLOSSARY

Some of the terms used in this book may be unfamiliar to persons who are new to either model railroading or to toy collecting. The following definitions (in layman's terms) are provided to assist in visualizing the descriptions of various pieces of railroad equipment.

CATENARY: A system of electric power lines suspended above railroad tracks to allow electric locomotives to receive current through their pantographs (which see).

CLERESTORY: The raised center section of a passenger car roof, normally containing small windows for ventilation.

COMBINE OR COMBINATION CAR: A coach containing seats for passengers in the rear section and a compartment for baggage at the forward end.

DIAPHRAGM: An enclosure connecting the end doors of two passenger cars, to allow safe travel between the cars.

DISTANT-CONTROL: Lionel's catalog description for a train equipped with a remote control reverse unit.

DRIVE WHEELS: The wheels of a steam locomotive which are connected to the pistons by drive rods, and which are rotated by steam power; the wheels of an electric or diesel-electric locomotive that are rotated by the electric motors.

ELECTRIC LOCOMOTIVE: Any of several locomotive designs powered by direct current electric motors. The electric current is drawn either from overhead power lines (see catenary and pantograph below) or from a third rail. Locomotives with a plain rectangular cab are called "Box Cab Electric" types.

ELECTRIC-OUTLINE LOCOMOTIVE: The appearance of a prototype electric-powered locomotive, commonly used in urban areas where coal burning steam locomotives were prohibited. The toy versions are normally powered by electricity, although Ives marketed a few clockwork electric-outline locomotives. The modifier "outline," when attached to the word "electric," refers to appearance, rather than the actual means of propulsion, although almost all of these toys were electric powered.

E-UNIT: Lionel's catalog description of its remote control reverse device; a common description among toy train collectors for any remote control reverse device.

HERALD: The logo of a railroad or business when painted on a piece of railroad rolling stock.

JOURNAL BOX: The area of a truck (see below) where the ends of a car's axles rotate in their bearings.

KNUCKLE COUPLER: The device by which two pieces of railroad equipment are hitched together, so named because they resemble the bent knuckles of two interlocked hands.

OBSERVATION CAR: The last car in a passenger train, with an open platform at the rear; this platform is sometimes fitted with seats for passengers.

PANTOGRAPH: A hinged, diamond-shaped apparatus on top of an electric locomotive, which can be raised to contact overhead catenary lines (which see) to gather electric current.

PICKUP ROLLER: A metal cylinder mounted beneath a toy or model locomotive or lighted car, used to collect electric current from the third (middle) rail.

GLOSSARY

PILOT: The front of the locomotive, analogous to the bumper on an automobile, and often called a "cowcatcher" on a steam locomotive.

PILOT WHEELS: Pairs or multiple pairs of wheels that are smaller than drive wheels and unpowered, mounted at the front of a locomotive to help support its forward end and to help guide it through curves and turnouts.

PROTOTYPE: In model railroading, the real thing; e.g., a genuine locomotive after which a toy locomotive is modeled.

PULLMAN: A passenger car fitted with sleeping berths, named for the Pullman Car Company which originated the design, and therefore usually capitalized.

STEAM-OUTLINE LOCOMOTIVE: The traditional appearance of a typical steam-powered locomotive, the toy versions of which are normally powered by electricity or clockwork motors. The modifier "outline," when attached to the word "steam," refers to appearance, rather than the actual means of propulsion.

TENDER: A specialized car coupled behind a steam locomotive that carries water for the boiler and either coal, wood or oil to fuel the firebox.

TINPLATE: The common term for antique stamped steel toy trains, although also used for plastic trains which are meant for operation on toy train track (as opposed to scale-type track); refers to the practice of tin-plating the steel that is used in fabrication.

TRAILING WHEELS: Pairs or multiple pairs of wheels that are smaller than drive wheels and unpowered, mounted at the rear of a locomotive to support its cab and/or firebox.

TRUCK: A swiveling frame containing two or more pairs of wheels that run in bearings (see journal box), mounted beneath and supporting a freight or passenger car or tender.

WHYTE CLASSIFICATION SYSTEM: A method of identifying steam locomotives by number of pilot, driving and trailing wheels. For example, a 4-6-2 locomotive has four pilot, six driving and two trailing wheels. Each wheel arrangement has a nickname. The 4-6-2 is a Pacific, for example, and a 2-8-4 is a Berkshire.

APPENDIX

SOURCES & ADDRESSES

Clubs and Associations

American Flyer Collectors Club
(AFCC), P.O. Box 13269
Pittsburgh, PA 15243

Train Collectors Association (TCA)
P.O. Box 248
Strasburg, PA 17579

Toy Train Operating Society (TTOS)
25 W. Walnut St., Suite 308
Pasadena, CA 91103

Lionel Collectors Club Of America
(LCCA), P.O. Box 479
La Salle, IL 61301

Lionel Operating Train Society
(LOTS), P.O. Box 66240
Cincinnati, OH 45262-0240

The National Toy Train Museum
300 Paradise Lane, P.O. Box 248
Strasburg, PA 17579

Manufacturers and Suppliers of Standard Gauge Products,
Past and Present

Antique Trains
1 Lantern Lane
Turnersville, NJ 08012
track

Clarke Spares & Restorations
(Tintown)
90 West Swamp Road,
Doylestown, PA 18901
bridge and station platform

Classic Model Trains
P.O. Box 179
Hartford, OH 44424
*train enamel and original design loco-
motives and cars*

Gargraves Trackage Corp.
8967 Ridge Road
North Rose, NY 14516-9793
flexible track and other track products

Joseph L. Mania
17 Douglas Road
Freehold, NJ 07728
*reproductions of Lionel Standard and
2-7/8" Gauge trains*

Moondog Express
P.O. Box 1707
Lompoc, CA 93438
road material

MTH Electric Trains
(formerly Mike's Train House)
9693 Gerwig Lane
Columbia, MD 21046
*reproductions of Classic Period Lionel
trains and accessories; track*

Pioneer Valley Models
P.O. Box 4928
Holyoke, MA 01041
scenic backdrops/cardstock buildings

Pride Lines Ltd.
651 W. Hoffman Ave.
Lindenhurst, NY 11757
*reproductions and original designs of
stations, trolleys and other tinplate
trains and accessories*

The Rich-Art Company
1714 Del Dios Highway
Escondido, CA 92029
*reproductions and original designs of
locomotives and rolling stock*

Ron Morris
2723 Beacon Drive
Sinking Spring, PA 19608
reproduction Lionel scenic plots

Rulon E. Taylor
5559 Kane Creek Road
Central Point, OR 97502
*reproduction Ives and American Flyer
tenders and parts*

Rydin Industries
26W Warrenville Road
Warrenville, IL 60555
track and switches

Scenic Express
1001 Lowrey Ave.
Jeannette, PA 15644-2671
landscaping supplies

Smith Metal Works
100 Colburn St.
Newark, NY 14513
engine house and roundhouse

Tintown
See Clarke Spares & Restorations

T-Reproductions
P. O. Box 5369
Johnson City, TN 37604

Williams Electric Trains
8835 Columbia 100 Parkway
Columbia, MD 21045.

BIBLIOGRAPHY

Carlson, Pierce. *Toy Trains, A History*. New York: Harper & Row, Publishers, 1986.

Claytor, W. Graham Jr.; Doyle, Paul A.; McKenney, Carlton Norris. *Greenberg's Guide To Early American Toy Trains*. Sykesville, Maryland: Greenberg Publishing Co., Inc., 1993.

Cowen, Lawrence. Address before the New York Society of Security Analysts, reprinted by *The Train Collectors Quarterly*, Vol. 34, No. 4, July, 1988.

Creswell, H. K. "600E Standard Gauge Hudson," *TTOS Bulletin*, Vol. 15, No. 7, July, 1980.

Creswell, Harlen. "Completing the State Set!", *TTOS Bulletin*, Vol. 16, No. 11, November, 1981.

"CTT Visits Mike's Train House," *Classic Toy Trains*, Vol. 7, No. 2, March, 1994.

"CTT Visits Williams' Reproductions Ltd.," *Classic Toy Trains*, Vol. 3, No. 3, June, 1990.

Fraley, Donald S., ed. *Lionel Trains, Standard of the World*, 1900-1943, Second Edition. Strasburg, Pennsylvania: Train Collectors Association, 1989.

Greenberg, Bruce C. *Greenberg's Guide To Ives Trains 1901-1932, Volume I*, Second Edition. Sykesville, Maryland: Greenberg Publishing Co., 1991.

Greenberg, Bruce C. *Greenberg's Guide To Lionel Trains 1901-1942, Volume I, Second Edition*. Waukesha, Wisconsin: Greenberg Division of Kalmbach Publishing Co., 1994.

Greenberg, Bruce C. *Greenberg's Guide To Lionel Trains 1945-1969, Volume II*. Sykesville, Maryland: Greenberg Publishing Company, 1991.

Greenberg, Bruce C., ed. *Greenberg's Lionel Catalogues, Volume I: 1902-1922*. Sykesville, Maryland: Greenberg Publishing Co., Inc., 1990.

Hall, George. "CTT Visits The Rich-Art Company," *Classic Toy Trains*, Vol. 10, No. 3, pp. 92-95.

Hertz, Louis H. *Messrs. Ives of Bridgeport*. Wethersfield, Connecticut: Mark Haber & Co., 1950.

Hertz, Louis H. *Riding the Tinplate Rails*. Ramsey, New Jersey: Model Craftsman Publishing Corp., 1944.

Hollander, Ron. *All Aboard*. New York: Workman Publishing Co., 1981.

Horne, Mark. *The McCoy Story*. Quartzsite, Arizona: The Main Event, 1992.

Hubbard, John. *Greenberg's Repair and Operating Manual: Prewar Lionel Trains*. Sykesville, Maryland: Greenberg Publishing Co., 1984.

Hubbard, John. *The Story Of Williams Electric Trains*. Sykesville, Maryland: Greenberg Publishing Co., Inc., 1987.

Kimball, Steven H., ed. *Greenberg's Guide To American Flyer Prewar O Gauge* Sykesville, Maryland: Greenberg Publishing Co., Inc., 1987.

Mallerich, Dallas J. III. *Greenberg's American Toy Trains*. Sykesville, Maryland: Greenberg Publishing Co., Inc., 1990.

McCoy, Margaret. "McCoy Manufacturing," *The Train Collectors Quarterly*, Vol. 25, No. 4, Summer, 1979.

McLaren, Jack. "American Flyer Wide Gauge--1926," *The Collector*, Vol. 19, No. 2, Summer, 1996.

McLaren, Jack. "American Flyer Wide Gauge--1927," *The Collector*, Vol. 19, No. 3, Fall, 1996.

On The Right Track, The History Of Lionel Trains. Published by Fundimensions Division of General Mills, Inc., 1972.

Riddle, Peter H. *Greenberg's Guide To Lionel Trains 1901-1942, Volume III Accessories*. Sykesville, Maryland: Greenberg Publishing Co., Inc., 1993.

Riddle, Peter H. *Greenberg's Wiring Your Lionel Layout, A Primer For Lionel Train Enthusiasts*. Sykesville, Maryland: Greenberg Publishing Co., Inc., 1991.

Riddle, Peter H. *Greenberg's Wiring Your Lionel Layout, Vol. 2, Intermediate Techniques*. Waukesha, Wisconsin: Greenberg Division of Kalmbach Publishing Co., 1993.

Riddle, Peter H. *Greenberg's Wiring Your Lionel Layout, Vol. 3, Advanced Technologies Made Easy*. Waukesha, Wisconsin: Greenberg Division of Kalmbach Publishing Co., 1996.

Riddle, Peter H. *Tips & Tricks For Toy Train Operators*. Waukesha, Wisconsin: Greenberg Division of Kalmbach Publishing Co., 1994.

Riddle, Peter H. *Trains From Grandfather's Attic*. Sykesville, Maryland: Greenberg Publishing Co., Inc., 1991.

Schuweiler, Alan R. *Greenberg's Guide To American Flyer Wide Gauge*. Sykesville, Maryland: Greenberg Publishing Co., Inc., 1989.

Sykes, J.B., Ed. *The Concise Oxford Dictionary of Current English*, Seventh Edition. Oxford, G.B.: Oxford University Press, 1989.

Thon, Bob. *"Making 'Em Like They Used To,"* Classic Toy Trains, Fall, 1987.

Train Collectors Association Directory of Information, Vol. 43, No. 2A. Strasburg, Pennsylvania: TCA National Office, 1997.

Williams, Nelson G. "Glenn Gerhard and the Trains He Built," *The New Century Limited*, publication of the Toy Train Collectors Society, Fall/Winter, 1996.

LIONEL ELECTRIC TOY 1923 *&"Multivolt" Transformers* TRAINS

Father and son enjoying Lionel's Standard Gauge electric trains—an established American tradition long before being depicted on the cover of the Lionel Corporation's 1923 consumer catalog.

INDEX

INDEX

INDEX

INDEX

ABOUT THE AUTHOR

Peter H. Riddle, a professor of music at Acadia University in Nova Scotia, ranks among the world's most prolific and respected authors on topics relating to toy train history, restoration, and operation.

Peter's dedication to thorough research, coupled with his abiding desire to help others increase their enjoyment of the hobby, has resulted in seven published books in the current decade alone.

Subject matter for Peter's books ranges from model railroad layout design and construction to toy train electronics and restoration; and from the history of toy electric train manufacturers to compilations of up-to-date value listings for contemporary collectors. He has also contributed as a writer and editor to more than 14 other books on various aspects of model railroading with toy trains, and has had more than a dozen feature articles published in *Classic Toy Trains* magazine and the Train Collector's Association's *Quarterly*.

Peter's love of toy trains is shared by his wife, Gay, herself an active train collector and operator, who assists in the development and editing of Peter's steady flow of books and magazine articles.

Other toy train books by Peter H. Riddle:
Easy Lionel Layouts You Can Build
Waukesha, Wisconsin: Kalmbach Publishing Co., Inc., 1997

Greenberg's Guide to Lionel Trains, 1901-1942, Volume III: Accessories
Sykesville, Maryland: Greenberg Publishing Company, Inc., 1993.

Greenberg's Wiring Your Lionel Layout, Volumes I, II, and III
Sykesville, Maryland: Greenberg Publishing Company, Inc., 1991, 1993, 1996

Tips & Tricks for Toy Train Operators
Waukesha, Wisconsin: Kalmbach Publishing Co., Inc., 1994

Trains From Grandfather's Attic
Sykesville, Maryland: Greenberg Publishing Company, Inc., 1991